STREETWISE

TIME
MANAGEMENT

Books in the Adams Streetwise® business series include:

Adams Streetwise® Business Forms (with CD-ROM)

Adams Streetwise® Business Letters (with CD-ROM)

Adams Streetwise® Business Tips

Adams Streetwise® Complete Business Plan

Adams Streetwise® Customer-Focused Selling

Adams Streetwise® Do-It-Yourself Advertising

Adams Streetwise® Finance & Accounting

Adams Streetwise® Hiring Top Performers

Adams Streetwise® Independent Consulting

Adams Streetwise® Managing People

Adams Streetwise® Motivating & Rewarding Employees

Adams Streetwise® Small Business Start-Up

Adams Streetwise® Small Business Turnaround

Adams Streetwise® Time Management

All titles are available through your favorite bookseller.

STREETWISE

TIME
MANAGEMENT

Get More Done with Less Stress by Efficiently Managing Your Time

by Marshall Cook

Adams Media Corporation
Holbrook, Massachusetts

Published by Adams Media Corporation
260 Center Street, Holbrook, MA 02343

ISBN: 1-58062-131-7

Printed in the United States of America.

J   I   H   G   F   E   D   C   B

Library of Congress Cataloging-in-Publication Data
Cook, Marshall.
Streetwise time management / Marshall J. Cook.
        p.   cm.
        Includes index.
        ISBN 1-58062-131-7
        1. Time management. I. Title.
        HD69.T54C6598   1999
        640'.43–dc21   98-50808
                                        CIP

This book was developed for Adams Media Corporation by CWL Publishing Enterprises, John Woods,
President, 3010 Irvington Way, Madison, WI 53713, www.execpc.com/cwlpubent.

This publication is designed to provide accurate and authoritative information with regard to the subject matter covered. It is sold with the understanding that the publisher is not engaged in rendering legal, accounting,
or other professional advice. If legal advice or other expert assistance is required, the services of a competent
professional person should be sought.
        — From a *Declaration of Principles* jointly adopted by a Committee of the American Bar Association
                                        and a Committee of Publishers and Associations

Illustration by Eric Mueller.

This book is available at quantity discounts for bulk purchases.
For information, call 1-800-872-5627 (in Massachusetts, 781-767-8100).

Visit our exciting small business Web site: www.businesstown.com

CONTENTS

CONTENTS

CONTENTS

Part V: Aerobic Exercise for Your Mind

CONTENTS

Part VI: Clutter Control

Contents

Part VII: Sound Mind/Sound Body

CONTENTS

Part VIII: Check Out Your Attitude

Preface

Don't read this book.

Use this book.

You'll change the way you live, reclaiming your power to make smart choices about the way you manage your time.

If you accept the challenges in the next thirty-five chapters, you'll learn how to get more done, without all the stress. You won't find time or save time. You'll *make* time for all the things you want and need to be doing.

Traditional time management stresses fitting more activity into a limited amount of time, primarily by "multitasking" and "doing more with less." Streetwise time management focuses on doing the right things, one at a time, and doing them well.

You'll start with "moment management," ways of taking care of the minutes, and move all the way up to techniques for ensuring that your life truly reflects your highest values.

You'll revisit the to-do list, that staple of all time-management programs, to make sure you're running the list rather than letting the list run you. You'll also decide whether you need a list at all.

You'll learn to make more time for the important activities in your life while eliminating time lost on the merely urgent activities that demand your immediate attention but really deserve little or no attention.

You'll identify the time snatchers in your life and learn how to avoid them, setting your agenda and sticking to it instead of letting other people set your agenda for you.

You'll take a hard look at the technology in your life to make sure the computer, the phone, the fax, and the beeper serve instead of drive you.

You'll eliminate three forms of clutter: the physical mounds of paper that threaten to bury you, the mental fog of confusion and noise, and the flood of raw information that makes knowledge impossible until you learn how to stem the flow.

If procrastination is an issue, you'll learn how much it's really costing you in time and energy, why you procrastinate now, and how to eliminate procrastination from your life. You'll also learn how to use your inevitable downtimes productively, without stress.

You'll focus on your body—learning the role sleep, diet, and exercise play in your streetwise approach to time management. You'll also focus on your psyche, eliminating anxiety and anger and honing your natural creativity.

Some of the techniques in this book will speak directly to you, offering you ways to improve your life dramatically. Others will be irrelevant to you. You decide. That's what this book is all about—reclaiming all the daily decisions that add up to the way you live.

Decide now that you're going to be an active participant in, rather than a passive consumer of, these ideas.

How to Use This Book

You'll encounter numerous "do-it-yourself" sidebars throughout these pages. These are your opportunities to apply techniques, evaluate your progress, and decide on the changes you'll make. Take time now to wrestle with these ideas. You'll create the time you need to live well for the rest of your life.

Actually take the speed sickness tests in Chapter 2, for example, so that you can accurately access your needs and begin to tailor a personal time-management program that will work for you. When I suggest that you log your activities to learn how you're spending your time now, take the time to do it. A bit of time spent now will return time and energy to you for the rest of your life.

Each chapter begins with an introductory list of the key ideas you should look for in the material that follows. Turn these points into questions and read searching for answers. That way you'll get the most out of every minute you spend with the book.

Then you'll encounter an anecdote describing someone who's grappling with the issues the chapter raises. See if you can relate to the dilemma described and think about your own specific needs.

The chapter will end with a continuation of the opening anecdote, with our case study a bit further along in finding solutions to time-management problems.

Finally, you'll find a summary of key *Streetwise Time Management* concepts from the chapter. Review them to cement them in your memory.

We've organized the book for you to read and work through sequentially, moving from general to specific and then taking a series of specific time and stress management issues in turn. But you can tackle these chapters in whatever order you want, starting with those issues that most affect you right now.

You'll enjoy a wonderful cumulative effect from your efforts. The more you begin to make decisions about how you spend your time, the better you'll feel about making still more positive changes.

Ready to get started?

Willing to commit a bit of time and energy now so that you can save time and energy later?

Able to take a serious look at your life and make creative changes?

Then the only time that really counts is right now. Let's get started.

Acknowledgments

The ideas in this book build on the ideas of Arnold Bennett, Stephen Covey, Frederick Franck, Alan Lakein, Juliet Schor, John Robinson, Hans Selye, Clark Stallworth, Steven Weber, Captain Augustus McCrae (who taught us to learn to love all the little every-day things), Satchel Paige, and a lot of other great thinkers.

John Woods, president of CWL Publishing Enterprises, brought this book into being and carried it through to completion.

Ellen Malloy Cook put up with a lot of grumbling on Saturday mornings as I sat at the kitchen table with my laptop. She has brought more to my life than I can ever say. This book, and all the books, are dedicated to her.

A New Way of Looking at the Way You Spend Your Time

Summary of Part I

1. **Decide how you spend your time. Don't let other people, circumstances, or habit decide for you.**

2. **Manage time your way. Develop a personal system that works for you.**

3. **Before you make a decision on what to do next, ask what and how much must be done and how fast you must do it.**

4. **Track how you really spend your time, and list specific ways you'll spend your time differently.**

5. **Make a decision, act on it, and move on.**

That's the premise of every time-management book, tape, or seminar you encounter. But *time* might not be the problem, and *manage* might be the wrong word for the solution.

You've got time, friend, the same twenty-four hours as all those movers and shakers who seem to get so much more done.

You can't really manage that time, but you can manage yourself better. If you don't, time will do a pretty good job of managing you.

This book will encourage you to explore the way you spend your time now and develop ways to spend it more effectively. We'll look at ways to fit more productive activity into your day, the focus of traditional time management, and also ways to be sure you're doing the right activities.

In this first section, we'll look at the way you're living now and figure out to what degree you're suffering from "speed sickness," the universal malady of the age. We'll begin to cure that speed sickness with "moment management," ways of keeping the minutes from getting away from you so they can't turn into wasted hours.

This is a do-it-yourself project. Don't just read about the techniques in this book. Apply them. When you do, you'll immediately begin to make more time for yourself—time for your work, of course, and time, also, for fun and for the people you love and the values you cherish.

Chapter 1

Can You Really Manage Time?

In this chapter, you'll learn:

■ **What time management can do for you—and what it can't do**

■ **How some elements of traditional time management can actually do you more harm than good**

Lon and Doris have gone on several diets together. They entered the "zone," they gave up carbohydrates, they ate nothing but carbohydrates. They charted every bite they ate, calculated the calories and the percentage of fat from calories, mapped the war between the forces of the good cholesterol and the evil empire of the bad cholesterol.

None of the diets worked. Oh, they lost weight on each regimen they tried. But when the diet ended, the weight returned, often with dividends.

Although they never thought to make the comparison, the various time-management systems they've tried have been a lot like the diets they've subjected themselves to. From the complicated day-planner system to the color-coded calendar, each time-management "diet" seemed to work—for a while—if for no other reason than they really paid attention to how they spent their time. But the systems themselves were time consuming and became burdensome, and they found themselves slipping back into feeling out of control of their lives.

> We define time management as a personal rather than a social issue in our culture.

If you're like Lon and Doris, constantly fighting and losing the battle of time, you need to take a new look at time management—streetwise time management, a system that will actually work for you precisely because you create your own system, based on conscious choices you make.

We define time management as a personal rather than a social issue in our culture. Stressed out? Too busy? That's your problem. Take care of it. Or don't. Just be sure to pay your bills and show up for work on time.

But let's think on a social level for a moment before we buckle down to the job of changing one single life: yours.

As a culture, could we establish a six-hour work day, a thirty-hour work week, and a paid vacation for every worker (maybe not Sweden's five to eight weeks, but something)?

Could we support alternative working arrangements such as flex time and job sharing? Could we acknowledge workaholism as a true social disorder instead of a badge of honor? If not, are we willing to count the true price we pay as a society for health care—

mental as well as physical—along with underemployment and unemployment?

Impossible, you say? In the 1950s, we decided that fighting the threat of a Communist takeover was our most important priority, and we completely restructured society to do it. (President Eisenhower created the interstate highway system, for example, as a means of evacuating our cities in the event of a nuclear attack.)

In the early 1960s, John F. Kennedy pledged that the United States would have a man on the moon within the decade, and we did it.

Check out the way social attitudes have changed toward cigarette smoking in the last twenty years. That didn't just happen. Folks worked hard to change those attitudes. Huge changes in social awareness and values are possible. What about changes in the way we evaluate our usefulness and care for ourselves?

But for now, you need to work on the one part of society you really can change—you.

Just What Can You Do about the Time Crunch?

Advertisers don't promote feelings or advocate lifestyles. They sell things by connecting with existing feelings and adapting their products and services to dominant lifestyles. The folks at Microsoft aren't saying we should feel out of control. They're assuming that we do—and offering a partial solution, an island of tranquillity in an ocean of chaos, one good product that works the way it should.

Let's examine the premise. Can you "control" your boss? (Would you want to if you could?) Is your workload totally beyond your control? You really can't do anything about your weight (diet and exercise), your backhand (practice, practice, practice—or give up the damned game), your weeds (pull 'em, hire somebody to do it for you, or take out the lawn and put in a nice rock garden), your dog (don't let my friend Patricia McConnell, a professional pet behaviorist, hear you say that).

Snapshot

"You can't control your boss,
your workload,
your weight,
your backhand,
your weeds,
your dog,
your life,
at least now
you can control
your cursor"

—Advertisement for
Computer Software

Picture the frenzied worker in another recent ad, obviously pushed to within an inch of her breaking point. "When you work late at the computer, do your contact lenses crash?" the headline probes. The solution: "They won't crash if you use Opti-Free."

I recently appeared on *The Oprah Winfrey Show* to talk about time and stress management. One of the other guests was a professional waiter. No, not the fellow who describes the special quiche of the day and keeps your water glass brimming. This patient fellow is working his way through college by standing in line as a surrogate for people willing to pay him to do it while they're off doing other, presumably more important, tasks.

These examples represent one dominant approach to time management. When you're too busy, buy your way out with a product or service to help get you through physically, mentally, and psychologically.

But here again, we should tally the true price for such conveniences, in time and money spent shopping, in increasing dependence, in the missed pleasures of cooking and smelling and savoring (and, in many cases, chewing) food. We have to count up the toll—on our eyes, stomachs, and psyches—when we push ourselves to work ever harder, ever faster, ever longer.

When you start keeping score right, sometimes you'll also start changing some of the decisions you make.

Limits to the Traditional Time-Management Approach

Getting up earlier seems to be a favorite solution. The folks who study our sleep habits estimate that Americans are now getting sixty to ninety minutes less sleep each night than they did ten to fifteen years ago.

You could try getting less sleep as a way of gaining control of time. You could make up a huge pitcher of "blender breakfast" and keep it in a cooler in your car, so you could drink your meal on the way to work.

You could take a waterproof tape player into the shower with you, so you could listen to a self-help tape (preferably on one of those compressed players that takes the "dead air" pauses out) while you're going at the grouting with your toothbrush. You could even wear your clothes into the shower, like the protagonist in Anne Tyler's novel, *The Accidental Tourist*, so you could wash your duds while you showered, grouted, and listened.

Personally, I'm not going to do any of those things. I'm not saying they're bad things. They might work wonderfully for some folks. But I personally would pay too high a price for the saved seconds.

I have to chew my breakfast, so I know I've really eaten; I'll have to live with the inconvenience and the irrevocable passage of time while I chomp my Grape Nuts.

I want and need the three-minute oasis of a steaming hot shower, my little morning miracle, a pleasure for body and soul, to start even the busiest day.

I do, however, get up at 5:00 A.M. and exercise for forty-five minutes to an hour and a half every morning before I chew my way through breakfast and wallow in that hot shower. That works for me. It might not work for you.

Lots of folks take a Walkman with them when they jog. I prefer letting my mind drift. Comedienne Joan Rivers reportedly has a speakerphone on her treadmill. More power to you, Joan. Whatever works. But that sounds awful to me.

Some of you need to impose strict order on your work space—a place for everything and everything in its place, with neat files, a clean desktop, a floor you can actually walk on. I'm in the compost heap school of desktop management, and I don't mind hurdling the piles of files and books and periodicals that inevitably collect on the floor.

I even found support for my slovenly workplace. In *How to Put More Time in Your Life*, Dru Scott extols "the secret pleasures" of clutter, calling messy folks "divergent thinkers" (which, you have to admit, sounds much better than "messy slobs").

The classic rules of time management don't work for everyone. You have to find your own way through the suggestions and exercises in this book. You may not be able to control some elements of your life—and you may not want to.

Snapshot

- "If you don't have time for reading, letter-writing, cooking or exercising, get up earlier in the morning."

- "Keep your breakfast fast and simple. Try a 'blender breakfast' consisting of a banana, fruit juice, granola, and a dash of honey."

- "If your bathtub needs a cleaning, do it during your shower. You can scrub as you finish washing or while your hair conditioner is working."

—Three of the *365 Ways to Save Time*, by Lucy Hedrick

There are lots of things none of us can control. If you drive a car anywhere more populous than the outback of Australia, you're going to get stuck in traffic. Manage the flow of traffic? You might as well try to manage the current of the river in which you swim.

If you make an appointment, somebody's going to keep you waiting. A phone solicitor will interrupt your dinner. Your boss will dump a last-minute assignment on you. Your child will get sick the same day you have to make that megapresentation before the board.

So that's where the time really goes!

You'll get interrupted seventy-three times a day, take an hour of work home, read less than five minutes, talk to your spouse for four minutes, exercise less than three minutes, and play with your kid for two minutes.

Nightmarish. Want to change that picture? Just as with poor Scrooge, scared into life change by the ghosts of Christmas past, present, and to come, it's not too late for you to refocus your life.

That's what time management is really all about.

But no matter what you do, you're still going to spend a lot of time waiting at red lights, idling in waiting rooms, and standing in line.

Some Initial Ways to Take Control of Your Time

You could make huge changes. You could quit your job, leave your family, move to a cabin in the Dakotas and paint landscapes. You could. But you probably won't and probably shouldn't.

You can make tiny changes without needing anybody's help or permission. You can, for example, learn to take four minibreaks a day, as I'll suggest in a later chapter.

You can explore the possibilities for some midsize changes, involving the cooperation of other people in your life. Could you, for example:

- Take your next raise in time rather than money or advancement?
- Work at least part of the time at home?
- Substitute barter and skills swapping for money to get work done for you?

As you work your way through this book, let yourself explore as many possibilities as you can. Some won't be practical. Some won't work for you. Some will be beyond your ability to do, for a variety of reasons. But by applying your creativity, initiative, and energy to this exploration, you'll find ways to create meaningful, life-affirming change.

No more prefabricated time-management systems for Lon and Doris. They're determined to learn how to get control of their time the streetwise way, making the day-to-day decisions that let them live the way they really want to, getting everything done that has to be done, and still having time left for the parts of life that don't fit on the to-do list but that make life worth living.

No more backsliding. No more "failing" to measure up to somebody else's system. Just applying street smarts to all those little daily decisions that add up to the way they live their lives.

How about you? Why not join them? If you're interested, read on.

> As you work your way through this book, let yourself explore as many possibilities as you can.

Time-Management Tips

1. Do it your way. Adapt time-management techniques to fit your personality and your life.
2. Concentrate your effort and energy on those elements of time management you can control. Focus on the possible.

Do You Have Speed Sickness?

In this chapter, you'll learn:

- How to define "time" in a new way
- How to diagnose your own speed sickness
- Why you really *don't* work better under pressure
- Why the "Age of Leisure" turned into the "Age of Anxiety"

Ned is constantly trying to save time. He drafts detailed to-do lists for each day, plans his errands so as not to have to double back or make a second trip, makes sure he's doing at least two things at once, listening to a self-help tape while driving to work, for example.

But despite all of his planning and scheduling, he feels himself falling further behind each day. Somehow he never quite finishes the tasks on the to-do list. He worries that, with all his frantic rushing around, his children are growing up without him, and he feels distant from his wife, Doris.

> He goes to bed each night exhausted and guilty.
> He's about ready to give up on time management.
> What he really needs to do is redefine his whole notion of "time." How? Read on.

Are you old enough to remember the plate spinner on the old Ed Sullivan variety show? This haggard-looking fellow would charge onto the stage, balance a plate on a pole, and set it spinning, repeating the deed with a second pole and plate and then a third. About that time, the first plate would slow down and start to wobble, so the spinner would hurry back to the first pole and rev up the plate, give numbers two and three a little goosing, and then start a fourth plate spinning.

The idea was to get fifteen plates spinning at once without letting any fall. This accomplished, the fellow would run down the line, snatching all the plates off the poles, to the thunderous applause of the audience.

I remember as a kid thinking how hard it must be to learn how to be a plate spinner. I also remember wondering why anybody would want to do something so pointless and nerve-racking.

We've become a nation of plate spinners. But unlike the pro on the Sullivan show, we seem to break a lot of plates, and we don't get any applause on those rare occasions when we manage to keep all the plates spinning.

How about you? Is the tape of your life stuck on fast forward? Is your game plan a perpetual two-minute drill complete with no-

How about you? Is the tape of your life stuck on fast forward?

huddle offense? Have you developed FedEx dependency because you're behind in your work?

You could be suffering from speed sickness—and not even know it. Read on.

Speed sickness isn't really new. Cracker-barrel philosopher Will Rogers defined it as well as anybody when he observed, "Half our life is spent trying to find something to do with the time we have rushed through life trying to save."

First Test to Diagnose Speed Sickness

Here's a simple test to see if you're suffering from speed sickness. All you need is a partner to keep track of time while you estimate how long it takes for one minute to elapse. Sit down and get comfortable. No fair peeking at a watch, and no fair counting off "One Mississippi, Two Mississippi...." Your partner says "Go." When you think a minute has passed, you say "Time's up!" Go ahead and try it. Then read on to find out how others did.

How far did you get? Did you underestimate the amount of time you had waited? If so, you're in the majority. In monitored tests, most folks called out "Time's up!" after only about fifteen seconds. At least one subject thought the minute was up after just seven seconds. Very few made it a whole minute.

If we were as bad at estimating space as we seem to be at estimating time, we'd be crashing into each other all the time.

Second Test to Diagnose Speed Sickness

Here's another test. Just sit still and do nothing for one minute, sixty little seconds, while your partner times you. How long does that minute of enforced inactivity seem to you? Are you uncomfortable with just one minute of stillness?

A minute has become an eternity. We measure time in nanoseconds now. (A nanosecond is one billionth of a second.) A supercomputer performs hundreds if not thousands of operations in one trillionth of a second. One trillionth!

If we were as bad at estimating space as we seem to be at estimating time, we'd be crashing into each other all the time.

Third Test to Diagnose Speed Sickness

One more test. It takes a little longer than the one-minute drill, but it isn't difficult, and it doesn't require a partner. Simply leave your watch at home when you go about your business tomorrow.

At the end of the day, reflect on these two questions:

1. Did you find yourself checking your wrist even when you didn't want or need to know what time it was?
2. Even without your watch, did you have any trouble keeping track of time?

If you answered yes to the first question and no to the second, you're again in the majority. Most of us have become accustomed to tracking time in ever-smaller increments as we drive ourselves from task to task, deadline to deadline, appointment to appointment. We even schedule the fun stuff. This constant checking has become habitual, so we don't even realize how time driven we've become.

I left my watch on the dresser one morning about four years ago and, with rare exceptions, have left it there ever since. I found myself glancing almost compulsively at my naked wrist for several days, a wave of anxiety washing over me each time I realized I didn't have my watch on. And yet I found that I always knew what time it was.

In our culture, the trick is to avoid knowing what time it is. Reminders are everywhere. Clocks leer down at us from office walls, and watches bob on the wrists of almost everyone we meet. The fellow on the radio chirps out the time constantly, in artless variations. ("It's seven sixteen, sixteen minutes after the hour of seven o'clock, forty-four minutes before eight....") Our computers blink the time at us when we log on and keep track of every passing minute while we work. Neon signs blink the time and temperature at us as we drive to our next appointment.

> Pause for just a moment to consider this: at one time there were no clocks and no watches.

Pause for just a moment to consider this: at one time there were no clocks and no watches. When the first public clock was erected in a village in England, folks flocked to the town square to view the wonder. And it had only one hand! You could tell time only to the nearest hour.

Can we even imagine life without the timekeepers? Probably not. We're not just aware of time, we're driven by time, besotted with time, engulfed in time.

"Time is on my side," Mick Jagger and the Rolling Stones told us in the 1960s, but time has become both the elusive prey and the hunter, chasing us through the day, the week, the year. "Slow down, you move too fast," a more mellow group, Simon and Garfunkel, advised, but we didn't listen.

Riding the Adrenaline High

Here's another simple test to diagnose a possible case of speed sickness. Just respond yes or no to the following statement: "I work better under pressure."

A lot of us seem to think so. We claim the trait on our resumes (along with "highly motivated self-starter"), and we brag about our ability to perform under the tightest of deadlines. I've written on deadline all of my adult life, and I've prided myself on my speed and accuracy under pressure. In my younger days, I even flirted with those deadlines, seeing how close I could cut it, getting that one last interview before sitting down at the keyboard and blasting off.

It wasn't just the constant caffeine creating that heady buzz. I was on an adrenaline rush akin to an amphetamine high. And in that giddy state, I honestly believed I was doing my best work while I rode the crest of my momentum.

You, too? Go back and look at that work after you've calmed down. Your best? If you're honest with yourself, you'll admit that the quality of the work suffers when you race through it.

And you suffer, too. You've got motion sickness—not the kind that causes queasiness when you react to the rolling of a ship, but rather a physical and psychological dependence on motion and speed that can become almost as powerful as a true addiction.

> "Leisure time" has become an oxymoron.

"Leisure time" has become an oxymoron. We experience one long work day, broken but not relieved by gulped meals and troubled sleep. Only the models in the clothing catalogs seem to have time to lounge.

Seven Common Symptoms of Motion Sickness

How about you? Have you got a case of motion sickness? Symptoms include:

- Nervousness
- Depression
- Fatigue
- Appetite swings
- Compulsive behavior (repetitive actions that are difficult or even impossible to stop)
- Unwillingness and even inability to stop working
- Inability to relax even when you do stop working

We Americans take shorter and fewer vacations, and we take our work with us, with our beepers and cell phones, faxes and e-mail. Home computers began to sell, remember, only when IBM had a Chaplinesque "Little Tramp" show us how to "take work home on your fingertips."

Leisure no longer rhymes with *pleasure* as we race through life, checking the "fun" items off the to-do list. Even our play has become purposeful (physical conditioning or enforced "relaxation") and competitive (who plays golf without keeping score?). I even read recently about a birdwatching competition. Birdwatching? Competition? Yep.

We all have to run the occasional sprint, meet the unyielding deadline, cope with the unforeseen emergency. And we can do so effectively and without long-term damage. It can even be exhilarating.

But keep driving in that fast lane until it becomes a way of life and you run the risk of:

- Hypertension
- Heart disease
- Drug dependency
- Stroke

Rushing through life suppresses the immune system, hampering the natural formation of T-lymphocytes (white blood cells). That, in turn, opens you up to a variety of ills, some categorized as psychosomatic (all in your head), but all very real.

Life in the fast lane can make you sick. It can even kill you.

Reports of the "Death of Work" Premature

In an article in a 1959 issue of the *Saturday Evening Post*, highly regarded historian and social commentator Arthur Schlesinger, Jr., warned Americans of "the onrush of a new age of leisure." Warned? In 1967, noted sociologists came before a U.S. Senate subcommittee on labor to predict with great confidence that Americans would soon be enjoying a twenty-two-hour work week or a twenty-two-week work year. Many of us would be retiring at thirty-eight, these experts said, and the big challenge, as Schlesinger indicated eight years earlier, would be in handling all that free time.

These prognostications remind me of the executive at Decca Records who turned down the chance to sign a garage rock band from England because "guitar music is on the way out." The band was The Beatles, and they did okay with three guitars and a set of drums. The only one on the way out was the Decca exec.

How could the "experts" have been so wrong? What happened? Why didn't our marvelous technology usher in the Age of Leisure?

We took the money. We opted for a higher material standard of living instead of time off. You don't remember making that choice? Perhaps it was never offered to you, at least not in those terms. But by and large, most of us decided to work more rather than less, and more of us went to work, so that instead of the Age of Leisure we created the Age of Anxiety and the norm of the two-income household.

Women, in particular, got caught in the time crunch. You were supposed to be able to have it all, a thriving family and a successful career. But too many superwomen came home from a hard day at the office only to find all the housework waiting for them. They wound up working, in essence, a double shift, all day, every day. And single mothers never had a choice. If they didn't do it, it didn't get done.

Whether or not we made the choice consciously, there was plenty of pressure on us to choose the money. Hard workers get and keep jobs as well as social approval. When the boss advises us to "work smarter, not harder," he or she really means "get more done," and that means working harder as well as smarter. "You can do more with less," we're told when asked to take over the workload for a departed colleague (no doubt a victim of downsizing, or even right-sizing). But it's a lie. You can't do more with less. You can do more work only with more time, effort, and energy, and that time, effort, and energy have to come from other parts of your life—like conversation, sleep, and play.

> When the boss advises us to "work smarter, not harder," he or she really means "get more done."

We Have Seen the Enemy, and It Is Us

Is it all the bosses' fault? Not really. In many ways, we've inflicted speed sickness on ourselves. We use our busyness as a measure of our self-worth and importance. We define our sense of purpose and our meaning in terms of our to-do list. We've internalized the clear social message that busy people are worthy people, even morally superior people. ("Idle hands are the devil's workshop.")

It isn't just peer pressure. Deep down inside us, stillness makes us nervous. Many of us actually dread free time and secretly look forward to Monday morning (although we'd never admit it). Unstructured time is threatening, and so we fill up the hours—all of them.

We abhor the notion of "wasting" time and speak of "saving" time, and "spending quality time," as if, as the adage has it, time were money, or at least a commodity like money, capable of being either stashed or squandered.

What Does Time Mean to You?

Here's a simple way to find out what time is to you. Jot down several phrases that use the word *time* in them. Make them descriptive of the way you relate to time. For example, you might write:

"I'm trying to learn to spend my time wisely."

"I've found that I can save time by making a to-do list every morning before work."

"I tend to waste time after dinner."

Go ahead and take a moment to write a few. (This is a workbook about you working out your relationship with time. I promise the exercise has a point.)

Now rewrite each of the preceding statements, but substitute the word *life* for the word *time* and see what you come up with.

"I'm trying to learn to spend my life wisely."

"I've found that I can save life by making a to-do list every morning before work."

"I tend to waste life after dinner."

The point to this little parlor trick? (Did you think of it as a "waste of time"?) If even one of your revised statements startled you, even a little bit, you got the point. We aren't talking about some tangible commodity when we discuss the time of our lives. We no more "have" time than we "have" inches of height.

We're talking about our very lives.

So where is that time you've saved? You can't see it. You can't hold it in your hands. You can't put it in a box and hide it for safe-keeping.

Just What Is Time, Anyway?

"If no one asks me, I know," St. Augustine once replied to this question. "If they ask and I try to explain, I do not know."

Time is nothing more (or less) than a way of measuring out that life. Other cultures measure time other ways, and some cultures don't measure it at all.

Here are how some other cultures speak of time:

"Think of many things. Do one." Portuguese saying
"Sleep faster. We need the pillows." Yiddish saying
"Haste has no blessing." Swahili saying
"There is no hand to catch time." Bengali saying
"Today can't catch tomorrow." Jamaican saying

And here's our own beloved bard, William Shakespeare, advising us from a long-gone time: "O, call back yesterday, bid time return!"

Can't be done. So, how much time do you really *have*? In one sense, we each have exactly the same amount. We have the moment we're living right now. That's all. And it's everything.

That's not to say we shouldn't learn from the past and plan for the future, even if we can't store it or hold it. We're going to do a great deal of learning and planning as we explore time together. However, although we remember the past and envision the future (both highly creative acts), we can't live in either one of them.

You can only live in the present moment as well as you can (by whatever definition of "well" you develop). This book is designed to help you do that, and you have more choice in the matter than you think. To a great extent, you get to decide how you live right now.

> You can only live in the present moment as well as you can.

Four Basic Questions to Help You Manage Time

You can use this checklist to help you make those decisions:

1. What has to be done?
2. How much of it has to be done?
3. How fast does it have to be done?
4. How much does it cost to do it?

The answers to these questions will enable you to decide what to do now. These decisions will add up to your whole life, well lived.

So, how about our poor friend Ned? Should he chuck the job, leave the wife and kids, and flee to Tahiti? Perhaps a less radical move will save him—like quitting his high-pressure job and opening up a small pottery shop. That kind of drastic reorganization of life is not only unnecessary, it's not really a cure for Ned's speed sickness at all. He'd simply take his hyperpace of life with him to Tahiti or to his new vocation as a potter.

Ned needs to take conscious control of his life, taming the workload and leaving time for something besides work. Instead of learning how to do more and more tasks at once, he'll learn how to do one thing at a time.

He'll get it all done—with time and energy left over for family and other important aspects of life he's now neglecting.

And if Ned can do it, you can do it.

Time-Management Tips

1. Time isn't money. Time is life. Live in the present moment.
2. Ask
   - What must be done?
   - How much must be done?
   - How fast must it be done?

Are You Really as Busy as You Think?

In this chapter, you'll learn:

- To account accurately for your time
- To discover the differences between how you think you should be spending your time and how you're actually spending it
- To create strategies for managing your time more effectively

In the second chapter, we met poor old nervous Ned, who found himself careening from task to task without ever getting to the end of the to-do list.

Now meet Ned's wife, Phyllis, wife and working mother of two—a description that qualifies her as among the most hard-working, time-pressured people in the world.

"Where does the time go?" She could tell you—if she had the time. Her days are a constant flow of activity from dawn to dusk, taking care of the house, getting the kids ready for school, getting herself off to work as a part-time computer systems analyst, somehow managing most days to be home when the kids get back from school and to have dinner ready when Ned gets home, exhausted, from his full-time job as a comptroller for a midsize corporation.

And yet, for all of her seemingly constant work, Phyllis really doesn't know where the time goes. For all the tight scheduling she has to do to get it all done, she feels out of control of her life.

Before she can *manage* her time, she needs to understand how she's actually spending that time now. This chapter will help her—and you.

Are you working longer and harder now than you used to?

You said yes, right? Most do—especially those who buy books on time management.

Juliet Schor agrees with you. In her 1991 bestseller, *The Overworked American*, Schor notes that the shrinking American work week bottomed out at thirty-nine hours in 1970 before it started to rise. She says we now work an extra 164 hours—one full month—each year. She also notes the rise in the two-income household in the last twenty-five years. While we're putting in those longer hours on the job, there's no one at home to clean and cook and plan a social life.

> The average American works two months a year more than do most Europeans, she adds.

The average American works two months a year more than do most Europeans, she adds. Four weeks of vacation a year are mandated by law in Switzerland and Greece, for example, and workers in France and Spain must have five weeks. Actual vacation time is often a lot longer (five to eight weeks a year in Sweden).

Schor blames the increase in working hours on the eclipse of unionism and a slowdown in economic growth, making it necessary for folks to work longer just to maintain their standard of living.

That seductive lifestyle has, in fact, trapped us in what Schor calls the "insidious cycle of work and spend." We work longer to make more money to buy more stuff. She concludes that we must "reclaim leisure."

In 1985, John Robinson thought we already had.

As head of the Americans' Use of Time Project at the University of Maryland Survey Research Center, Robinson had been keeping track of how we spent our time since 1965. In that time, Robinson says, we actually experienced a steady increase in free time. Men gained an average of seven hours of leisure each week, up to forty-one hours, and women were right behind them with a six-hour gain to forty hours each week to call their own.

We think we're busier, he notes, but it just isn't so. "The perception of a time crunch appears to have gone up in the period of time where free time has increased," he concludes.

Surprised? So was Robinson, since his findings run counter to what we say about our lives. How can we have more leisure time but feel more rushed? Watching television eats up 37 percent of the average American woman's spare time and 39 percent of a man's, Robinson reports.

Perhaps time spent passively absorbing those flickering images somehow doesn't register as leisure, and we subconsciously subtract it from free time, the time we feel we can choose to spend as we wish.

John Robinson is, by his own definition, an omnivore. Along with a rigorous work schedule, he makes time to go to jazz festivals, search for old miniature golf courses, and test locally brewed beers.

So who's right? Are we Schor's worker bees or Robinson's couch potatoes?

Recent findings reported in *American Demographics* magazine for June 1996 back both conclusions. A whopping 45 percent of people reported having "less free time than five years ago," after keeping time-use diaries in 1995, backing Schor's contention. But that figure was down from 54 percent in 1990, bearing out Robinson's assertion.

Are You a Doer or a Sitter?

Time researcher John Robinson expected to be able to categorize folks according to the way they spend their free time. One man would be likely to work on his car engine, he reasoned, whereas another would rather go to the ballet.

But that's not what Robinson found. It isn't a matter of either/or. It's much more a case of all or nothing. The split Robinson uncovered is between the doers and the sitters. The same folks most likely to attend cultural events, for example, are also more likely to fix their own carburetors. Others seem unable to report having put their free time to any particular use.

Robinson explains this split between the doers, or "omnivores," as he calls them, and the do-nothings in terms of one of Newton's laws of physics: bodies in motion tend to stay in motion; bodies at rest tend to stay at rest.

The same article cites the increasing popularity of cats over the more dependent and time-intensive dogs as evidence of our busyness, by the way.

Even Robinson agrees that, whatever the reality, we *feel* busier. His Use of Time Project survey in 1985 reported 32 percent of us "always feel rushed." By 1992, the figure had risen to 38 percent in a survey by the National Recreation and Parks Association. Think about that. Almost two out of every five of us report always feeling rushed.

The numbers soar for certain categories. It is not surprising that working mothers topped the charts in the 1992 survey with a 64 percent "too busy" self-rating. No matter what Robinson says, I suspect working mothers feel they're too busy because they are too busy.

A Nation of Watchers and Shoppers?

However much free time we have, a two-year Gallup Poll bears out Robinson's contention that we spend a lot of it in front of the tube. Watching TV ranks way ahead of any other leisure-time activity, from 26.2 percent on Sunday to 34.1 percent on Thursday. Reading and socializing vie for second place, with 8.9 percent (or 5.29 hours a week) for socializing on Fridays.

If you can't find us in front of the television, Schor suggests you try the shopping mall. We spend three to four times as many hours a year shopping as do Western Europeans, she reports, and the United States now contains 16 square feet of shopping center for every man, woman, and child in the country.

All that shopping takes money, of course, and we've got it. The average American's yearly income of $22,000 is about sixty-five times the incomes of half the world's population, Schor notes.

We work to earn to spend. When not earning or spending, we relax in front of the tube. And we say we don't have enough time.

How Are You "Spending" Your Life?

This book is about you. So how about it? Are you too busy? Are you wasting too much time? That's not up to Robinson or Schor or Cook

> Almost two out of every five of us report always feeling rushed.

or anybody else to decide. You get to decide what's a waste of your time. And you get to decide how you're going to spend that time.

First, you need to know how you're spending your time now—not the "average American" from Robinson's surveys, and not some hypothetical wage-slave in Schor's studies—you. Are you willing to take a close, honest look at the way you spend your time (which is to say, the way you live)? If you don't like what you find, will you use the results to redirect your efforts and energies?

To do so takes effort and self-awareness. It also takes courage.

Get yourself a notebook just for this exercise. Make sure it's portable, fitting in your purse, coat pocket, backpack, or attaché case. You'll want to have it with you all the time. On the first page of that notebook, list the major categories you want to track. Your list will be different from mine or anybody else's.

Certainly we'll all include the same basic categories, such as "sleep." (I've never met anyone who doesn't sleep, at least some of the time, although a lot of us don't sleep as much as we'd like to or think we should. More on that in a later chapter.) But you may want to differentiate between "bed sleep" and "nap-in-the-living-room-recliner sleep," for example.

We'll all have "eat" on our lists of basic time-consuming activities, but again, you may want to split food time into regular sit-down meals, eat-and-run drive-through raids on nutrition, and foraging (or snacking or noshing or whatever you call it).

Is "work" specific enough for you? It depends on how much you want to learn from this self-study. I suspect most of us will want to keep closer tabs on exactly what we're doing at work, breaking time into categories such as "meetings" (perhaps also differentiating between "productive meetings" and "total-waste-of-time meetings"), "report writing," "responding to telephone inquiries," "commute time" (possibly a major and previously unnoted time-consumer), and even "break time." (Don't be afraid to chart breaks. You may well discover that you take too few rather than too many.)

The more categories you create, the more precise and helpful the information, and the more annoying keeping track will be. The more you decide to put in, the more you'll get out later. Err on the

> Are you willing to take a close, honest look at the way you spend your time?

> Err on the side of overscrupulous data keeping. The information you collect here is going to serve you well.

side of overscrupulous data keeping. The information you collect here is going to serve you well.

Let your list sit overnight and take another look at it, adding and deleting as you see fit. Have you forgotten anything? You can, of course, add items during your survey week if you haven't anticipated everything here. The key is to note the items you're interested in tracking and to be sure your system enables you to account for your time fairly accurately. (It will do no good to list two hours a day as "miscellaneous.")

Give each item on your list a number, a letter, or both. "Work" (as in job) could be 1, for example, and "going to waste-of-time meetings" could be 1-A. But keep it simple. The system should help you gather data, not get in your way.

You're almost ready to start your self-study. First, write down your estimate of how much time per week you spend in each category. You can do this in total hours, in percentage of time spent, or both. When you're done, you'll probably want to convert hours into percentages anyway.

For example, if you figure you average seven hours of sleep a night, you can write "49" (7 x 7) next to that category on your list. Since there are 168 hours in a week, 49÷168 computes to 29 percent. (Actually, 29.167 percent, if you need to be that precise. Or "about 30 percent" may suit your purpose.)

Next to your estimate, write the number of hours/percentage you think you ought to be sleeping each week. If in your heart of hearts you believe that Mom was right, for example, and that you really do need eight hours of sleep, you'd write in "64/33.3 percent" next to your "49/29 percent."

Now keep your time log for a full week. Try to pick a "typical" week (if there is such a thing), neither a vacation nor a business trip, one relatively free of major crises. If a crisis does erupt in the midst of the week you've chosen, you can always start over another week. It is important that you be persistent and precise.

Can you do two activities at once? Of course. In fact, traditional time-management books insist you do two, three, even four things at a time. But for the purpose of this survey, you're going to decide on the dominant activity at any given time. For example, if you're listening to a book-on-tape while driving to work, your dominant activity is driving to work. The book-listening is incidental. If you're reading a book with the television on, you need to decide whether you're mostly reading a book or watching television.

Start your log when you wake up on Day One.

> *6:15 A.M. Lay in bed, semiconscious, listening to "Morning Edition."*

Make your next notation when you significantly change your activity.

> *6:32 A.M. Dragged carcass out of bed. Bathroom. Shower. Dress.*
> *6:58 A.M. Breakfast.*

The smaller the increments, the more precise the results (and the more work the gathering of them).

> *6:59 A.M. Worked crossword puzzle.*
> *7:02 A.M. Stopped working crossword puzzle to let dog out in backyard.*
> *7:02:15 A.M. Resumed working crossword puzzle.*

Too precise? I doubt you'd find this level of precision desirable or helpful. I also doubt you'd keep recording that way for a full week. Make your notes in a way that will tell you what you want and need to know about yourself at the end of the week.

Be honest, even if it hurts. Folks tend to fudge downward on time spent watching television and upward on time spent exercising, for example. You want a true picture of your activities in a typical week. Then you can decide if you want to change anything.

Allow enough time at the end of your survey week to do the math. (No, you don't have to note this time on your log. You're finished with that.) Go back to your first page, where you made your list and created your Estimate column and your "should" (Ideal) column, and write in the Actual numbers. Each entry should now have three sets of numbers after it.

If you're reading a book with the television on, you need to decide whether you're mostly reading a book or watching television.

	ESTIMATE	IDEAL	ACTUAL
Sleep	49/29%	64/33.3%	52/31%

If you've been rigorous and honest, you may get some surprises.

	ESTIMATE	IDEAL	ACTUAL
Internet/ E-mail	7/4.2%	7/4.2%	68/40.5%

OK. You're not likely to get that big a surprise. But you may note some relatively large discrepancies among estimates, ideals, and actuals. If so, rejoice. You're a perfect candidate for time management. You may find that by adjusting actual times to conform more closely to your ideal, you'll improve your life significantly.

You may also find that you need to rethink some of your ideal times and your reasons for having established them.

If an adjustment leaps out at you now, note it in a fourth column, New Ideal, or Time-Management Goal.

	ESTIMATE	IDEAL	ACTUAL	NEW IDEAL
Internet/ E-mail	7/4.2%	7/4.2%	68/40.5%	14/8.4%

Then write the adjustment you intend to make in the form of a declaration.

> *"I will surf the Internet and answer e-mail no more than two hours a day,"* or *"I will average no more than fourteen hours online each week."*

Congratulations. You've taken the first big step in successful time management. You've accounted for your time. You've perhaps uncovered areas where you may be spending too much of that time and areas where you aren't spending enough. You've made some initial declarations concerning your future activities. If you did nothing else, this new level of self-awareness and resolve would be extremely helpful to you.

But there's much more you can do, if you're willing, to help yourself spend time wisely and well–not to satisfy the numbers on the chart, but to create a joy-filled as well as productive life.

Phyllis's time inventory revealed several surprises. Like most of us, she actually watched more television than she was aware of. In fact, when she wrote it down in her time log, she was embarrassed, not only by how much, but by what she was watching. She also isolated time spent working crossword puzzles–a benign addiction she picked up even before she married Ned.

Does this mean Phyllis has to give up TV, word games, and any other activity that relaxes her and gives her pleasure? Not at all. She gets to decide if these are ways she wants to spend time or if she'd be better off doing something else. But she wouldn't have been able to make those decisions about time until she became aware of how she really spent that time.

Phyllis–as well as the rest of us–can begin to gain the control she needs over her life by practicing effective "moment management," the topic of our next chapter.

But there's much more you can do, if you're willing, to help yourself spend time wisely and well.

Time-Management Tips

1. Keep a log to track how you really spend your time–especially noting passive time-eaters like watching television.
2. Use your log to make a list of specific ways you'll reallocate your time.

Chapter 4

Moment Management

In this chapter, you'll learn:

- How small amounts of wasted time may be adding up to a big time-management problem

- How to apply three basic principles of moment management to your own life

- How to become more aware of the choices you make every day

- How to make choices rapidly and effectively

- Why the only wrong decision is the one you refuse to make

"What choice do I have?"

Ned and Phyllis have started to look at the way they spend their time—which is to say, their lives—with an eye to working more efficiently and effectively, certainly, but also to freeing up time for other areas of their lives, the relaxation and leisure activities they never seem to find time for.

But they've both found that much of their day seems to be prescheduled so that they really don't have a lot of choices about time management until the end of the day, when they're often too exhausted to do much of anything anyway.

They need to learn to practice *moment management*, the fine art of taking control of some of the many small decisions they make—often without even knowing it—during each day.

Perhaps you've heard the expression "penny wise—pound foolish."

Some of us are pretty good at keeping track of our pennies. We control day-to-day expenses carefully, shopping around, for example, for the best price on toilet paper. We clip coupons from the Sunday paper and wait to shop on "Double Coupon Day." We'll drive the extra six blocks to save two tenths of a cent on each gallon of gas we pump ourselves (to save the service charge, of course).

But some of us might also fall into the "pound foolish" category, squandering all those carefully saved pennies and a whole lot more on a large impulse purchase, or worse, failing to plan properly for retirement.

With time, many of us are the opposite—pound wise but penny foolish.

You might be quite careful about making large time commitments, shying away, for example, from a promise to serve on a committee (a well-known black hole for time), no matter how worthy the cause. You might be so good at this sort of time management, in fact, that you have a hard time understanding why you still wind up with too much activity to try to fit into too little day. If you fall into that category, your primary problem might not be the "pounds"—the major time commitments of weeks, days, even hours. It's those pesky "pennies," the unnoticed minutes each day you spend doing something

> With time, many of us are the opposite—pound wise but penny foolish.

you don't want or need to be doing or doing nothing at all while you wait for someone or something.

"Penny time" doesn't count because you don't bother to count it. But it adds up. If you could somehow save all those pennies of time that are slipping through the holes in your life pockets now, you'd find yourself with extra hours and with breathing space between times.

Even our "penny wise" money examples illustrate the point. How many "time pennies" does a coupon clipper spend clipping all those coupons? If you divided the money you saved by the time you spent clipping, would you be paying yourself minimum wage?

But time isn't really money. We only think it is. Time is life. If you enjoy clipping coupons, if it relaxes you, if you do it with your life mate while the two of you are watching a television show you enjoy, then you're getting paid in more than money, and coupon clipping is probably a good time investment for you. If coupon clipping is onerous—if you hate it, dread it, put it off, resent it—then it just isn't worth the $4.15 you saved doing it. You decide.

That's the whole point of this book. It's your call. Make enough good calls, and you'll find yourself with time dividends. Take care of the minutes, and the hours will take better care of themselves.

> Time isn't really money.
> We only think it is.
> Time is life.

Three Basic Principles of Moment Management

1. Decide, Don't Drift.
2. Review Your Options.
3. Practice Instant Response.

Let's look at each principle in turn.

Decide, Don't Drift

How many decisions do you make each day without even noticing? Probably a lot more than you think.

When the alarm goes off, will you leap right out of bed (yeah, right) or roll over and grab an extra ten minutes?

Let's list a basic half dozen you might make every work day before you even leave the house in the morning—along with a few of the dozens of subdecisions these simple six involve.

Alarm

Actually, it starts the night before. Will you set the alarm or let yourself wake up naturally? If you set the alarm, what time will you set it for? When it goes off, will you leap right out of bed (yeah, right) or roll over and grab an extra ten minutes?

Exercise

Yes. Of course. But today? First thing in the morning? In this weather? With my bum knee acting up?

Shower

Or bath? Wash the hair or skip it this time? Deodorant? Which brand?

We haven't even mentioned toothbrush (hard or soft bristles, manual or electric?), toothpaste (plaque remover? whitener? paste? gel? powder?), or brushing motion (up and down, side to side?).

Wardrobe

Even the fashion challenged (I put myself in this category) spend some time thinking about clothes—no, not whether to wear them or not, but which, and what goes with what. Heavy coat or windbreaker? Umbrella?

Breakfast

Yes, it's the most important meal of the day, but who has time?

If breakfast, what kind? Mom used to serve us bacon and eggs, toast with gobs of butter, and whole milk. Now we're supposed to gnaw on tree bark. What's really best to eat?

Transportation

Most of us need to get ourselves someplace else to start the work day. Do you walk? (How many of us live close enough to work to actually walk there?) Bike? Take the bus? Join a car pool? Drive by yourself (by far the popular choice in southern California, where I grew up, and in Madison, Wisconsin, where I live now)?

And these are the normal days. We haven't even gotten to those days when the kid's sick and can't go to day care, or the boss calls a 7:00 A.M. staff meeting, or you wake up to ice-covered streets, or the bus drivers go on strike.

It's a wonder any of us get to work at all. (Try telling the boss that the next time you're late, right?) How do we do it?

Because we don't really *decide* all those decisions at all.

How much conscious thought do you give to your morning routine? If you're like most of us, your wake-up call, your wardrobe, and your breakfast menu don't really change much from day to day. In fact, these mundane parts of the day—and lots of others—have probably become so much a matter of habit and routine, you'd feel funny doing things any other way, and you'd have a hard time changing your pattern (as we all find out when we go on a diet, try to get up half an hour earlier to exercise, or give up donuts for Lent).

That's a good thing. If you spent a lot of time pondering your teeth-brushing technique every morning, you'd really have a time-management problem. Putting all this stuff on autopilot frees up your brain cells for more complex activities, such as negotiating rush-hour traffic.

Autopilot is fine—that is, so long as your routine is serving you well. But you may be unknowingly wasting precious time and energy in rituals so ingrained they take on the force of natural law.

You get to decide which of those rituals, if any, and other parts of your daily life you want to examine, with an eye toward streamlining or even eliminating some functions while perhaps incorporating other, more worthwhile activities.

This all takes time, of course, and time is precisely what you haven't got enough of. But a little bit of time and effort now can save you uncounted hours in the long run. And despite the urgencies of the day, you are living for the long run.

Do It Yourself

How many decisions do you make between the time you wake up and the time you take off for work or begin your work-at-home routine? Carry a notepad and pencil with you one morning and note the decisions, forcing yourself to become conscious of "choices" you make without even thinking about them.

Are there any you might like to modify or even delete from your routine? If so, you've created the beginning of your personal moment management program.

Review Your Options

"What choice do I really have?"

That question often prevents us from even attempting meaningful change in the way we live. It really does feel as if much of the day, the week, life itself is prescribed for us. Of course, we have to get up and go to work, pay taxes, gain weight as we age, dislike our mothers-in-law, and become estranged from our teenage children.

Not true. You always have a choice.

Say it again. It's the most important statement you're likely to run across today: you always have a choice.

If it doesn't feel that way, it's because the consequences are so dire—perhaps even unthinkable—that you refuse to consider them.

Which brings us to the bad-news corollary and to the good news about choices: you always have a choice, and you always have to pay the price for your choices.

Blow off work today? Yeah, you could do that. But...

> You always have a choice, and you always have to pay the price for your choices.

- You've used up all of your vacation and sick time, and you'll get docked a day's pay if you don't show up.
- Worse, you've used up all the boss's good will. If you don't show, you're history.
- You have the most important presentation of your career. If you aren't there, the deal falls through.
- Seven associates are counting on you.

Which is to say that you'll pay a price, in loss of wages or job, loss of the esteem or confidence of those you work with. The price is probably much too high for a day's frolic in the park. But you do have that choice. Affirming that you do helps you regain a sense of control over your life, essential to any real attempt at streetwise time management.

The existence of that choice becomes clear when something happens that overshadows the importance of the day's work and the consequences of not doing it. Such occurrences include:

- Your child waking up with a raging fever
- One aging parent calling to tell you that the other is failing and calling for you
- Your water breaking

You always have a choice.

Choose not to pay your taxes? You could do that. You could also go to jail, of course, or pay a fine, or escape detection but lose sleep and psychic energy worrying about that knock on the door.

You get to decide when and how you'll exercise your freedom to choose.

Often the hardest part will be perceiving that you have a choice at all. Then the trick becomes seeing all the options available to you. You may have brainstormed for solutions to a problem at work; you can do the same sort of process yourself about your life decisions.

Many of the specific time-management techniques in this book begin with a rapid but wide assessment of choices. Stress the word *rapid* in that last sentence. None of this makes any sense as time management if it takes you too long to do it.

Practice Instant Response

In one sense, those earth-shattering events we just talked about make decision making easy. Your father is dying 2,000 miles away. You hop on a plane. No agonizing. No comparison shopping for the best air fare. You just go—and worry about picking up the pieces later. Terrible emergencies give you a great gift—clear focus.

Smaller choices may give you greater difficulty, especially when the consequences seem to be nearly equal and nearly equally bad—one of those "damned if you do and damned if you don't" deals.

You had planned to bike to work, but the morning brings heavy rain. You can drive—and put up with the hassle and expense of downtown parking—or take the bus and endure the waiting and the walk from the bus stop to the office.

Do It Yourself

Think of an experience when an emergency exploded, blowing your schedule to bits. Recall how you felt at the time and what thoughts went through your mind. What action did you decide to take?

What happened to all those must-do jobs and A-1 priorities you had planned to be doing?

Caution

One of the symptoms of clinical depression is an inability to make even seemingly simple decisions. If you seem to be struggling too hard to choose a breakfast cereal, and you exhibit any of the other symptoms of depression—weight loss or gain, trouble sleeping, listlessness, for example—you might want to check it out with your doctor.

You don't especially like either option, but neither one's going to kill you, or even, truth to tell, make that much difference. You shouldn't waste a lot of time deciding. You make the call, and then you act.

And you shouldn't spend even one second second-guessing—not even if the sun breaks through the clouds while you're standing at the bus stop, making you wish you'd taken a chance and rode your bike after all.

To become a streetwise and effective minute manager, you need to practice the art of instant response—recognizing the options, making the call, and acting quickly. It's the new three Rs:

- Read (the situation)
- Reflect (on the choices)
- Respond (with decisive action)

You need to do this all in minutes, or even seconds, and without the fourth R:

- Remorse (over choices made)

What if you make the wrong choice?

Wrong choices fall into one of two categories: your choice either didn't actually make any significant difference or it did.

If it didn't really matter, even if, with the magic clarity of hindsight, you now see that another choice might have in some sense been better, let it go. Banish the second-guessing from you mind. It's a waste of time and energy.

If your decision did matter and now seems wrong to you, a mistake, admit the mistake, accept the blame and the consequences, make it right in any way you can, and move on.

And know this: no matter how it looks at the moment, most decisions, even some of the large ones, fall into the first category. Most of the time, you can't really make a mistake. The only mistake you can make is not making a decision.

"I took the road less traveled," the poet Robert Frost said, "and that has made all the difference." Sure. The decision to get married (or not, or to someone else, or later), to move from the country to the city (or the city to the country, or from one city to another, or to stay right where you are), to take the job (or not, or pursue another career) makes a huge difference. But you can't see the consequences when you make the decision. And whatever decision you make, you'll have suffering and elation, pain and pleasure, growth and learning. In that sense, no decision can ever truly be a mistake.

Phyllis has stopped cooking the traditional big breakfast for Ned and herself. She discovered that she likes cold cereal and fruit just fine, thank you, and Ned really feels better with a large glass of orange juice when he gets up and a granola bar or some other mid-morning energy snack to carry him to lunch.

Phyllis had grown up with the attitude that you needed a good breakfast ("good" involving lots of work for her mother) every morning. She had never consciously considered starting the day any other way.

Now that she does, Ned and she have extra time in the morning, Ned has lost a couple of unwanted pounds, and they both feel better—except for the occasional flush of guilt Phyllis feels for not doing things the way her mother did.

She has taken an important first step, simply by questioning her assumptions about the way things have to be. In the days ahead, Ned and Phyllis will find many other ways to make time available to them through effective moment management.

Do It Yourself

Think of a major life decision you made at least five years ago. Such decisions include:

- Getting married or divorced
- Moving to another area of the country
- Making a major career choice
- Deciding to have or to adopt a baby

Try to remember the factors you weighed in making that decision.

Now list all the unforeseen consequences of your decisions, the results you didn't and probably couldn't anticipate when you made the call.

If you could go back in time and remake your decision, would you do anything differently?

Can you in any sense call your decision a mistake?

What evidence do you have that another decision would have worked out better?

Time-Management Tips

1. Hoard the minutes so you can better spend the hours.
2. Decide how you spend your time. Don't let others decide for you.
3. Read the situation, reflect on the choices, and respond with decisive action.
4. Don't waste a second second-guessing.

PART II

Great Ways to Get More Out of Your Days

Summary of Part II

1. Unless you schedule rest and play and plan time to nurture relationships, you may neglect these vital areas.

2. Don't wait until you're too tired to rest. Rest when you need to, with short vacation breaks all through the work day.

3. Don't take on too much, and build in a cushion of time to accommodate the inevitable delays and interruptions.

4. Figure out what you don't need to do and then stop doing it.

5. It doesn't matter where you start. It only matters that you start.

6. When life seems overwhelming, take a moment to relax and get your bearings.

If you're like most folks, you use some kind of to-do list to help get you through the day.

Some folks use fancy day planners. Others rely on a pocket calendar or computer valet. Some assign priority values to their tasks, whereas others just scribble down the stuff they dare not forget.

But even if you only keep the list in your head, you've probably got a list. The more hectic your day, the more complicated your list, and the more that list drives you through the day.

That may be a problem. It could be that the list is running you instead of the other way around.

In this part, we'll take a look at that task list and determine how—and even if—you should be using one to help you become a streetwise time manager.

Knowing that startup time often involves a lot of wasted time, we'll look at specific ways to get a fast start on every project.

Streetwise time management is about more than speed. Sometimes it's about stopping altogether. We'll look at ways to consciously break momentum and get you the rest you need—when you need it—to keep you working efficiently.

Do You Run the List, or Does the List Run You?

In this chapter, you'll learn:

- How to prioritize the tasks that must get done
- How to make a to-do list, not a wish list
- How to create a format for your list that suits your needs
- How to include long-range goals in your scheduling
- Why you can't afford to be over-organized

Chapter 5

Ever since he took a time-management seminar three weeks ago, Jason has been getting up fifteen minutes earlier each morning to prepare a to-do list for the coming day. After listing all the necessary tasks he can anticipate, he rates them by priority: A-1 for the most crucial, A for important, B for useful but not essential, C for worth doing but least important. Except that he does seem to wind up a flurry of A-1 notations with a smattering of As and no B or C ratings.

In the three weeks, he's never once managed to accomplish all the items on his list. He has gotten grouchy from the lost sleep and frustrated by his sense of failure. He's ready to chuck time management and go back to muddling through the way he was before. At least that way, he doesn't have a written record of all the things he didn't do.

There's nothing new about the to-do list. Folks have been jotting down lists of things they need to do and then checking each item off the list as they do them for a long time. The more you need to do, and the more pressure you feel to do it, the more helpful keeping a list can be.

Alan Lakein spelled out the uses and misuses of the to-do list in his groundbreaking 1973 book, *Time Management: How to Get Control of Your Time and Your Life*. He showed us how to prioritize those to-do items, making sure we tackled the essential items first. Lakein's idea was to use the list to get everything done, starting with the most important. But the overall goal was to live a happy, healthy, well-rounded life. Lakein had the wisdom to consider rest, recreation, and relationships as important components of the full life.

Subsequent time-management coaches seem to have lost Lakein's gentle wisdom and sense of proportion. The to-do list has become a means of fitting ever more work into the same limited twenty-four-hour day. The list has become a tyrant, pushing us to *do more* instead of helping us to do *better* and to do *right*.

Time-management consultant Anne McGee-Cooper identifies the resulting sense of frenzy in her book *Time Management for Unmanageable People: The Guilt-Free Way to Organize, Energize and Maximize Your Life*. When you try to get more done in the same amount of time, she counsels, you run the risk of overload, a

> The to-do list has become a tyrant, pushing us to *do more* instead of helping us to do *better* and to do *right*.

phenomenon known in computer lingo as "thrashing," when the computer gets too many commands at once and gets stuck trying to decide what to do first.

There are other dangers inherent in developing a list of tasks for the work day. To illustrate those dangers, let's look at a sample to-do list, one that makes just about every possible mistake.

The To-Do List from Hell

We'll impose a midlevel of organization, less than a minute-by-minute script but more than a simple list of tasks.

To Do Before Work

- Exercise: 100 sit-ups, 50 push-ups, 25 squats
- Review agenda and materials for staff meeting
- Read *The Wall Street Journal*
- Morning commute (seventeen minutes)
- Listen to motivational self-help tape on time management

Morning

- Answer faxes, overnight mail, voice mail, e-mail (8:00–9:00)
- Staff meeting (9:00–10:30)
- Organize research for quarterly report (10:30–11:45)
- Drive to lunch meeting (fifteen minutes)
- Lunch meeting (noon–1:30)

Afternoon

- Write draft of quarterly report (1:30–3:00)
- Meet with committee on workplace expectations (3:00–4:30)
- Afternoon commute (eighteen minutes—pick up dry-cleaning)

That's it. There's your work day, all laid out. Do all that and you'll likely be laid out, too.

Do It Yourself

Recall a day when you got thrashed, overloading a day with too much to do and too little time to do it. Don't use a day when an emergency erupted. Choose instead one of those "typical" disaster days.

What factors caused you to try to do more than you could?

How much of the overloading came from outside sources?

How much was a result of your own overambitious scheduling?

At any point in the day did you perform a task you could just have easily put off until later in the day or another day altogether?

In hindsight, do you see any activities that seemed important at the time but that, as it turns out, didn't really need doing at all?

Notice that your ability to accomplish all the tasks on your list depends on split-second timing. Everything must go perfectly—no traffic jams, no emergencies, no interruptions. When's the last time you had a perfect day—no traffic jams, no emergencies, and no interruptions? That's what I thought.

The Day as You Really Live It

You sleep through the snooze alarm twice. (You're exhausted from your wrestling match with yesterday's to-do list.) No time for exercise or, for that matter, breakfast—which didn't even make it onto the list. You're down two, feeling guilty and grouchy before you've even gotten started.

You glance at your meeting notes, skim the left-hand column on the front page of the *Journal*, and sprint to the car. You're in luck. The car starts, even though you've put off getting it serviced—no time. No idiot ruins your day by getting into an accident ahead of you, and traffic flows fairly smoothly.

Even so, the commute takes 18.5 minutes, so you're already running ninety seconds behind. You didn't get to listen to your motivational tape, either, because the tape deck in the car jammed. (Better put "get tape deck fixed" on your future to-do list.)

You can anticipate the rest. (You don't have to anticipate it. You've *lived* it.) You don't get anywhere near through the voice mail, let alone the e-mail. The meeting starts late and runs long—don't they always? It's too late to tackle the quarterly report, and you spend the rest of the morning answering the phone and battling faxes, most of which could have just as well come by snail mail—or pony express, for that matter. (What makes us think our stuff needs to be communicated instantly?)

After a lunch you didn't taste and a meeting you didn't need, you finally get a few minutes for those notes for the quarterly report. You're tired, grouchy, full of a chicken enchilada that refuses to settle down and let itself be digested, and preoccupied with the meeting you've got to get to in a few minutes. No wonder the report refuses to organize itself.

> When's the last time you had a perfect day—no traffic jams, no emergencies, and no interruptions? That's what I thought.

Another meeting (starts late, runs long), another snarling, gut-wrenching commute, a wasted stop at the dry-cleaners (in your rush this morning, you left your claim ticket on the bureau).

Another day shot.

And now it's time to start the second shift, the work day put in at home sweet home.

Pretty dismal scene, isn't it?—and not really that much of an exaggeration.

Did the to-do list help? Sure. It provided a record of what you didn't get done while you were doing other things, and it helped you to go to bed guilty and frustrated by every unchecked item. What went wrong? You failed to plan for the unplanned. You weren't realistic about your own capacities or about the real time required to do things. You left stuff off the list that nevertheless needed to be done.

In short, this wasn't a to-do list. It was a wish list, a fantasy, an unattainable dream, an invitation to frustration and fatigue.

Ten Ways to Create a Healthy To-Do List

1. Don't put too much on it. This is fundamental. Master this one, and everything else falls into place.

Be realistic in your expectations and your time estimates. Make a real-world list, not an itinerary for fantasyland. Otherwise, you'll spend the day running late, running scared, just flat-out running to catch up. You won't even have time to notice how your efficiency drops as you become cranky and exhausted.

Don't jam the list. Let it help you organize, keep on task, and get the job done.

If by some miracle things take less time than you had allowed for, rejoice! You've given yourself the gift of found time, yours to spend however you want and need to.

To help follow rule 1, follow rule 2.

2. Put some air in it. Overestimate the commute time—allowing for the idiot dawdling in the fast lane and the cautious creep who makes you miss the left-turn arrow. Factor in the wait before the meeting and the time spent bouncing around in voice-mail limbo.

> What went wrong? You failed to plan for the unplanned. You weren't realistic about your own capacities or about the real time required to do things.

3. List possibilities, not imperatives. This speaks more to your frame of mind when you make the list than to the specific items on that list. You're listing those tasks that you hope, want, and, yes, need to finish during the day. You're not creating a blueprint for the rest of the universe, and your plans don't have the force of natural law.

What happens if you don't get to everything on your list? What happens, for example, if you wake up simply too ill to crawl out of bed, let alone tackle the crammed work day? I'm talking serious sick here, not the borderline sore throat and headache that might keep you in bed on a Saturday but never on a Monday. In a way, the serious sickness is easier because you don't have to decide whether or not to attempt to go to work, and you don't have to feel guilty about staying in bed while the rest of the world tends to business. (Depending on your tolerance for pain and your level of guilt, you might have to be near death to achieve this state.)

Let's suppose you're sick enough to have to stay flat on your back in bed for two days, and you can barely wobble around the house in bathrobe and slippers on the third. In all, you miss an entire week of work.

Meanwhile, what happened to the stuff on your to-do list?

The meetings went on without you. Folks figured out they could live without the quarterly report for another week. (It was that or write it themselves.) You've got 138 unheard messages on the voice mail (62 of them from the same person); 178 items in the e-mail box (52 of them the result of a list server getting "stuck" and sending out the same message multiple times); and a desk awash in memos, faxes, overnight letters, and other unnatural disasters. You take stuff home for a week, trying to get caught up.

That's bad. It isn't that bad. You didn't die. You didn't lose a loved one. Western civilization did not grind to a halt. Commerce and government managed to struggle on without you. It's too late to respond to some of those urgent memos and messages, but it turns out they really didn't need a response after all.

Try to remember that the next time you're relatively healthy but nevertheless falling behind on the day's tasks. We say things like:

> Let's suppose you miss an entire week of work, what happened to the stuff on your to-do list? Western civilization did not grind to a halt. Commerce and government managed to struggle on without you.

"Don't sweat the small stuff...and it's all small stuff."
"In a hundred years, who'll know?"

But we don't really believe or act on such adages. This is not to suggest that what you do isn't important—at least as important as playing baseball. I'm simply saying that you, and I, and everybody else, need to keep things in proper perspective.

4. Don't carve the list on stone tablets. When I first started making a to-do list each day, I'd type the list into my computer and run it off on the laser printer. What a beautiful and impressive document it was, with crisp black letters on clean white stock, a regular work of art.

That was the problem. I wouldn't draw a mustache on the Mona Lisa, and I wouldn't cross out or rearrange anything on a laser-printed to-do list.

Your list has to be flexible if it's going to do you any good. You have to be able to change it, digress from it, flip it on its ear, add to it, wad it up and toss it in the recycle bin if it's really going to help.

Find a flexible format that works for you. If you like an intricate grid system, with squares for every five minutes during the day, go for the grid. If crayon on butcher paper is more your style, start scrawling.

Don't try to fit a format. Find or create a format that fits you.

5. Order creatively. Make sure the most important tasks get done before you drown in a sea of relative trivia. Answer the e-mail first if it's the top priority on your list. If it isn't, schedule it for later in the day. Don't do it first simply because it's there, demanding attention, or because it's relatively easy, or because you've gotten in the habit of doing it first.

Vary your pace, alternating difficult and easy, long and short, jobs requiring creative thought with rote functions. Change activities often enough to keep fresh.

Attack mentally taxing jobs when you're most alert and energetic. (We'll talk about your biorhythms in a later chapter.)

6. Break the boulders into pebbles. When I first started editing my newsletter, *Creativity Connection*, I boxed off an entire after-

For Example

Think you've had a bad day at the office? Consider former Los Angeles Dodger center fielder Willie Davis, who faced disaster during the second game of the 1965 World Series against the Baltimore Orioles. In the top of the fifth inning of a 0 to 0 tie, with Dodger ace Sandy Koufax on the mound, Davis managed to make three errors in one inning, including two on the same play, to blow the game. The Dodgers never recovered, losing the series in four straight games.

After his record-setting game, Davis was philosophical. "It ain't my life," he told a vast radio and television audience. "And it ain't my wife. So why worry?"

Another baseball player/philosopher, Satchel Paige, put it this way: "Don't look back. Something might be gaining on you."

noon on my calendar to "Do newsletter." I had carefully counted backwards from the publication date to allow for printing and mailing, and I figured four hours was plenty of time to write and edit the material and lay it out in PageMaker.

I was, of course, an idiot. Folks didn't get their copy in on time. I didn't get mine written on time either. When I finally got the first page laid out, it vanished into the ether. (Where does all that stuff go after it disappears from the computer screen?)

The longer and later I struggled, the deeper into the mire I sank. When I finally got done, I was a mess. So was the newsletter.

I no longer schedule one session to "Do newsletter." I schedule several sessions, one to write, edit, and lay out the reviews; another to select and edit reader letters; another for the writer profile; and so forth. I prepare the market updates relatively close to final deadline to keep them current, let the finished pages sit and cool off for at least a day, make my final read through, and send it to the printer. I've even gotten so I rarely launch a page layout into the cosmos.

The newsletter comes out in much better shape. So does its editor.

7. Schedule breaks, goofs, time-out time, and little rewards. Most of us schedule "rest" for last—if we schedule it at all. By the time we get to it—if we get to it—it's too late to do us any good.

If you don't put rest on the list, you won't rest. So put it on the list. And don't save it for last. Plan the rest for when it will do you the most good, before you become too tense or exhausted. Brief rests at the right times will help you maintain a steady, efficient work pace.

Instead of waiting until the end of the day for that fifteen minutes of pleasure reading, for example, schedule three five-minute reading breaks during the day. You may even want and need to schedule that game of catch with your kid or that walk around the neighborhood with your spouse.

I know—that sounds awful. What kind of monster has to schedule things like that? Lots of us monsters. Instead of calling yourself names, start planning a balanced, fulfilling life.

8. Schedule for long-range as well as short-range goals. You know you should do some serious financial planning. You know you

> If you don't put rest on the list, you won't rest.
> So put it on the list.
> And don't save it for last.

should have a current will. You know you should create a systematic plan for home maintenance and repair.

If you know all that and never seem to get to it—put it on the schedule.

9. Be ready to abandon the list. "If you only write the story that is planned," writer and teacher Ellen Hunnicutt tells her students, "you miss the story that is revealed."

The same goes for the story of your life. The most important things you do probably never appear on any to-do list or show up on the day planner. Never become so well organized and so scheduled that you stop being alert to life's possibilities—the chance encounter, the sudden inspiration.

Not all surprises are bad surprises. It just seems that way sometimes.

10. You don't have to make a list at all. The to-do list is a tool. Techniques for creating an effective list are suggestions, not commandments. If they help, follow them—adapting and modifying them to fit your own circumstances and inclinations. If they don't help, make your own kind of list, or don't make any list at all. You won't have "failed time management." You'll have simply discovered something that helps some folks and not others, and that doesn't turn out to be helpful to you.

Bonus Suggestion: Create a Not-To-Do List

Along with noting and organizing the tasks you'll do, you might also want to write down those things you *won't* do.

I'm not talking about the sorts of epic life-pledges that appear on lists of New Year's Resolutions, stuff like: Stop smoking, Don't nag, and Cut consumption of chocolate. You can certainly make that kind of list if you find it helpful. I'm referring here to day-to-day tasks that have fallen to you by custom, habit, or lot but that should properly be done by someone else or not done at all.

Examine large tasks (serving on the school board) and small ones (responding to every memo from the district supervisor) to make sure (1) they need to be done and (2) you're the one who needs to do them. If the task fails on either count, put it on the not-to-do list.

Just for Fun

For a delightful depiction of the dangers of developing list addiction (which surely must have its own twelve-step programs and support groups by now), read "A List," one of Arthur Loebel's delightful "Frog and Toad" stories.

"I have many things to do," Toad realizes one morning. "I will write them all down on a list so that I can remember them."

He writes down "wake up" and, realizing that he's already done that, crosses it off—a great momentum-builder.

Other items include "getting dressed," "eating breakfast," and "going for a walk with Frog."

Disaster strikes, as it must in any great work of literature. While Frog and Toad are on that walk, a gust of wind snatches the paper from Toad's hand. Like Dumbo, who thinks he can't fly without his "magic" feather, poor Toad finds himself incapable of acting without the list to guide him.

Toad's story has a happy ending, but I won't spoil it for you. You'll just have to make the time to read it for yourself.

Do It Yourself

If you don't already keep some sort of to-do list, create one now for the upcoming work day. If you've been keeping a list, use the ten tips we've just discussed to modify the way you make your next list if any of the suggestions seem appropriate.

Be as specific as you feel you need to be. Some folks use a detailed chronology, with each fifteen-minute segment of the day accounted for. Others simply list major projects with rough estimates of how much time they ought to take. Some list tasks in the order of importance. Others use some sort of code (A-1, A, B, C) to weight the importance of tasks.

As you live the day you've mapped out for yourself, write notes to yourself on the success or failure of your planning strategies. If you aren't able to get to all the items on your list, try to account for the gap between the real and the planned.

Do you need to modify the way you make your list?

Is list making a useful tool for you?

Streetwise time management isn't just or even primarily about doing more things in the same amount of time or doing the same number of things in less time. Time management also involves choosing to do the right things.

Jason decided to stick with the to-do list for another three weeks, modifying the way he made the list so that it could serve as a useful guide instead of a stick he could use to flog himself. He made a particular effort to be more realistic about how long tasks were likely to take and how many interruptions he was apt to have to contend with.

He found two immediate and unexpected dividends. First, he came to see that the "interruptions" he had been resenting were in fact an important part of his day and his workload. He was accomplishing a lot with these impromptu discussions but not giving himself any credit for them.

Second, he found that he had an easier time saying no to last-minute demands on his time since his time was already accounted for with a reasonable schedule.

He actually found that, by putting less on the list, he was winding up getting more done—and feeling a lot better about it.

Three weeks isn't quite long enough for the better to-do list to really take hold. Jason will need to keep at it for at least three more weeks to make constructive list management a healthy habit.

Time-Management Tips

1. Don't neglect the three Rs: Rest, Recreation, and Relationships.
2. Avoid task overload.
3. Allow time for the unplanned in your plan.
4. Be realistic about how much you can accomplish.
5. Create a not-to-do list of tasks you need to delegate or simply stop doing.

Getting Started

In this chapter, you'll learn:

- How to eliminate start-up rituals
- How to prepare mentally for any job
- How to silence the mental critics
- When to break off a work session

LaVonne has a terrible time getting started.

She works out of her home, transcribing audiotapes of interviews into typed notes for a variety of clients. She doesn't really mind the work and, in fact, even enjoys it most of the time, once she gets going. But she fiddles and diddles before every work session, finding jobs around the house to do, going for that second cup of coffee, finding an article in the morning newspaper just too fascinating to skip.

When she finally settles in at her workstation in her second-floor office, she invariably finds that she's left her earphones or some other vital piece of equipment someplace else.

"I'm a real procrastinator," she admits with a rueful grin.

She knows she's wasting a lot of time. She doesn't feel good about it–or herself. And she doesn't really understand why she does it.

And there's the key to this particular bit of streetwise time management for LaVonne, and for anybody who has a hard time getting started. Before you can begin to solve the problem, you have to figure out what's holding you up.

> "When the going gets tough, the tough get going."
> –Dwight David Eisenhower

A lot of us just find it tough to get going.

Most of us suffer to some extent from work aversion. Some of us like our work, and most of us at least don't hate it, but we'd still rather be doing something else most of the time. That's why they call it "work," right?

That aversion makes getting started the hardest part of any job. "Writer's block" gets the most attention, but folks encounter "meeting facilitator's block" and "plumber's block" and "computer programmer's block," too–that state of semiparalysis brought on by fear and pain and just plain old lack-of-want-to.

We all have to learn to work through the aversion if we want to maintain the habit of eating regularly. But some of us perform time-consuming start-up rituals before we start to work, and many don't really work effectively for several minutes even after starting.

You may not even be aware of your rituals, which makes them hard to get rid of. Some of your warm-ups may actually help prepare

> Most of us suffer to some extent from work aversion. Some of us like our work, and most of us at least don't hate it, but we'd still rather be doing something else most of the time.

you to work, but others may simply postpone the inevitable confrontation. Those are a waste of time, and you need to get rid of them.

Seven Ways to Get a Fast Start

1. Prepare mentally. Back at the turn of the century, a philosopher named Charles Haanel called the subconscious mind "a benevolent stranger, working on your behalf." For all of our subsequent research on the way the brain works, I've yet to encounter a better description.

You can get that subconscious stranger working for you on any job you have to perform. The night before the job, tell your subconscious exactly what you want to accomplish the following day. You're not issuing orders here. You're not telling the subconscious how you intend to do the job. That's part of the conscious planning stage.

You're simply planting the idea, giving that larger mind that exists outside of conscious thought time to mull and sift, combining images and ideas, amassing energy and positive attitude.

Instead of letting the subconscious disaster tapes play, visualize yourself performing exactly as you wish. This is particularly helpful if you're going to speak to a group or otherwise put yourself before an audience.

This isn't a matter of "wishing will make it so." Positive visualization won't cast a magic spell over your audience or make a difficult report any easier to write. But it will affect your behavior, helping you call forth your best effort by concentrating energies and consciousness.

For some great athletes, this ability seems to be a natural gift, no less than speed, strength, and coordination. They talk about actually seeing themselves hitting the home run, intercepting the pass, or returning the backhand baseline volley before they make the play.

What comes to some as a natural gift, you can develop as a tool.

2. Prepare physically. You should have your tools assembled and accessible before you begin the job. Stake out a specific place for the work, where you can keep everything you need within easy reach and leave stuff out between work sessions. That way, you eliminate time spent pitching camp and then tearing it down again each time.

Do It Yourself

Remember the last time you got ready to do a difficult job? How did you prepare yourself? Were you able to get right to work, or did you find yourself casting about for other things to do first? Did you actually welcome interruptions?

If you found yourself stalling, puttering, idling, or simply starting very slowly, this chapter will be especially useful for you.

Also, when you become accustomed to doing a job in a specific place, you'll be focused and ready to work as soon as you enter that place. It doesn't have to be fancy or even private. It just has to be yours, and it has to have the tools you need.

3. Map the terrain. Before you begin the trip, figure out where you want to go.

Remind yourself of your purpose. What's in it for you? For your organization? For the client or customer? If you can't answer these questions, save yourself time and effort—and ensure that you'll do a better job—by taking a few moments now to get the information you need and to focus on what you hope to accomplish.

If you still aren't sure, seek out the authorization, approval, or verification you need. Again, a few minutes spent here can save hours later. And you'll work more efficiently and confidently.

If the work involves several stages, write them down first. Don't try to create the sort of orderly outline only an English teacher could love. Just jot down the steps or ideas in the order they occur to you. Then number the items in proper sequence.

4. Start anywhere. If you aren't ready to start at the beginning, start someplace else.

You can't escape certain sequences. A plumber has to turn off the water before disassembling the pipes. But jobs often contain flexibility. The finished product has to be assembled in the proper order, but you don't necessarily have to tackle the components in that order.

When you're thinking your way through a problem, it doesn't matter where you start. It matters only that you start.

5. Start anyway. I've known lots of writers who have suffered from blocks at one time or another. Poets seem especially susceptible to the disease.

But the reporters who write on deadline for a daily newspaper never seem to get blocked. They often write when they feel lousy. They worry that lack of time has forced them to do a lousy job, but they write anyway. Folks who can't afford to get writer's block don't get it.

The same goes for plumber's block, CEO's block, and bus driver's block.

For Example

A movie director shoots the scenes in the most practical sequence, getting all the location shots before returning to the studio for the interiors, for example. These separate scenes become the raw material for the finished movie. If the director and the editors do their jobs well, the viewer can't tell (and doesn't care) in what order the scenes were shot; the movie tells a coherent, entertaining story. The seams don't show.

The poet can afford to wait for inspiration. The rest of us do the job, inspired or not. If you're good at your work and you give it honest effort, your mood won't show in the finished product. Nobody can tell whether or not you felt like doing it. Fact is, they don't even care. They're interested in the results, and the results can be just as good regardless of the mental anguish you felt while dragging yourself to the task.

6. Lock out the critics. We all make mistakes. Writers get to make theirs in private, and we can give ourselves the chance to fix them before anybody else sees them. But when Green Bay Packer quarterback Brett Favre throws an interception, half the known universe sees him do it (or so it seems in football-crazy Wisconsin), and there's no way he can pull the ball back and take the play over.

I know of lots of writers who compose their rough drafts as if a Lambeau Field full of rabid fans and multiple millions of TV viewers were watching. Even worse, they write with their editors perched on their shoulders, ready to pounce at the first sign of a dangling modifier.

Maybe you're doing your job that way, too, feeling the eyes of editor or boss or critic while you try to think your way through a challenge.

It's a two-step process: first the doing, and then the judgment. Just as an NFL quarterback has to shut out the howling of the mob and concentrate on the receiver, you have to shut out concerns about judgment during the process of creation. If you don't, you won't take a chance, try out an idea, or risk a "failure" in the eyes of the invisible judge.

You might even be afraid to start—and getting started is the only way you'll ever finish.

7. Stop before you need to. "Don't stop me. I'm on a roll."

Momentum is a wonderful feeling, especially when you've got a lot to do and not much time to do it. The last thing you want when the job is going well is an interruption. Common sense tells you to keep working until you're finished. If you can't finish the job in one sitting, you work until you're exhausted or until you run into a snag you can't work your way through.

But it actually makes a lot more sense to stop before you get too tired and before you reach a snag. If you stop because you're

Do It Yourself

Who's the harpie in your head?

Many of us carry around the voice of doom in our heads—a critical murmuring that makes us wary of tackling any job.

It could be the voice of a well-meaning parent warning you to "be careful," a teacher admonishing you to start living up to your potential, a boss counseling you to "work smarter, not harder" (whatever that means).

How about you? Do you have a naysayer whispering sour nothings in your subconscious? If so, isolate this nattering, and write down the negative message so you can talk back to it and dismiss it. You may have to do this several times over a period of weeks. If you stick with it, you'll still the voice, robbing it of its power.

When you do, you'll find yourself a lot less reluctant to take on a challenge.

stuck, you carry that "stuckness" with you until the next work session, building up an aversion to the task. That aversion is the stuff that mental blocks are made of.

But if you stop in midstride, sure of the next step you'll take, you'll come back to the job confident and even eager. You won't have to waste any time getting back into the groove because you won't have gotten out of it.

> By learning to take regular breaks when she needed them and to stop each day's work session knowing exactly how she was going to start up again tomorrow, she was able to wipe out much of her work avoidance.

When she examined the way she was working, LaVonne was able to figure out why she had such a hard time getting started. Since she had such a hard time starting, she tended to work in marathon sessions, not daring to stop for fear she'd lose too much time starting up again. She worked until she was tired and hungry, her back ached, and other demands on her time really began pressuring her.

But these long and painful work sessions were in fact contributing to the procrastination, causing LaVonne to subconsciously dread beginning a process that would invariably make her feel terrible before she stopped.

By learning to take regular breaks when she needed them and to stop each day's work session knowing exactly how she was going to start up again tomorrow, she was able to wipe out much of her work avoidance.

The fiddling and diddling are still a habit, which she consciously has to force herself to break, but it seems to be getting a little easier each time.

Time-Management Tips

1. Use positive visualization to call forth your best effort.
2. Map the terrain before you start the journey.
3. Start anywhere. Start anyway. Just start!
4. Stop short of frustration, to ensure a smooth start-up next time.

Chapter 7

Is Your Life a Constant Two-Minute Drill?

In this chapter, you'll learn:

- How to tell when you're overcommitted
- Why you should take several vacations every day—and how you can do it
- Six specific relaxation techniques for the office or anywhere else

Do It Yourself

You know you're running your two-minute offense when:

- You charge from meeting to meeting, appointment to appointment, with no time to gather your thoughts.

- You've taken lunch at your desk so often, your keyboard gets clogged with bread crumbs.

- The ringing phone makes you jump.

- You feel one bad surprise away from throwing up your hands and screaming.

- A long-time friend calls to tell you she's coming to town and would love to see you, but you make excuses because there's just no way you can spare the time.

- You aren't getting any exercise, but you feel exhausted.

- You crawl into bed at last—and can't fall asleep.

Edie feels herself running faster and faster just to stay even.

She careens from crisis to crisis, unable and unwilling to slow down. She's sure there's a better way. She doesn't like dropping into bed exhausted at the end of every marathon day. But who has time to plan ahead? Edie can barely cope with the moment.

Worse still, lately she finds herself having a hard time falling asleep, despite—or perhaps because of—her exhaustion. She's becoming concerned about her health and figures she should probably talk to a doctor, but she hasn't been able to find the time to schedule an appointment.

It's the most exciting and the longest two minutes in football. The trailing team has the ball and hope but no timeouts. The quarterback (we might as well put John Elway or Brett Favre in there; they're the best at pulling the game out in the last minute) drives his team down the field, working the clock and the sidelines, eating up yardage while preserving time. There's no time to huddle or even to take a breath. It's just take the snap, drop back, and throw.

For a football fan, the two-minute drill is a joy to watch. But as a way of living, it has its drawbacks.

You've had days, even weeks, like that. For short spells, it can be exhilarating—as long as you can keep one jump ahead of disaster. But the longer you sustain this killer pace, the more you suffer and the less efficient you become—not just in your work but in every aspect of life.

If you wait for life to ease up and for the bad surprises to stop coming, you may wait too long. You have to call an end to the two-minute drill, for yourself, your loved ones, and your colleagues.

But the more you worry about relaxing, the more tense you become. What now?

Let's move from the football field to the beach to illustrate a coping mechanism when the stress level gets too high. I grew up in southern California, and so, of course, I surfed. The ocean gave me a few scares and taught me humility. I remember one time in particular when I went body-surfing when the lifeguard was flying the yellow flag for caution.

The waves didn't look so bad from shore. But one of them took my measure, sucking me toward it with a savage undertow. I managed to catch the wave, but the curl at the crest drove me straight down and under. I hit bottom and spun completely around. I hadn't gotten much of a breath before I was pulled under, and my lungs were already fighting for air. I realized with what was left of my wits that I literally didn't know which way was up.

I started thrashing desperately, fighting the current and exhausting what was left of air and energy. All of my thrashing was actually holding me in place against the current and my body's natural tendency to rise in salt water. Had I kept struggling, I might not be here to tell you the story. Some instinct or impulse (or possibly just simple fatigue) stilled me. I went limp—and immediately began to rise toward the surface.

I had saved myself by doing nothing.

And that's what I suggest you do to save yourself when the surf gets scary. Relax mind and body and let the current carry you for a couple of minutes, four or five times a day. It will save you from the undertow.

Putting the Power in the Pause—Taking Minivacations Every Day

Take your break before you need it. Don't wait to be exhausted, and don't wait to be stuck. Break your momentum—and the buildup of stress and fatigue—with a sanity break in the midst of the chaos. Make the break a good habit, three or four times a day.

Here are seven ways to go on vacation without leaving your desk. After you read them, jot down three or four more of your own.

1. The breath break. This is about the simplest, cheapest vacation you'll ever take. For two minutes, just breathe. Take air way down into your belly. You should actually be able to feel your stomach rise with the intake of breath.

Haven't you been breathing already? Sort of. But as you hurry, and as you feel the pressure build inside you, your breath becomes shallow, and you don't get the oxygen you need. You'll especially notice this when you have to speak in front of a group. Your voice rises and gets squeaky, and your throat becomes dry and sore.

> Take your break before you need it. Don't wait to be exhausted, and don't wait to be stuck.

Do It Yourself

Complete this sentence: "Life is a pain in the..."

Where do you take out your stress? Shoulders, neck, and lower back are favorite targets, but you may have another body part you tend to beat up on, without realizing you're doing it.

To find your pressure point, take time out during a tough day. You'll want some privacy for this. Tense every muscle in your body. Make yourself into one big clenched fist. Then begin relaxing, starting with your toes and working your way up your body. The area that hurt the most when you clenched and that gives you the most relief as you relax is your hot spot.

If that doesn't work, take bodily inventory as you lie in bed at the end of a difficult day. The place that hurts is the place you should relieve during the day, before the hurting starts.

To combat the ill effects of this oxygen debt, you don't have to empty your mind or chant a mantra or wrap yourself into a yoga position. All you have to do is breathe deeply and slowly for a couple of minutes three, four, even five times a day. In private, with your feet up and your eyes closed would be nice, of course, but you can take a breath break in the middle of a meeting, behind the wheel of the car, or on the phone. Nobody needs to know you're sneaking oxygen.

2. The continental drift. Think of a place where you felt peaceful and content, "your own special island," as Bloody Mary sings in *South Pacific*. Harken back to a time when you were truly relaxed. Or create an imaginary oasis.

Then go there for two minutes.

Shut everything else out, close your eyes, and create the scene in your mind. See, hear, feel. Let warmth and peace wash over you.

You'll return refreshed after just a couple of minutes, and you'll know you can go back again soon.

3. Picture it and get rid of it. Something bothering you? Expel it from your mind.

Create a mental image of your nemesis, hot branding iron in hand, ready to poke and prod you. If your anger and frustration has an abstract source, give it specific shape. Lack of time making you crazy? Picture a clock gone berserk, its hands spinning out of control. Or make time into a huge Indiana Jones–style boulder, rolling toward you with desperate speed.

Then put the image into a bubble and imagine that bubble floating slowly up and away, becoming smaller and smaller until it finally disappears.

Action-movie alternative: forget the gentle bubble stuff; blow your troubles to smithereens.

Hey? Are you starting to enjoy this? Good. That's what vacations are for.

4. The shoulder shrug. We tend to take out our tensions on specific parts of our bodies. The shoulders are my favorite targets. Without knowing I'm doing it, I tense my shoulders as I work. If I don't catch myself at it, I end up with a sore neck and shoulders and a pounding headache.

I can break the tension, save my shoulders, and avert the headache by remembering to relax my shoulders and rotate them slowly and gently for a couple of minutes. On particularly bad days, the results are dramatic. My shoulders seem to drop several inches, and a soothing warmth flows up my neck.

I never even realize how tense I am until I unclench my muscles and relax. How about you? Are you tensing and clenching while you work?

5. The thought for the day. This one takes a bit of preparation, but it's well worth the effort. Collect pithy bits of wisdom, interesting observations, intriguing fragments of ideas, funny phrases, anything that snags your fancy. You can catch them everywhere—from the media, from conversation, from your own boundlessly creative and endlessly curious mind. Get in the habit of jotting them down as you run across them.

When it's time for a break, pull one of your gems out, read it a couple of times, and let yourself chew on it for two minutes. Don't direct your thoughts. Just let them wander where they will.

6. The object of your affection. Hold a picture of a person you treasure, an object that has special meaning for you, or a talisman (like that lucky silver dollar you've lugged around with you for years). Spend two minutes with it, again letting your thoughts roam.

7. Advanced resting technique, for the gifted and talented. Combine the breathing with any other relaxation activity.

It's a little like patting your head and rubbing your stomach at the same time, but with practice, you can master this advanced technique.

While taking that minivacation in the Rocky Mountains or pondering a pithy saying from your favorite philosopher, consciously slow and deepen your breathing.

This double dose of relaxation can work wonders—as long as you can relax while doing it. If it starts to become work, stop!

Do It Yourself

These six techniques work for me. What works for you? Take a two-minute break right now and write down several two-minute breaks you could take and enjoy on the job.

Why the Two-Minute Break Works

Will a two-minute break really do you any good?

Yeah. It really will. But you may feel uncomfortable breathing from your tummy the first few times, and you may not notice the effects right away. But if you stick with it, you'll feel the difference.

Here's why. As you come under fire in the daily wars, your body reacts instinctively, tensing muscles and doling out emergency rations of adrenaline and other natural uppers, getting you ready to fight your enemies or run away from them. These automatic responses work against you when you've got no one to fight and nowhere to run.

These reactions build on themselves, and you can get caught in a dangerous loop. You sense danger, and your body responds. That response in turn seems to verify the perception of danger and triggers more response.

No wonder you can't relax at the end of the day!

But the cycle can work for as well as against you. If you can relax your body—slowing your breathing, calming your heart—by taking a two-minute break, your panic will subside. You'll regain focus, clarity, and energy.

Free Twenty-One-Day Satisfaction-Guaranteed Tension Trial

I can assure you that these techniques have helped me greatly. You can prove they work for you by trying them for twenty-one days before drawing any conclusions about their effectiveness. Break up each work day with three or four of these short breaks for three weeks and see if you notice the difference.

How about it? Are you willing to try? You have nothing to lose but tension and that "quiet desperation" Thoreau warned us about so many years ago.

Edie's been taking minivacations several times a day for several weeks now, and she's starting to feel the difference!

Caution

You'll probably need help remembering to rest. You'll need to build breaks into your daily routine, and you'll probably need to plant reminders, in the form of a note in the briefcase, a Post-it on the refrigerator, an alarm clock. (Setting an alarm to remind you to rest? Whatever works.)

If you hang around a computer most of the day, as I do, you might be able to program your inanimate partner to remind you, with a beep or a scroll line ("Don't forget to relax!") or some such.

At first, she felt stupid when the self-programmed reminder to "Breathe!" crawled across the top of her computer screen. Sometimes when the work was going well, she even resented the notion that she should break the momentum.

But she was desperate enough, tense enough, driven enough to try anything, even something as radical as forcing herself to take a break.

After a couple of weeks, she stopped feeling stupid and started feeling good.

Now she's falling asleep faster and sleeping better at night, and she's noticed she has more energy and is more alert during the day.

She's discovering the power in the pause.

Time-Management Tips

1. Stop thrashing, so you can float to the surface in a crisis.
2. Take frequent, short rests when you need them to restore energy, clarity, and enthusiasm.

Putting Your Priorities in Order

Summary of Part III

1. Don't schedule "Lose weight." Schedule "Work out at the gym for forty minutes three times a week." Then do it!

2. Balance every addition to your schedule with a deletion of equal time.

3. Don't expect results immediately, and don't quit just because you backslide. A change in behavior takes time and practice.

4. Don't let the merely urgent push out the important. Schedule important activities that you aren't making time for now.

5. Ask the Lakein question: "Is this what I want or need to be doing right now?"

6. Follow the Pareto principle: do more of what works and less of what doesn't.

Activity doesn't equal productivity. You need to be sure you're doing the right things.

In this part, you'll get help in establishing clear goals and designing your activities to help you reach those goals.

You'll learn to focus on important tasks rather than letting the merely urgent eat up precious time and energy.

You'll also learn the ancient art of doing the possible instead of squandering time on unreachable goals and intractable people.

Learn How to Get Organized

In this chapter, you'll learn:

- If you're a TP, a CL, or some of each
- How to combine the best elements of both character types
- How to create specific action plans to achieve long-term goals
- Why you'll never *find* time to pursue long-term goals—and how you can *make* the time you need.

Not too many years ago, Jenny was an athlete. She has the volleyball trophies and the track ribbons in the closet to prove it. But these days, she can't seem to find the time for fun and games or any kind of exercise.

She drives to and from work and spends the day chained to a computer. By the time she shops, runs errands, cooks, and cleans, there's no time or energy left for jogging.

She watches what she eats, but her weight is still creeping up, and she feels sluggish, old, and slow.

For some of us, trying to get organized is neither easy nor natural. But it's necessary for anyone who wants to use time effectively.

Are You a TP or a CL?

To keep things simple—a must for streetwise time management—we'll separate everyone into two categories of organizers, the TPs and the CLs.

TP stands for *tidy and punctual. CL* indicates *cluttered and late.*

TPs keep a neat work and home space. They don't drop it on the floor; they put it in its place. If a CL drops it, the TP will probably pick it up.

A place for everything, and everything in its place—that's the TP motto. Socks get neatly folded and put in the drawer designated specifically for socks and nothing else.

TPs tend to be detail-oriented perfectionists. They'll see a project through step by step, checking and rechecking as they go. They have a tough time going on to the next step until the one they're working on is completed to their satisfaction.

TPs are punctual. If they say they'll be there at 1:00, they arrive at or before 1:00. Because they place such a high value on being on time, some TPs tend to become impatient with folks who don't, which is one reason interaction between TPs and CLs is not always pleasant.

> *TP* stands for *tidy and punctual. CL* indicates *cluttered and late.*

If you like a TP, you'll describe him or her as "conscientious," "well organized," and "meticulous." If you don't like the TP, you'll use words like "picky," "uptight," and "rigid."

Everything the TP is, the CL isn't. Where the TP likes a well-regulated buffet, the CL makes stew. CLs get excited about ideas but tend to flame out when it comes time to implement them. When the CL makes an appointment for 1:00, it's a rough estimate.

But the portrait of the CL isn't all negative. Some CL traits tend to correlate highly with creativity and divergent thinking:

- Tolerance for chaos and ambiguity
- Ability to accept failure
- High energy and enthusiasm
- Willingness to laugh, especially at himself or herself

If you like the CL, you probably think of him or her as "laid back," "easy going," and "flexible." But if you're the one who has to pick up after the CL, your descriptors might be "slob" and "inconsiderate jerk."

In Neil Simon's *The Odd Couple*, Oscar Madison is the classic CL trying to coexist with super-TP Felix Unger.

You remember the fable of the grasshopper and the ant, right? The TP ant prepares for winter, while the CL grasshopper plays. He'll have to rely on the kindness of strangers when the snow starts to fall.

From our descriptions, it might seem pretty clear that the conscientious TP is a much better citizen than the flighty CL. But this isn't about right and wrong, moral or immoral. One way isn't right (thus implying that the other must be wrong). One group isn't better than the other. They're just different. We see and evaluate life differently, and we react out of our perceptions.

To thrive, most organizations need a mixture of types, folks with the TP's virtues of conscientious, sustained effort and precision, and folks with the CL's creative flair for innovation.

And like the successful organization, the efficient, effective individual blends TP and CL traits, with organizational skills that don't dampen zeal and playfulness.

Do It Yourself

You're not all TP or all CL. You've got elements of each. Take a few minutes to find your place on the TP/CL spectrum.

Very TP   Balanced   Very CL

Take a look at the bathroom after you get done with it in the morning. Have you squeezed the toothpaste tube carefully from the bottom, and did you remember to recap it when you finished? Did you rinse off the toothbrush and hang it up in its place? For that matter, have you replaced that toothbrush within the last three months (the way dentists say we should)?

Or did you swish a little water around in your mouth and spit (assuring yourself that you'd brush extra well next time)?

The first description is very TP and the second very CL.

You wouldn't think of using the last of the toilet paper and not replacing it with a fresh roll, would you? A CL might ("I'm in a hurry here!"), but a TP never would.

How many rolls of toilet paper do you have in reserve? A TP will have plenty of tp.

Is your bathroom routine unvarying from day to day (always done at the same time, in the same order)? Or is every morning a catch-as-catch-can adventure?

Do It Yourself

Focus on your basic goals, those ultimates that underline your life and give it its meaning. What's really important to you? Family? Spiritual growth? Financial security? Health? Phrase these values, your personal mission statement, as precisely as you can. No one has to ever see, much less judge, these statements. This is just for you. Use your CL skills here to see the scope of your life. It's quite a mural.

To the extent that you're able to organize your life around these fundamentals, you'll be able to achieve satisfaction.

Your basic "very TP" personality is superb at handling the details, tying up the loose ends, keeping the train on track and running on time.

The "very CL" sees the big picture, focusing on where those tracks lead and whether he or she really wants to go there.

In shaping your life, scheduling your activities, and planning how you will spend your time, you need to take care of both the details and the overall direction those details lead you in.

If you're to achieve your goals, you need to break those goals into specific steps, steps into activities, activities into a schedule that invites and facilitates action.

And that brings your TP skills into play.

Breaking Goals into Steps

Let's suppose one of your basic life goals is to "maintain good health and physical fitness." We know that physical well-being bears directly on mental health, mood, and ability to work and play. So, what, specifically, are you going to do about it?

After a bit of concentrated brainstorming, let's suppose you come up with these steps:

1. Lose 25 pounds.
2. Exercise regularly.
3. Drink alcohol only in moderation.

Good start. But now you have to define these steps much more clearly.

"Lose 25 pounds" seems straightforward enough, but even this goal needs refining. Why do you need to lose weight? Why 25 pounds? How fast is safe? How will you maintain the loss when you achieve it?

And, of course, losing weight comes down to the day-to-day matter of what and how much you put into your mouth. Are you going to try a prescribed diet or a weight loss program with prepackaged foods? Or are you simply going to "cut down" or "give up dessert"? You need to get specific.

"Exercise regularly" is also vague.

Define "exercise." Does it have to hurt to be good for you? Will parking the car at the far end of the lot and taking the stairs instead of the elevator make enough of a difference?

What does "regularly" mean? Every day? Twenty minutes with your heart rate at 80 percent of its maximum three times a week? (Such precision appeals much more to the TP, as does the record keeping that may go with it.) A little jogging when you have a chance? (More in line with CL thinking.)

Whatever your personality, you need to break your goal of regular exercise into specific activities, based on a realistic appraisal of your capabilities, your options, and your tolerance for various forms of exercise. (You can say you're going to swim laps for an hour a day, but you'll never do it if you aren't at least an adequate swimmer, if you don't have easy access to a pool, or if lap swimming bores the daylights out of you.)

Considering such factors, suppose you develop this exercise regimen:

1. Work out on the treadmill for thirty minutes three times a week.
2. Ride the exercise bike for thirty minutes three times a week (alternating with the treadmill).
3. Do light-weight, aerobic weight lifting for thirty minutes twice a week.

Now you've got a specific plan. All that remains is the doing. "All," he says!

Get out the calendar or the day planner.

Work around your work schedule, of course, but don't automatically assume that you can't move some of your work obligations to accommodate your exercise.

Also factor in family and other personal obligations and rhythms. Missing dinner at home for that workout at the Y will help you achieve your fitness goal but rob you of vital family time.

Accommodate your biorhythms as much as you can. I exercise first thing in the morning, which suits me fine and gives me energy

Caution

If you decide to add a half hour of exercise to your daily routine, you also need to decide what you won't be doing while you're lifting weights or riding that exercise bike. You aren't getting an extra thirty minutes. You have to take that time from someplace else.

Will you get up a half hour earlier, skip lunch, shun your daily session with Dan Rather, Peter Jennings, or Tom Brokaw?

for the rest of the day. But my regimen might be all wrong for you and might cause you to abandon your exercise program before you've given yourself a fair chance.

When you've settled on appropriate times for exercise, write them down on the calendar, and train yourself to consider these "appointments" to be as important as any others you make. That means that the sort of emergency that would cause you to miss a doctor's appointment or a board meeting would also keep you from your exercise session. So would significant illness or injury. But if "I don't feel like it" or "something else came up" wouldn't keep you from your performance review with the boss, it must not keep you from your self-made appointments to exercise, either.

When you begin your new routine, give yourself plenty of reminders. In addition to the notations on the calendar and the day planner, you might want to plant Post-it note "land mines" where you're sure to stumble over them during your normal work routine. Again, you may be able to program your computer to remind you. Give yourself visual clues—like a sweat band next to your wallet or purse in the morning.

Be firm in your resolve. Soon the exercise—or any other addition to your schedule—will become a happy habit.

Evaluation

How will you know if it's working?

Give yourself enough time. It takes at least three weeks to get over the novelty and discomfort of breaking patterns and beginning to establish a new routine.

Record your reactions in a notebook. You'd be surprised how much those reactions will change in just a few weeks, so much so that you might forget how you felt when you started.

Keep referring to your specific goals. Are you losing that pound and a half a week? Is your new exercise regimen giving you the increased energy and sense of well-being you hoped for?

Evaluate, too, how the change is fitting into the rest of your life. How are your loved ones reacting to the new demand on your

> It takes at least three weeks to get over the novelty and discomfort of breaking patterns and beginning to establish a new routine.

time? What have you had to give up to create time for the new activity? Is it a fair tradeoff?

Decide to stick with the plan for another three weeks, make necessary alterations, or scrap the plan and develop a new one. These are your goals, and you have the power to achieve them through specific planning and disciplined action every day.

Jenny still hasn't *found* the time for exercise. She *made* time.

Taking advantage of her basic TP love of structure and order, she signed up for an aerobics class at the local Y three days a week. She can go right after work, so it doesn't disrupt her schedule too much.

At first, she dreaded the sessions. She felt awkward and clumsy, and muscles she hadn't used in years protested in ways that made getting out of bed the next morning a real challenge.

But dread is already giving way to bemused tolerance, and she even catches herself some afternoons actually looking forward to the workout.

Better still, she finds that she has more energy during the day, and she's lost 6 pounds she'll never miss.

Time-Management Tips

1. Break long-term goals into small steps and small steps into specific activities. Then do them!
2. When you add something to your schedule, figure out specifically what you're going to drop.
3. Give yourself three weeks to begin to establish a new routine.

Is It Really Important—or Merely Urgent?

In this chapter, you'll learn:

- How to become more conscious of the choices you make
- How to separate important activities from the merely urgent
- How to get more of the important stuff done
- Why we tend to waste time on trivial activities— at the expense of essential ones.
- The one question any effective time manager must ask—several times a day
- When time-management decisions aren't really a matter of time at all

When you're ready to retire, will your retirement be ready for you?

The question has been nagging at Paul for months, maybe even years. He has a rough—very rough—idea of what he can and can't expect from Social Security. He's scanned the pages of small print outlining his options for drawing on his retirement pay from the company, but actually calculating all the variables looks about as much fun as doing the income taxes—without the urgency of an April 15 deadline to make him do it. He's having $50 taken out of each paycheck for an IRA but doesn't really know if it'll be enough.

He knows he should sit down and do the heavy calculating now while he still has time to do something about it. It bothers him—but it hasn't bothered him enough to force him to actually do it.

Paul is bumping up against one of those "important but not urgent" activities in life that never seem to get done.

What next?

You face that question hundreds of times each day, from the moment you wake up until you lapse back into sleep. Your answers to those questions determine how you live your life. The sum total of all those answers are your life.

Many of the questions are pretty basic yes/no decisions, the sort we looked at when we talked about making decisions in the chapter on moment management.

The answer to a simple question can branch into a more complex set of choices. If you decide to eat breakfast, your next question is, of course, "What shall I eat?" A Spartan bowl of oatmeal, no brown sugar, no butter, no syrup? A chocolate glazed donut? Two eggs fried in bacon grease? Cold meatloaf between two leftover pancakes?

Take the matter of clothes. Almost everybody in our culture wears them, at least in public. This is a matter of law and custom. Where I live (Wisconsin), it's also a matter of survival during several months of the year.

You do have a choice, however. The negative consequences of going naked may far outstrip (sorry, couldn't resist) any potential benefits, but you could still make the choice.

More obvious is the choice of what clothes to wear. Your clothes make a statement about your position in society and your

> Paul is bumping up against one of those "important but not urgent" activities in life that never seem to get done.

attitude toward others. If I wear a suit, tie, and wingtips, I announce that I'm a solid and productive citizen on my way to business. If I wear a ragged sweatshirt and cutoffs, I still might be a solid citizen, but I'm planning on doing some gardening or washing the car. Black leather, lipstick, and spiked heels make an entirely different statement—especially when worn by a male.

Proper business attire is a matter of social convention. But you still have a choice. At some point, you made that choice consciously. You may now be choosing your level of clothing (if not the specific tie or earrings) by habit or default, but you're still performing an act of free will. I insist on this point (and have by now probably beaten it nearly to death) because becoming more conscious of the choices you make and learning to reclaim some of these choices is the essence of streetwise time management.

The Dilemma of the Ringing Telephone

I'm going to ask you to spend a little time now to save a lot of time later. I want you to devote conscious thought to everyday choices you may not be thinking about now. The more uncomfortable you are with this exercise, the more potential it has to help you.

Imagine for a moment that you work in an office and that your office has a telephone (not too much of a stretch there). Imagine that the phone rings (again not a real feat of creative visioning, I suspect). Will you answer it? Yes, you do have a choice (especially if you have voice mail or can let the call ring through to another phone), although most of us automatically snatch up a ringing phone. (Remember Pavlov and his salivating dogs?)

You usually have to make the decision to answer a ringing telephone without the most important piece of information, namely, who's on the other end. That's one reason why most of us answer the phone most of the time, even when it rings just as we sit down to dinner. It *could* be important, although it's more than likely somebody soliciting a donation or trying to sell you something.

Who's calling you right now? I could make it easy and tell you it's a financial planner making a cold call to solicit your business.

> I want you to devote conscious thought to everyday choices you may not be thinking about now. The more uncomfortable you are with this exercise, the more potential it has to help you.

Who's calling you right now? I could make it easy and tell you it's a financial planner making a cold call to solicit your business. But that wouldn't be much of a test case.

But that wouldn't be much of a test case. Let's suppose, instead, that it's your significant other (hereafter referred to as the SO), the man or woman you share your life with, the single most important person to you on the face of the planet. Now do you want to answer the phone?

Well, sure, of course, except that you *are* at work, and you're awfully busy, right in the middle of something important, on deadline, and, well, truth to tell, you wish you could know what the conversation was going to be about before you committed to getting into it, right? Even caller-ID can't help you there.

But through the magic of the hypothetical case, I'm going to tell you exactly what your SO wants to talk to you about, and then you can decide whether to pick up that phone or let it ring through.

To avoid having to resort to "he or she," we'll let the SO be male in this case. Obviously, it works either way.

- **Case A.** Your SO just got off the phone after a long talk with his sister, Robyn, out in Oregon. She's having a terrible time with her oldest, Andrew, who just got expelled from school for getting caught with marijuana in his locker. Robyn's upset, and so's your SO, who doesn't know what he can do to help. He wants to talk to you about it.
- **Case B.** SO is calling to tell you that he seems to have lost all feeling on the left side of his face, and he feels as if he might pass out any minute.
- **Case C.** He wants to talk about your relationship. You had a fight last night, and you were both still upset when you went to work this morning. Some things need ironing out right now.
- **Case D.** Nothing special. He just wants to chat.

So, are you going to pick up that phone? It's your call (literally). I promise they'll be no repercussions; your SO will never know if you choose to duck him.

No question about Case B, right? You'll not only take the call, but you'll drop whatever you had going at work and race home to take him to the emergency room. You don't even have to make a decision. You just act.

Given the circumstances, Case D might be a fairly easy call, too. You'll talk later.

Case A is a little tougher. Of course you care about Robyn and Andrew and the whole unfolding soap opera out in Oregon. You care even more that your SO is upset and embroiled in a family problem. But there's nothing you can do about it now, and you do have that big meeting in fifteen minutes to get ready for.

Do I hear that phone ringing through?

Case C is probably tougher yet. Your relationship with your SO is the most important thing in your life. But this isn't the time, the place, or the medium for a heavy discussion. Rehashing last night's argument now probably won't do any good and might even do some harm. And to tell the truth, you're at least a little angry that he'd call now, knowing how busy you are. And yet...

Maybe it's just as well we can't always know who's calling and what they're calling about.

Is It Important or Merely Urgent?

Something is important to you if it touches your core values, the basic motivations that guide your life. Something is urgent if it demands your attention right now.

To become a streetwise time manager, you need to learn the difference.

In our phone call exercise, Case B was an easy decision because the call was both important and urgent to you. The health and safety of a loved one is at stake (or at least seems to be, and there's no way you'd take a chance with something like that), and the situation demands immediate action. A challenge that is both important and urgent demands a lot from you, but it doesn't require any decision making.

Case C, the discussion about relationship, is also clearly important but lacks a sense of urgency. (Why now?)

Case A, with poor Robyn and Andy in Oregon, seems somewhat less important and perhaps even less urgent.

Do It Yourself

Before reading on, list three or four activities in your life that fall into each category:

Urgent and important

Important but not urgent

Urgent but not important

Neither important nor urgent

Case D carries with it the least sense of urgency.

And that cold-calling financial planner is neither important nor urgent, a real easy call to skip.

To understand the key distinction between important and urgent and to learn to apply that distinction to your own life, take a few minutes to sort out some of your own activities.

The Four Categories of All Life's Activities

1. Urgent and important: relates to your core values and needs immediate attention
2. Important but not urgent: no sense of immediacy
3. Urgent but not important: doesn't touch core values
4. Neither important nor urgent: all the other stuff in life

Here are a few samples to help you sort:

Urgent and important
Call from day care—your child is throwing up
Big presentation to make in two hours
Car swerves in front of you

Important but not urgent
Regular exercise
Long-range financial planning
"Quality" time with family

Urgent but not important
Colleague needs to "talk with you right away about that Hansen deal"
Department meeting started four minutes ago
E-mail icon is blinking

Neither important nor urgent
Working a crossword puzzle
Catching up on office gossip
Reading the baseball box scores

There really is an important, maybe even urgent, point to all this. Take a look at the two categories "important but not urgent" and "urgent but not important." You might be doing too much of C and not enough of B.

The Secret of Streetwise Time Management Revealed: Why We Waste Time on Trivia and Don't Spend Enough Time on Essentials

Life is full of urgencies that really don't make any difference in the long run (or even in the short run, for that matter). Yes, you're four minutes late for that department meeting. But the department meeting is a fat waste of everybody's time (including the person running it), ninety minutes of plodding through announcements you could have read for yourself (or chosen to ignore).

Getting to that meeting is now urgent but not particularly important.

Technology has increased our sense of urgency. An overnight letter cries for more immediate attention than something sent bulk rate or even first class. A fax outshouts an overnight letter. E-mail outscreams them all.

But the delivery system has no bearing on the importance of the content. That e-mail message may be no more important to you than the letter informing you that "YOU MAY ALREADY BE A WINNER!" in the big sweepstakes.

We also have extremely important choices that don't carry with them any sense of urgency. Of course you should exercise regularly. You know it's good for you, mentally as well as physically. You'll do it. You absolutely will. Just not right now. Hey, you're four minutes late for the department meeting.

Unless you take conscious control of your decision making, you'll respond to the urgent, even if it's relatively unimportant, and shun the important, unless it also carries a sense of urgency.

> Take a look at the two categories "important but not urgent" and "urgent but not important." You might be doing too much of C and not enough of B.

Asking the "Want to/Need to" Question

If all this business of dividing activities into four quadrants on an important/urgent grid seems like a lot of work, here's an easier way to begin to gain control of your daily life.

Again, you're going to need to develop a way to interrupt yourself several times a day. These interruptions can coincide with your minivacations, but they don't have to.

Simply stop what you're doing, take a breath, and ask yourself the following question:

"Is this what I want or need to be doing right now?"

You can, of course, modify the question to fit your own circumstances and your approach to life. (I've created this version by modifying the "Lakein Question" proposed by Alan Lakein in his 1973 book.) But be sure to touch on the three key elements:

Is this what I *want*
or *need*
to be doing *right* now?

Note that it's "or," not "and." Obviously, a task can be a long way from what you'd really like to be doing and still be the thing you need to do.

If the answer to this question is yes, go back to what you were doing. You'll have affirmed your choice of activities and made your decision consciously, the key element in streetwise time management.

If you want or need to do it but not right now, put it off and do something with a higher degree of urgency. That way, you'll avoid getting caught in deadline pressure later.

If you neither want nor need to be doing it, now or ever, *stop*.

It may seem amazing to you, but if you stick with the "want/need" question for twenty-one days (same satisfaction-guaranteed deal as with the vacations), you'll catch yourself doing things you can't justify, and you'll be able to shift activities to better serve your needs.

This simple question can make a tremendous positive difference in the way you live.

Knowing When Time Isn't Really the Problem

To get the whole picture, we need to throw in one more element here:

Time management isn't always a matter of time at all.

Going to that department meeting and sitting in a passive stupor is neither important nor particularly pleasurable (unless you're a gifted daydreamer), but it is a lot *easier* than exercising.

Confronting the office deadline may be a lot easier than trying to iron out the kinks in a relationship. Often we will take the path of least resistance, especially if we can justify the choice on grounds other than ease. (I *have* to go to the meeting. It's my job.)

Sometimes we don't do things because they're difficult or they make us feel uncomfortable. But we use the excuse that we don't have enough time. Time management won't help you with such tasks.

You have to uncover the real cause of your failure to act and then choose to act despite your fear or reluctance.

Why You'll Never Be Able to "Find" Time

Time needs "managing" only because we don't seem to have enough time to do everything we want and need to do. In particular, we never seem able to find time for those important but not urgent activities.

Stop looking. You'll never *find* time. It isn't lost. You're living it. You have to consciously decide to live it in certain ways and not others. You have to make time by taking it away from one activity and giving it to another.

Conscientious and creative use of the to-do list can help here. If you want to exercise three times a week, if you need to do some long-range career and financial planning, if you care enough about another human being to want to nurture your relationship, you will schedule time for these things. Otherwise, you may not get to them,

> You'll never *find* time. It isn't lost. You're living it. You have to consciously decide to live it in certain ways and not others. You have to make time by taking it away from one activity and giving it to another.

and even if you do, you'll give them only your leftover time, when energy and focus are at their lowest.

You can also create time for yourself by slicing some of that "urgent but not important or even a lick of fun" stuff out. In upcoming chapters, we'll work on ways to do just that.

When Paul took a hard look at his priorities, he realized that "retirement planning" fell into the "important but not urgent" category. That partially explained why he hadn't done anything about it–but only partially.

A little self-searching revealed that he was also avoiding working the numbers because he hates that kind of stuff, always has, always will.

"No time" and "Don't want to" had led him to avoid doing something important.

Paul made an appointment with a financial planner to go over his situation. That gave him a deadline, a sense of urgency. Then he made a second appointment, with himself, to pull together all the information he'd need to make the planning session productive.

It wasn't fun, but the sense of relief he felt when he finally sat down to do the work actually made it a pleasure. The task turned out to be not nearly as difficult or unpleasant as he had feared, and now, with some workable modifications in his money management, he feels fairly confident that he'll be able to retire when he wants to.

Time-Management Tips

1. Schedule time for activities that are important but not urgent and do fewer of the merely urgent activities.
2. Several times a day, ask yourself, "Is this what I want or need to be doing right now?"

The 80/20 Principle Meets Streetwise Time Management

In this chapter, you'll learn:

- How the Pareto 80/20 principle operates
- How to adopt the 80/20 principle to your personal time-management program

Like many modern parents, Nancy and Tom both have jobs outside the home, and both participate actively in raising their two children, Jessica, six, and Artie, four.

And, like many of us, they find themselves in a nearly constant frenzy, trying to find time for the kids—and for each other—while performing on the job, shopping for and preparing meals, and keeping the house and yard reasonably clean.

They plan their time carefully, keep an elaborate family calendar, chart out their commutes and errands like officers handling the logistics of a complicated military campaign. That enables them to get the work done, but they both feel guilty about not spending more time with their children and with each other.

"Quality time is a myth," Nancy concludes. "We need *more* time!"

Direct mail marketers have something important to teach us about time management.

The folks who send you all those catalogs, official looking "immediate response requested" letters, and "you may already be a winner" sweepstakes entries, know exactly how many yes answers they have to get for every 100 times they ask the question. To make sure they get the response they need, they test everything, from the wording of the headline to the terms of the offer.

The most important variable turns out to be getting the stuff into the right hands. They don't dump their brochures out of airplanes—although it seems like it sometimes. They target their mailings, by demographics (age, sex, income), psychographics (political affiliation, preferences as indicated by other purchases), and geography. They can rent mailing lists that zero in on left-handed Virgos who bowl at least three times a month and live in a neighborhood with an average household income of $35,000 to $50,000. (It isn't quite that precise, but almost.)

They find out which ZIP codes pay off and which ones don't. Then they drop the lists that don't produce and intensify their efforts on the lists that do.

These findings echo a bit of folk wisdom known as the Pareto principle, which states that 80 percent of the result will come from

> These findings echo a bit of folk wisdom known as the Pareto principle, which states that 80 percent of the result will come from 20 percent of the effort.

20 percent of the effort. In direct mail marketing, that means that 80 percent of your sales will come from 20 percent of your mailing lists. Some ZIP codes, for example, will pay off big time, whereas others will yield sparse results.

Advertisers, of course, keep track of such things. Note well what they do with this information. Rather than pouring more money into the nonproductive ZIP codes, trying to bring them up to a profitable level, they drop the losers and spend still more on the lists that pay off.

You should use your time the way they use their money. Put it where it's most likely to pay off for you, based on past experience.

The 80/20 Principle in Daily Life

The Pareto principle applied to labor states 80 percent of your labor problems will come from 20 percent of your employees.

In employee management, 80 percent of the work gets done by 20 percent of the workers. (Note that it isn't necessarily the same 20 percent causing the trouble and doing the work—but it certainly could be.)

At school, teachers will spend 80 percent of their time on 20 percent of their students (usually the "problem" students, sometimes the "gifted and talented," almost never the "average").

In research, 80 percent of the usable information you get will come from 20 percent of your sources.

In sales, 80 percent of your repeat business will come from 20 percent of your customers.

If you only knew which 20 percent, right?

The trouble with the Pareto principle, as with most principles, is that it works a lot better as a description after the fact than as a prescription beforehand. You seldom know going in which 20 percent will yield the big results. If you did, you could cut or even eliminate your efforts on the unproductive 80 percent and focus on the 20 percent that will really pay off.

> You seldom know going in which 20 percent will yield the big results. If you did, you could cut or even eliminate your efforts on the unproductive 80 percent and focus on the 20 percent that will really pay off.

The 80/20 Principle Applied to Streetwise Time Management

Do you buy the Pareto principle?

Direct mail marketers know exactly what percentage of those sweepstakes entries come back with magazine orders attached. They can quantify results and plan future campaigns accordingly. But how can you put exact numbers to things like "trouble" from "problem employees"?

Here's what the Pareto principle might look like as applied to your life: 80 percent of your satisfaction will come from 20 percent of your activity.

Is that true? How do you measure "satisfaction"?

If we toss out the numbers and keep the underlying principle, 80/20 might look like this: *a great deal of your satisfaction will come from relatively few of the things you do.*

Does that work for you? Why not find out?

> If we toss out the numbers and keep the underlying principle, 80/20 might look like this: *a great deal of your satisfaction will come from relatively few of the things you do.*

How to Put Your Time Where It Pays

Carry your time-management notebook around with you for a week or so. Keep a list of those activities that yield high satisfaction by contributing, directly or indirectly, to your sense of well-being. List them when you do them, of course, but also note them when they occur to you (when, for example, you find yourself wishing you had time for an activity but don't).

Your list might include items like:

- Talking with your life partner, both the focused, productive conversations and the chats about "this and that"
- Taking the kids for a walk to the park and pushing them in the swings
- Reading mainstream fiction—not the mystery novels you gulp down because you can handle them even when you're tired, and not the classics that everyone is supposed to have read

but few actually do—just good, thought-provoking, well-written books

- Singing "take me out to the ball game"—and then actually going (though you'll always have to "care if you never get back")
- Luxuriating in a whirlpool (something that you haven't actually done since your honeymoon, but you caught yourself wishing you could, so you wrote it down anyway)
- Visiting Belgium to see where your ancestors came from (Hey! You can dream, can't you?)

Now take a look at your typical to-do list, or review a week's worth of activities, starring items that consumed time but contributed nothing on the "satisfaction scale." These items might include:

- Mowing the lawn
- Shopping for groceries
- Paying the bills
- Attending the weekly staff meeting

You could probably keep your list of unsatisfying activities going for pages. Why bother? You have to do all this stuff—or else you wouldn't be doing it now, right?

Not necessarily. There may be lots of ways to apply the Pareto principle to your daily living.

Moving Beyond Prioritizing

We've already talked about building time into your schedule for important but not urgent activities like financial planning and regular exercise. We talked, too, about scheduling regular minivacations four or five times during the work day to break the vicious stress cycle.

Caution

This hypothetical list isn't meant to suggest that there's anything wrong with mowing the lawn or doing the grocery shopping—or anything wrong with you if you actually enjoy and gain a sense of accomplishment from these activities.

When I mow the lawn, I get a decent workout and at least a faint trace of the feeling that I'm tending to the little parcel of land entrusted to my care. I also enjoy sitting on the porch and looking at the newly manicured carpet. (Oh, OK. It's hardly a manicured carpet, but at least I've hacked down the week's growth.)

The point of making these lists is to note the activities that truly do and do not give you satisfaction—not those you think are supposed to do so. For some folks, having the neighbors in for a block party is fun and satisfying. For others, it's stressful and frustrating. Same goes for golf, painting by the numbers, or joining a gourmet cooking club.

As with everything else in this book, you make the call.

Now we're ready to move a step further by applying five simple words that will make the Pareto principle work for you: do more of what works.

Talking with your partner and playing with the kids in the park gives you satisfaction? Do more of it. Carry that good book around with you and make time to read it. Start working now to make time—and money—for that visit to your ancestral homeland. Set a date and make a plan.

But you can't do any of this unless you look at the reverse side of the proposition. If you want to do more of what works, you have to do less of what doesn't.

Stop throwing good time after bad.

Your lawn needs mowing. You don't want to mow it. If you do, you won't have time to take the kids to the park.

But the lawn doesn't care who mows it. You can trade a little money for a little time, while swapping an item from your "bad stuff" list for one on your "good stuff" list by hiring a neighborhood kid to mow the lawn.

You say that kid won't do as good a job as you do? Maybe not. But he can do it, whereas he can't be your kids' parent and walk them to the park. Can you lower your lawn-care standards a tad to buy you time and increased satisfaction?

Now we're ready to move a step further by applying five simple words that will make the Pareto principle work for you: do more of what works.

Can't Get No Satisfaction?

The satisfaction scale is only one way to rate the value of the ways you're spending your time. There are many others. For you, a good way to spend your time might mean it:

- Enhances your financial security
- Helps to spread your value system
- Aids your advancement up the career ladder
- Promotes physical fitness

The important thing is that you define what constitutes a good use of your time, and then you take steps to put more time where it will yield the most positive results.

Since applying the Pareto principle to their lives, Nancy and Tom have created a variety of ways to spend more time with their children.

Tom did indeed buy his way out of mowing the lawn, trimming the hedges, cleaning the rain gutters, and a variety of other household tasks he really didn't enjoy but thought he had to do.

Tom took over the grocery shopping, an activity he does enjoy, from Nancy, and often even takes Jessica and Artie with him, whereas Nancy now pays the bills and then reviews the finances with Tom each week, just before they go out on a weekly Saturday night date.

They also get take-out twice a week. Yes, it costs more than preparing the food themselves. They've had to make cuts in the household budget elsewhere, but when they actually sit down and talk about the money versus time spent with their kids and with each other, it seems a very small price to pay, a fairly inexpensive way to buy time for the truly important things in life.

Time-Management Tip

1. Do more of the activities that yield the best results.

Working Well with Others

Summary of Part IV

1. Don't promise anybody a minute until you know what they want it for.

2. Don't schedule or call a meeting until you're sure you need one.

3. Never waste your employees' time.

4. Tell workers why when you tell them what. Help them see the big picture and the purpose for their work.

5. One thing at a time—for you, and for everyone who works with you.

6. Don't just add; swap. Give something up every time you take on something new.

7. When you say no, you've given a complete and sufficient answer.

8. You may never be certain, and you'll never know everything. Act anyway.

If a teacher wrote "works well with others" on your report card in grammar school, she probably meant that you tended to cooperate and share your toys, while causing little or no trouble.

But for the streetwise time manager, getting along isn't a matter of going along.

You need to get tough about setting and sticking to your own agenda rather than letting others determine your priorities for you. This section shows you how.

You also may need to learn how to say no to tasks you shouldn't take on. (You may even find that you're shouldering others' work without even being asked.) And you need to learn how to make your no stick.

If you supervise other peoples' time as well as your own, we've included tips for helping those working with you to make efficient use of their time, thus freeing you to make more efficient use of your own.

Who's Setting Your Agenda?

In this chapter, you'll learn:

- How the words "Got a minute?" can eat up huge chunks of your time—and what you can do to prevent it from happening

- How to manage your calendar by leaving spaces

- When to practice—and when to abandon—time-management practices

Chapter 11

Deborah has just about day-planned herself to death.

She elaborately plans out her days and weeks—ironically, she finds that she has to schedule time to do it—and is conscious about making every appointment and meeting she commits herself to attend. Since she's in personnel, people are literally her business. She places a high priority on being responsive to peoples' requests on her time. She figures, rightly, that that's what she's getting paid to do, and she doesn't resent it when folks ask for her help, even if she's busy.

The problem is, she's become so swamped that she's not able to attend to all the people making those requests, much less keep up with the reading she needs to do to keep current on regulations and policies affecting her coworkers.

She needs more than time management. She needs people management, too.

If anybody should be used to dealing with frantic folks, it's Bill.

Bill runs a lock and key shop near my office in downtown Madison, and has for decades. In that time, thousands of folks have come to him in advanced stages of panic, locked out of the car with, of course, someplace to get to and no time to get there.

I'll admit to having had need of Bill's services a couple of times over the years, which is how I know about the sign he keeps next to the cash register on the counter, the one that announces: "Your lack of planning does not constitute my emergency."

Bill always gets us into our cars and on our way. He just doesn't get worked up about it.

How about you? Are you able to keep your head above water when other folks start making waves, or do you tend to catch their stress?

> How about you? Are you able to keep your head above water when other folks start making waves, or do you tend to catch their stress?

The Three Little Words That Can Eat Up All of Your Time

The phone rings. You snatch it up before it can ring again.

"Are you busy?" the voice on the other end asks.

No! I'm just sitting here waiting for your phone call.

"Is this a good time to talk?"

There's never *a good time to talk!*

"Got a minute?"

I've got the same minute you do! What do you want to do with it?

Maybe you've been tempted to answer that way. But you're a conscientious and caring human being. You've learned that the customer is always right and that everybody, including your colleagues, is in one way or another your customer. So, instead of sarcasm or confrontation, you probably reply with something along the lines of, "Now's fine" or "Fire away" or "How may I help you?"

You've just signed a blank check. Now the caller gets to fill in the amount.

Those three little words, "Got a minute?" may be stealing your life, a few minutes at a time.

You can stop this time erosion, and you can probably do it without hurting anybody's feelings. But hurt feelings or not, you need to take back control of your day, one minute at a time.

Let's take it from the top, from the moment somebody asks "Got a minute?" and see if we can work out a response someplace between "Why, sure. Take all you want" and "Buzz off."

What's wrong with "Buzz off"?

It won't win you many friends—or customers—and influence people, of course. But beyond that, it may be inappropriate. You may want and need to have the conversation being offered you. You have the right to decide.

That's the key to streetwise time management in a sentence. You get to decide how you spend your time, which is to say that you get to decide what you'll do right now, this minute.

To make a smart decision about the "Got a minute?" telephone question, you need two critical pieces of information:

1. What does the caller want to talk about?
2. How much time does the caller want?

When you have this information, you can decide *if* you'll talk and, if so, for how long.

> You have the right to decide. That's the key to streetwise time management in a sentence.

Do It Yourself

Think back to the last time a phone call disrupted your work flow. Specifically:

- How did the caller make his or her demand on your time?

- How did you respond?

- How could you have responded better?

Develop your strategy now for handling that sort of call next time.

You have the right to ask. In fact, you're not managing your time well if you don't.

There are lots of nice ways to do it. "How may I help you?" is a good one, since it focuses on the needs of the caller while eliciting the information you need. You can no doubt come up with several more to fit various situations. If you need to, write them down on a 6-by-9-inch card and keep them by the phone as a reminder and a cue card until you feel natural asking.

What about that old standby, "No"? Is it ever OK to answer "Got a minute?" with simply "No"?

Of course. You get to decide, remember? If you really don't have a minute, "No" is the right as well as the accurate response.

You can follow it up by buying a little time ("Can I get back to you in about half an hour?") or by setting a specific time to talk. That way, you've asserted control over the situation and your schedule. Note, though, that you've still signed a blank check; you've just postdated it. You still don't know what the conversation is to be about, and so you still don't know if you really want or need to have the conversation at all.

The Golden Rule Applied to the Three Little Words

If you practice effective responses to "Got a minute" long enough, you'll train some of your frequent interrupters to ask the right question in the first place, a question that will supply the information you need to answer it.

"I need about five minutes to discuss the Aarons project with you. Is this a good time?"

How about you? Is that the way you open a conversation, or are you just as guilty of the "Got a minute?" question as everyone else? Get in the practice of asking others as you would like them to ask you. You'll get a lot better response.

Recovering from the "Take a Meeting" Syndrome

Somewhere along about the middle of the 1980s, folks stopped merely talking to each other. Whenever two or more people gather in the workplace, it's a meeting. We don't even just meet anymore. We "have a meeting" or "take a meeting." Raise the level of rhetoric and you raise the apparent value. "We need to have a meeting" somehow sounds much more important than "Got a minute?"

But summit conference or casual chat, you still have the same basic right to decide whether you want to have, or take, or do it.

We've all got itchy trigger fingers when it comes to our calendars and day planners. We hear the word *meeting* and practice our fast draw, whipping out those schedules.

"How about next Tuesday?"

"No good. I'm on the road."

"Wednesday?"

"What time?"

"2:00?"

"No good. I've got the Benson meeting."

"How long will that take?"

"At least until 4:00."

"How about then?"

"Can't do it. I have to be in Milwaukee by 5:00."

So it goes, until you find a common hole in the wall of appointments. You often have to extend the work day to do it.

"OK. We'll meet at the donut shop at 4:00 A.M."

Before you wind up with crumbs on your chin at four in the morning, assert your right to ask questions and decide based on the answers you get before you commit. You need to know:

1. What's the subject matter?
2. Does it really require a meeting? (Maybe you can talk about it for two minutes right now and avoid having to meet later.)
3. Are you the person to do the talking, now or later? (Actually, Phyllis is handling that account. You'd better talk to her.)

Caution

Don't bother trying to teach the rest of the world to practice proper telephone etiquette. You're in charge of your life, not theirs. Besides, you probably won't convert anybody, and the effort won't make you very popular.

It may be somebody else's fault for asking the wrong question, but it's your responsibility to take care of your own time. No matter what the question, answer in a way that serves you well.

It's OK to Draw a Blank

Where is it written that the calendar always has to be full?

Even if you're doing a great job of asking for the information you need before committing to a meeting or even a conversation, you still may be winding up with a crammed calendar and a ton of work to lug home each night.

If so, it may be that you're just not comfortable saying "enough" until you've filled every slot on the day planner. If so, you've given up control of your time to others (and to the number of slots on your day planner).

Repeat after me:

"You don't have to fill every space on the calendar."

Say it long enough and you'll believe it. Believe it and you'll do it. You don't have to give away every scrap of the day. Save some for yourself. If you aren't able to leave space blank, then box out time slots for yourself before someone else takes them.

What sorts of things go into those blank slots?

- Time to do the paperwork you've been doing nights and weekends
- Time to initiate instead of just reacting
- Time to think
- Time to read

Yes, thinking and reading are permissible in the workplace, even if you seldom see much of either going on. They're also two of the most important tasks you can perform to keep yourself effective and productive.

And one more activity you can use to fill that slot:

- Nothing

You can and should schedule downtime. If an emergency butts its way into your carefully planned day, your downtime becomes the buffer zone, saving you from meltdown. If nothing comes up, you'll have no trouble finding a good use for that time.

> You can and should schedule downtime. If an emergency butts its way into your carefully planned day, your downtime becomes the buffer zone, saving you from meltdown.

Here's another tip for effective calendar maintenance: if good calendar management is a problem for you, get a calendar with wider time slots. If your planner gives you ten-minute increments during the business day, get one that gives you fifteen-minute slots. If that doesn't help you, consider going to thirty-minute slots. The fewer slots you have to fill, the less likely you'll be to overfill the day.

Planning by the Colors Instead of the Numbers

During a discussion on calendar management at a recent seminar, a parish priest shared his method for controlling his calendar. Before deciding how he should be spending his time, he needed to create an accurate picture of how he was already spending it. Using felt marking pens, he went over several recent weeks in his day planner, color-coding various activities: yellow for meetings, for example, blue for sermon preparation, red for couples' counseling, and the like. When he stepped back to survey his masterpiece, he was struck by the dominance of yellow. He was simply spending too much time in meetings, which explained why he wasn't able to get to other activities.

Then he did something about it.

He color-coded the next several weeks in advance, assigning some "yellow times" for meetings but also plenty of blues and reds, to create what he judged to be a proper balance of activities. Then he scheduled meetings until he had filled all the yellow spaces. Then he stopped scheduling meetings. No more yellow; no more meetings.

I pass his system along to you, not only because you might want to try it, or modify it to your own circumstances, but also as an example of creative and bold streetwise time management.

Who Really Has a Claim on Your Time?

All people are created equal, but some of the people in your life are a lot more equal than others.

Here's another tip for effective calendar maintenance: if good calendar management is a problem for you, get a calendar with wider time slots.

When a business associate calls, you're likely to activate your time-management skills, finding out what he or she wants to talk about and how much time it might take. When a loved one calls, you're much more likely to abandon time management and just talk.

Some people have a much higher priority in your life than others do. These folks also have a much stronger claim on your time. You've entered into relationships with loved ones and friends, based on love, respect, and affection. You've entered into relationships with colleagues and bosses, too, based on a social contract.

The problem comes when we fail to discriminate, when we grant "most favored person" status to everyone who wants to "trade" with us. Do so, and you have less time for the ones who want, need, and deserve it.

If you fail to discriminate, you've ceded control of your life to others. You've also opened yourself to the possibility that you're neglecting important people in your life who aren't willing or able to demand your time.

When You Should Chuck Time Management: A Morality Tale

You can effectively control your interactions with others, reclaiming large portions of your life to live as you want to. But that doesn't mean you always should. I need to tell you a story to illustrate the point. It's a true story, but I'll change the name of my costar.

Right about the time I was mastering the time-management technique of "getting rid of the time wasters," a former colleague, since retired, appeared at my office door one morning.

Thank you, Lord, I remember thinking. You've sent me a test.

Dave is surely one of the dearest men on earth, unfailingly kind, gentle, and conscientious. But he functions in a different time zone than I do. His sense of pace seems to be a lot slower than mine. I figured he would provide a perfect opportunity to try out my new time-management skills. I would manage Dave right out the door, and he wouldn't even know what hit him.

I immediately stood up. That's rule number one. I moved toward the door, cutting him off so that he couldn't violate my space. That way, I'd keep him standing. Bodies in motion tend to stay in motion, after all, but once the butt hits the chair, you're stuck with a conversation.

I had all of my best kiss-off sentences cued up and ready, stuff like, "I know how busy you are, so I'll let you go."

But something about the way he stood before me set off a quiet warning in my mind. "Don't do it," a voice seemed to whisper. "Don't brush him off." (It wasn't like Kevin Costner out in that cornfield in *Field of Dreams*. I just had a feeling.) I heard myself inviting him in and asking him to sit down—even as my yammering conscious mind was screaming "No! Don't do it!" I was seeing my entire carefully planned day destroyed, appointments falling like dominoes.

Uncharacteristically, Dave came straight to the point. He had cancer. He needed an operation. He had told family but hadn't told anyone else at work. He was telling me because he considered me to be his friend. He was scared.

I expressed my concern and offered what comfort I could. Mostly, he just needed to tell someone, to let someone carry a crushingly heavy weight with him a little way. He had honored me by choosing me for the job.

A few minutes later, he stood up, gripped my hand in both of his, thanked me, and left. The whole exchange took no more than five minutes.

After he left, I was literally shaking, not only because of his news, but because of my awareness of how close I had come to giving him the bum's rush, leaving him alone with his fear.

There was nothing on my to-do list that day nearly as important as spending five minutes listening to Dave and caring about him. In fact, the encounter probably makes my short list of truly important encounters. We have to remain open to the moment and to the people who need us in life. It can't all be schedule and work.

The story has a happy ending. Dave came through the operation fine and is enjoying his retirement. He has moved away, and I haven't seen him in a long time. I miss him. If he shows up at my office door again, he'll get a warm welcome—no matter how busy I am.

> There was nothing on my to-do list that day nearly as important as spending five minutes listening to Dave and caring about him.

Deborah is recovering from her meeting "addiction." She's no longer a "girl who can't say no."

Those three horrible little words, "Got a minute?" no longer strike fear in her heart. Before she answers, she can hear herself thinking, "It depends." Then she gets the information she needs to make the right decision.

Although she occasionally backslides, reflexively pulling out the day planner at the first hint of a meeting, for the most part, she's teaching herself to practice effective people management—and to do it without offending anyone.

She has liberated time for the reading she used to have to take home for evenings and weekends. And she's even been able to seek out and talk with a few people who needed some guidance but who weren't assertive enough to ask to meet with her.

Time-Management Tips

1. Get the information you need before deciding whether you've "Got a minute."
2. You're always responsible for managing your time.
3. Leave your calendar in your pocket until you're sure you really need to schedule a meeting.
4. Don't give away the whole day.
5. Schedule downtime.

Seven Time-Management Tips for Managers

In this chapter, you'll learn:

- How to help your staffers manage their time well
- When technology saves time and when it just increases pressure
- How to conduct effective meetings

Chapter 12

"What if I called a meeting, and nobody showed up?"

The question has occurred to Mark many times since he took over as unit manager. Attendance at the "mandatory" monthly meetings has been sparse. (They're "mandatory," except that everybody has obviously figured out that nothing happens to you if you skip.) Those who do show up straggle in late, sit with eyes glazed, and shuffle out without seeming to take any interest in the announcements and information Mark distributes.

Mark knows he's no entertainer, but he's considered learning how to juggle flaming torches to keep folks' interest during meetings. Meanwhile, he dreads going to the meetings as much as and probably even more than anybody else in the unit.

He attributes the problem to "lousy staff attitude." He needs to consider a more compelling cause: "lousy staff meetings."

The Seven Tips

Managing people takes time. It may take an inefficient or ineffective manager longer to plan, supervise, and evaluate someone else's work than to just do it himself or herself.

The answer isn't to fire the staff. The answer is to manage them effectively. Here are seven time-management tips that will help you do it.

1. Never waste their time. Does the sight of one of your workers standing idle threaten you? If so, resist the temptation to assign busywork just to keep them moving. You waste their time, of course, and you also waste your time, thinking up the work, explaining and supervising it, pretending to care about it when it's done.

You'll also be eroding their trust in you and your decisions. They know it's busywork!

Don't fill their time for them. Show them what needs doing. Show them how to do it. Make sure they have the tools they need. Then get out of the way.

2. Make sure the time savers are really saving their time. I recently conducted a time-management seminar at a large Wisconsin company. As my host led me through the bullpen office area to the class-

Do It Yourself

List several tasks you routinely assign your workers to perform. Beside each task, briefly state your reason for assigning it.

Now go through your list of reasons, starring any reasons that relate to the worker's use of time (to keep Ken busy between rush times) rather than the ultimate outcome of the task (to keep the salad bar properly stocked).

Some of those starred items might constitute busywork. If so, think about alternatives you can assign.

room, I noticed two folks standing by the fax machine, their bodies tensed with anticipation. As the machine started to whir, one reached out and actually tugged on the sheet of paper to make it come out faster.

The fax is supposed to save time, right? But we soon learn to fax letters that could have (should have?) gone by good old pony express, and we put off writing the letter until it has to go by fax. That doesn't save time; it just increases pressure.

Somebody has to choose the fax, repair the fax, maintain the fax, and replace the fax with the new, improved, faster fax, bought with money somebody had to spend time to produce.

Have we "saved" time here? Not really.

I'm not advocating a retreat to the Stone Age. I don't even want to think about trying to write without a computer, research without the Internet, or handle phone calls without voice mail.

But these good slaves can make terrible masters, driving your staff to distraction with their bells and beeps and buzzers. Make sure the machines work for the people and not the other way around.

We'll take a closer look at ways in which our machines can help or hurt us in Chapter 17.

3. Separate the important from the merely urgent for your staff. For your staff, as for yourself, you need to distinguish between truly important activities, those that serve the central mission, and the stuff that seems to demand immediate attention without really meriting any attention at all.

Do you and your staff ever engage in long-term planning, skills training, or needed conflict management? Or do these things get lost in the daily clamor?

You'll never "find" time to do these important (but seldom urgent) activities with your staff. As a good manager, you must be sure to make the time.

Ask "Why?" for the phone calls and memos and faxes demanding your staff's immediate attention. Can you relieve some of the pressure and release your staffers to more important work?

4. Tell them why. "How come I have to do this?" If that question from a staffer feels like a threat to your authority, if you become

Do It Yourself

Ask the people who work with you to fill out an Important/Urgent chart for their daily activities. Then sit down with them, singly or in a group, and discuss jobs they need to do more and less of. Let them take an active part in shaping the day's work. You'll gain their trust, their involvement in the process, and their valuable insights into their work.

Do It Yourself

You already thought through reasons for many of the tasks you assign to staffers. Using that list, practice simple explanations you can give to them when you give the assignments. The more you do this, the easier it gets.

defensive when you hear such a question, your staffers will learn to keep the questions to themselves.

But they'll still wonder.

They have the right and the need to know the purpose behind your assignment. When you ask them to do something, also give them the reason.

You'll have a more motivated and more efficient work force.

5. Allow them enough time for the task. Be realistic in your demands. Don't overstress the staff. If you do, you'll get shoddy work. You might even get less work. Even a conscientious, willing worker doesn't perform well under unreasonable pressure.

6. Encourage them to do one thing at a time and do it well. Watch your staff at work. Are they on the phone, jotting notes, eyeing the computer screen, all while trying to grab a fast sandwich?

Getting a lot done? Probably not. And they're probably not getting anything done well.

If your coworker is on the phone with a potential client, you want that worker's total attention on the task at hand, not thinking about the next project or the last project or the work that isn't getting done. They'll work faster and better, with less need for clarification or revision.

This seventh and final tip is so important, it has been the subject of whole books.

7. Cut down on meeting time! If you asked your staff to list "urgent but not important" and "neither urgent nor important" activities in the workplace, chances are "go to a meeting" will appear on most lists.

Most of us hate meetings. We avoid them if we can; resent them when we can't; and complain about them before, during, and after. And we have good reason to feel that way. We've all sat through too many painfully dull, obviously meaningless meetings.

So, our first tip here ought to be obvious but apparently isn't: don't have a meeting if you don't have a good reason to meet.

That means never, right? Wrong. You really do need meetings. You can create a productive interaction that can't happen with a memo or e-mail or phone call or one-on-one conversation. People get a better grasp of the whole operation. Names become faces, and faces become individuals. You can develop and maintain a sense of shared purpose and cooperation. In a meeting:

- Everyone hears the same thing at the same time, removing some (but not all) miscommunication.
- If people don't understand, they can ask for clarification.
- The speaker can note nonverbal clues (crossed arms, frowns, glazed eyes, eager nodding) to determine how people are responding.
- Most important, when people interact, they create ideas that never would have occurred otherwise.

Schedule regular meetings. If you don't have a reason to meet, or if you have reasons not to meet, you can always cancel. Nobody ever complains about a canceled meeting.

But every time you do have a meeting, make it worth their time and energy to be there. Here's how.

Before the meeting

1. **Get ready.** You really have to know your stuff to explain it to others. Do your homework. Review your reason(s) for holding the meeting and the outcome(s) you want.
2. **Get the meeting place ready.** Make sure you've got the flip chart and markers and overhead projector. How about visuals? Refreshments? Seating arrangements? Put them in rows facing front if you want them to sit quietly and listen passively. Put them around a table if you expect them to take an active part in the discussion.
3. **Get them ready.** Don't pass out copies of a thick report to start the meeting and then expect folks to read and react on the spot. Even the most willing worker won't be able to do a good job.

   What do they need to know before the meeting? Get information to them at least two working days ahead of time.

> Every time you do have a meeting, make it worth their time and energy to be there. Here's how.

Sure, some won't read it. But many will, and they'll come prepared.

4. **Get out an agenda.** Whatever else you send them before the meeting, be sure to circulate an agenda. Emphasize action items and spell out recommendations you plan to make. If they need to bring something with them (like their calendars so you can plan yet another meeting), tell them now.

Be sure to include the day, place, and time for the meeting.

During the meeting

5. **Get rid of bad talk.** Don't let your meeting degenerate into personal attack or disintegrate into multiple sidebar discussions.

Here are a few ground rules other groups have found helpful:

- Use "I" statements in sharing your perceptions.
  Not: "This meeting is a stupid waste of time."
  But: "I feel like we're wasting our time here."
- Talk about issues, not personalities.
  Not: "Your idea is idiotic."
  But: "I don't think this idea will work because..."
- Come prepared.
- Listen actively. Don't interrupt.
- Don't yell, pound the table, or curse.

You might not want or need these guidelines. Develop your own that work for your group.

Now What Do We Do?

How will you use all this time you've saved for your staff? You probably won't have trouble filling the time. But if you don't plan for it, existing jobs will simply expand to fill it.

Your final task as an effective time manager for your staff must be to consider how time really ought to be spent. Are there other important activities that haven't been getting done?

> Whatever else you send them before the meeting, be sure to circulate an agenda.

Before you spend all of their time, though, consider giving a little time off as a reward for a job well done. You can't give them anything they'll appreciate more or that could motivate them better.

Mark cleaned up his act, without having to take up juggling or tap dancing.

Rather than trying to force people to attend staff meetings, he started calling them "optional" (which simply recognized the truth)—and making them worth attending.

He circulated a short agenda ahead of time, along with a list of announcements, one brief paragraph per announcement. He started the meetings by asking for questions but no longer read through the announcements. He also doled out responsibility for most of the agenda items to the people closest to the areas involved, turning it into their meeting instead of his.

The discussions are lively, and they matter. Real decisions get made. Nobody will admit it, but Mark suspects some folks even look forward to the meetings now. He certainly does.

Before you spend all of their time, though, consider giving a little time off as a reward for a job well done. You can't give them anything they'll appreciate more or that could motivate them better.

Time-Management Tips

1. Never waste your employees' time.
2. Make sure the machines are working for the people—and not the other way around.
3. When you tell workers what to do, also tell them why.
4. Encourage your staff to do one thing at a time—and be sure you do the same.
5. If you must call a meeting, make it worth everyone's time and energy to attend.

Does Your No Really Mean No?

In this chapter, you'll learn:

- **Why you say yes too often when someone asks for your time**
- **Four tips to help you say no**

Chapter 13

"If you want something done," the adage goes, "ask a busy person."

Dan is surely one of those busy people. And sure enough, folks are always asking.

He can always be counted on to take on that additional job. He'll not only serve on the volunteer board, he'll chair it, take the meeting notes, edit the newsletter, and head up the recruitment subcommittee.

"I just don't know how you do it all," folks tell him.

Neither does Dan. And he hasn't stopped to figure out just how much that extra work is costing him.

"I just don't have your energy," folks tell him, or "I can't ever seem to find the time"—right before they ask him to take on another job.

"We can always count on you!" they gush when he says yes.

Dan is wearing out. He doesn't want to let folks down, and he really doesn't know how to say no.

It's time he learned.

Your willingness to serve speaks well for you. You help because you believe in the cause and because you want to make your family more secure and your workplace and your community better places to work and live in. You're a helper, a problem solver, a doer. You're community minded, a team player, in sports parlance the "go-to person."

But you may be doing more than you should—for your own physical and mental health, for the well-being of your loved ones, and for your ability to be effective and efficient.

The Not-So-Nice Reasons for Being So Nice

1. Looking for love in all the right causes. You earn the gratitude and approval of your peers when you shoulder their burdens. That approval and acceptance may in part fuel your need to say yes. Behind this desire may even lurk the fear that, if you don't work so hard, those around you will stop accepting you.

2. The guilt syndrome. "It's difficult to say 'no' when someone asks you to serve on a not-for-profit board, or chair a committee, or

Do It Yourself

Why do you say yes?

Write down your reasons—all of them—for saying yes to a recent request for your time. Hang on to this list as you read the next section.

attend a fund-raiser for a very worthy cause," writes Jan Benson Wright, editor of *The Peoria Woman*. "When we decline, we are often inclined to shoulder a subsequent burden of guilt, because 'superwoman' failed to come through as expected."

3. The myth of indispensability. Rather than kindness, your effort may in part be motivated by arrogance. Perhaps you don't let others do the job because, deep down, you don't believe anyone else can do it or do it as well as you can. You've taken to heart the adage, "If you want a job done right, do it yourself."

4. The fear of expendability. What if you didn't show up for work and nobody noticed? On some basic, subconscious level, you may be afraid that the moment you stop all of your efforts, people will discover that they don't really need you at all.

Reasons three and four seem mutually exclusive. They're not. It's quite possible to feel both ways at the same time. Just as you can be in a "love/hate relationship," you can feel both indispensable and expendable.

Do It Yourself

Now take out your list of reasons why you accepted that last optional burden. Do any of the four reasons we just explored apply to you? If so, you may be saying yes because it's easier than saying no.

Understanding this about yourself is the first big step in summoning the courage to say no.

Why All That Yes Sneaks Up on You

Glaucoma is a gradual hardening of the eyeball, which, if left untreated, can cause blindness. It's an especially insidious disease; because the impairment is so gradual, the victim is often able to make subtle, unconscious adjustments to a slowly shrinking field of vision, becoming aware of the disease only when it's too late to treat it.

Making too many commitments can be like that, too.

"The problem with clutter in our lives, like clutter in our closets, is it arrives one piece at a time, never in basketfuls," Benson Wright notes. "It's not too difficult to refuse a huge, overwhelming load of additional responsibilities; it's tough, however, to decline 'just one more.'"

How many extra tasks do you perform, anything above and beyond what's required? Here's the start of one person's list:

Do It Yourself

Draw up your list of optional extras. Chances are the items on your list are all good, worthy endeavors, too. You probably genuinely enjoy doing them. We tend to enjoy the things we do well and gravitate toward these tasks when we have a choice. I'm a word person and often find myself as recording secretary and/or newsletter editor for any committee I serve on. My sister-in-law the CPA lands on a lot of budget and finance committees.

Time management would be a lot easier if there were obvious time wasters on your list and tasks you dreaded doing.

Hang onto this list as you read the rest of this chapter.

- Coach a Y basketball team.
- Chair the workplace expectations committee at the office.
- Coordinate United Way fund-raising in the department.
- Serve as recording secretary for the church council.

These are all good things to do. Somebody should do them. But does it have to be you in every instance?

He Ain't Heavy, He's My Colleague

Your list of extra commitments may not be complete. You also need to figure in jobs you've taken on that rightfully belong to someone else—not some generic "other" who could take over as committee chair if you stepped down, but the specific person whose job you've shouldered.

For Example

Connie hates to write up the required sales reports at the end of each day. She'd much rather be out in the field making more sales. Karl really doesn't mind the paperwork and is actually quite good at. Yes, it's an extra hour or so at the office, but he really doesn't mind.

So Karl winds up doing Connie's work.

Everyone is supposed to take a turn making the coffee at the office, but Jeff makes it too strong. Sylvia never washes out the pot when it's empty. Nora leaves the machine on overnight. Gloria forgets when it's her turn. Jill figures it's easier if she just goes ahead and makes the stupid coffee.

So Jill takes on permanent kitchen duty, without even being asked.

A Qualitative Method for Computing the True Cost of All Those Extras

You probably have a good idea how much money you give to charitable causes (if for no other reason than that you have to come up with a fairly precise number to report to Uncle Sam every April 15). When you make this yearly calculation, you have a good opportunity to make adjustments in next year's giving, bringing the level up or down to where you think it ought to be and redistributing funds according to shifting priorities.

But most of us aren't nearly as conscious of how much time we're donating. This lack of awareness makes it much harder to change that level of involvement or redistribute your energies.

Money has value only in terms of what it will buy (possessions, comfort, status, entertainment, freedom). Same with time; you'll truly appreciate its value only in terms of what you can do with it. What would you be doing if you weren't doing some of the activities on your list? We each carry around a lot of "if only" sentiments, things you say you'd do if only you could "find" the time. Here are some examples from a recent time-management workshop.

If only I could find the time, I would:

- Learn how to play golf.
- Read the complete works of Mark Twain.
- Get more sleep.
- Master conversational Spanish.
- Write my memoirs.
- Have people over for a meal at least twice a month.

Take a good look at your list. It represents the true cost of your commitments. Line up the two lists, commitments on the left, yearnings on the right. Decide which activity on your wish list you'd most like to start. Then pick the item on the commitment list you could quit to free up the time you need.

Then do it.

Do It Yourself

Take out that list of extra activities you prepared a few minutes ago and put some numbers next to the items. Estimate the amount of time you spend in a week, a month, or a year. You don't need mathematical precision here, but you do need honesty. Don't fudge.

When you add up those numbers, you begin to get a sense of how much your perpetual motion is costing you.

Do It Yourself

Spend a few minutes sketching a list of activities you'd like to do "if only...." Distinguish between things you really want to do and effects you'd like to have. For example, maybe you really want to study Spanish, or maybe you just wish you knew how to speak or read it. The first desire is active and belongs on your list; you'd really like to do the activity. The second is passive; you wish you already had the benefit of the activity. It doesn't belong on this list, unless you're willing to do the work to get the benefit.

Another Subjective Method for Trimming the Activity List

Go through your activity list twice more. On the first pass through, assign a number from 1 to 10 for each on the enjoyment scale, 10 being "highly pleasurable," and 1 being "pure drudgery." Then go through again, assigning a number from 1 to 10 on the importance scale, 10 being "crucial to the survival of the human race" (well, maybe not quite that important), 1 being "who really cares?"

Our hypothetical list of activities might look like this.

ACTIVITY	ENJOYMENT	IMPORTANCE
Coach a Y basketball team	9	7
Chair the workplace expectations committee at the office	2	4
Coordinate United Way fund-raising in the department	1	8
Serve as recording secretary for the church council	5	5

Just looking at the numbers, it seems we've got ourselves a basketball coach here. If you give it a 9 on the enjoyment scale, you're probably also good at doing it. (That correlation doesn't always work, but it's an awfully strong indicator.) If you like it, you're good at it, and you think it's important, do it!

Want something to trim? I think it's time the workplace expectations committee found itself a new chair, don't you?

The United Way job is tougher to call. It may be extremely important, but you may not be the person to do it. The cold truth is, someone else who enjoys coordinating and fund-raising will probably do a much better job than you will.

The "Something's Got to Give" Theory of Streetwise Time Management

The next time someone asks you to take on a new activity...
The next time you find yourself starting to take over a task
without even being asked...
The next time you're tempted for any reason to take on a new
commitment...

Write the task on your commitment list and, next to it, write
the specific activity you're going to give up to do it. You must be
honest here; the time it took you to perform the old activity must
equal the time required for the new one.

Here are some examples.

NEW ACTIVITY	OLD ACTIVITY
Exercise on the treadmill (Forty-five minutes every morning)	Forty-five minutes of sleep
Chair the neighborhood recycling committee	Play with my kids on those Saturday mornings
Join a book discussion group	Watch television

The first tradeoff, exercise for sleep, may not be a good deal
(although it's one I've made). Exercise is surely good for physical,
mental, and emotional well-being. But so is sleep. Are you getting
enough? Too much? Not enough (more likely)? We'll explore the
issue of sleep in detail in Chapter 29.

If you decide you need the sleep, that doesn't mean you can't
also do the exercise. It means you have to figure out another trade.

The second tradeoff is even more problematic. You may believe
strongly that recycling is our last best chance to save the planet. But
you also place high value on spending time with your kids, especially
if you don't get to see them much during the week. Can you work
another trade? You'd have to find a way that would also fit the kids'
"schedules," of course. (Don't decide to give up watching *Saturday
Night Live* to play with your four-year-old.)

> If you decide you need the sleep, that doesn't mean you can't also do the exercise. It means you have to figure out another trade.

Can't find a way to do the recycling without abandoning the kids? Then you might have to leave the recycling to somebody else.

The third example looks like a terrific swap. Instead of wasting time on mindless television, you'll be exercising your critical skills and absorbing great literature. Maybe. But television and print are simply media. The content should factor into the equation. Are you giving up reruns of *The Gong Show* to read genuinely stimulating books? Go for it. But swapping *Masterpiece Theatre* for the complete works of Danielle Steele may not be a great deal. (I'm not saying it isn't. I neither watch *Masterpiece Theatre* nor read Danielle Steele.)

To do this right, you should figure in the quality of that two-hour group discussion, too. Are you having a good time in the company of stimulating conversationalists, or do you come home fuming over all those "stupid blockheads" in your reading group?

All this computing of relative worth may seem cold and calculating, and you do risk squeezing all the spontaneity out of life if you always draw up a list before you act. But the heartless figuring is in fact a way to heed your heart by giving more time to activities that support your core values.

You would never consciously choose to neglect your kids. But you might choose to spend less time with them by default, without realizing you were doing so, when you take on the socially worthy work of being your neighborhood recycling czar. Well-meaning resolutions to "make it up to them" might quiet your conscience, but they probably won't translate into actual time spent.

How to Say No

All this figuring and calculating and deciding won't do you a bit of good if you aren't able to act on your decisions.

The moment is at hand. The outgoing chair (desperate to find a replacement) has asked you to shoulder the burden. What do you say?

1. Beware the automatic yes. You may have gotten into your time trouble because you have a very hard time saying no. But you've learned by bitter experience that it's much harder to get out of something later than to turn it down now.

> Can't find a way to do the recycling without abandoning the kids? Then you might have to leave the recycling to somebody else.

2. Buy time. Unless you're already certain of your response one way or the other, ask for time to think about it. This is both a reasonable and a truthful response. You really do want and need time to think about it.

3. If the answer is no, say no. Say it gracefully, but say it.

"I'm really flattered that you'd think of me. Thank you so much. But I'm going to have to turn the opportunity down."

And then shut up!

4. You don't have to give a reason. This may come as a shock. We're reasonable people. We like to think we're motivated by reason, and we want others to understand and agree with our rationale for our decisions. We want people to continue to think well of us. So we give reasons. And when we do, we open the issue to discussion.

"I'm just too busy right now."

"I know how busy you are. But actually this doesn't take very much time at all. And besides, you're so efficient and well organized..."

"I really don't think I'm the best choice for the job."

"You're just being modest. You're perfect for the job. Why, with your way with people and your ability to handle a meeting..."

You'll lose this debate. You're arguing the negative position, a much harder stance to support. You can be rationally talked out of something you feel strongly to be right and talked into something you know instinctively to be wrong for you.

If you "lose" (meaning you fail to get them to say, "You're right. Sorry I asked"), you've got two alternatives, neither of them good. You can acquiesce and agree to take on the task. Or you can stick to your guns and continue to say no, leaving both of you much more upset than necessary.

Decide, based on your informed understanding of your motives and the true costs and benefits of the activity. Then stick to your decision. You'll find yourself with a great deal more conscious control of your life, and that control will buy you a lot more time to do what you want and need to be doing.

Dan's only half the man he used to be—and he's a lot happier!

> Unless you're already certain of your response one way or the other, ask for time to think about it.

He took a hard look at all the extra commitments he had made, tallying up what they really cost him in time and in opportunities lost. Then he cut out half of those commitments.

The first no wasn't easy. In fact, it was one of the toughest phone calls he ever made. He could hear the hurt and the disappointment in the voice at the other end of the line.

He persevered, learning not to get drawn into debates about decisions that rightly belonged only to him.

He's taking a computer class—something he had been wanting to do for a long time—and started a light aerobics workout three mornings a week—something he had felt that he should do for an even longer time—and still feels a lot less hurried than he used to.

His friends are still his friends, though he did lose a couple of users. He has more time to nurture the true friendships now, too.

Time-Management Tips

1. Before you take on a new commitment, decide what activity you'll have to give up. Then see if you want to make the trade.
2. Just say no. You don't have to give a reason.

How to Make a Decision and Stick to It

In this chapter, you'll learn:

- What indecisiveness really costs you
- Three fears that stop you from making up your mind
- Why a wrong decision is better than no decision
- Seven tips for making good decisions fast
- What to do when you make a mistake

Chapter 14

Do It Yourself

If you want to work on your ability to make good decisions rapidly, spend a few moments figuring out what's holding you up now.

Imagine a recent time when you were under pressure to make a decision. Note specifically what created the sense of urgency. A project deadline is an obvious source but not necessarily the only one. Expectations—your own as well as others—can also play a role. Fear of potential consequences can paralyze your will. The more specific you can get about the factors weighing on you, the better able you'll be to act more decisively the next time.

"Don't just do something. Stand there!"

That motto doesn't really hang over Frank's desk, but the people who work for him think it should. It seems to be his guiding principle.

He's a nice enough guy, and he has a lot of good ideas. Maybe that's the problem. He has so many good ideas, he can never seem to pick one and act on it.

The whole office burns while Frank fiddles. His failure to make decisions is affecting productivity and morale.

But folks are either forceful or they aren't, right? Is there really anything Frank can do to teach himself to be more decisive?

"It's not always so important what you decide," the CEO of a fairly large company confided to me recently. "It's just important that you decide."

And often, it's important that you do it in a hurry.

Indecision may be costing you in ways you haven't even thought of. When you delay making a decision, you also delay taking action based on that decision. You spend additional time weighing the pros and cons, you lose focus on the task at hand, and you squander precious psychic energy worrying (a topic we'll take up in detail in Chapter 32).

You may be paying in terms of how others view you, too. If you're chronically slow to reach a decision, the people you work with may learn to place little trust in you. Although you might think of yourself as thoughtful and deliberate, they may see you as indecisive and even weak and incapable.

It works the other way, too, of course. When you think of yourself as decisive and resolute, others may view you as stubborn—a potential problem we'll take up later in this chapter.

"To be or not to be. That is the question."

Thus begins one of the most famous soliloquies in all of literature.

William Shakespeare wrote those words almost 400 years ago and put them in the mouth of one of his most fascinating characters, Hamlet, Prince of Denmark. As you may recall, poor Hamlet was trying to decide whether it was better to live with the burden of avenging his father the king (slain and replaced by Hamlet's dastardly Uncle Claudius) or to end it all by killing himself.

Fortunately for the play, which needed five acts, Hamlet couldn't decide on anything. Brilliantly indecisive, he could see the wisdom in both sides of any argument, but he couldn't take any course of action.

If you can't decide whether or not to act, inaction wins by default. In the case of Hamlet's soliloquy on suicide, such indecision kept him alive for another couple of acts.

Your everyday conflicts need and deserve a firm decision, not a decision by default. Even though many conflicts require that you first generate a variety of potential options, as long as you fail or refuse to decide, nothing gets done.

> If you can't decide whether or not to act, inaction wins by default.

Three Fears That Prevent You from Making Up Your Mind

Can't decide? One or more of these common pitfalls could be getting in your way:

1. The fear of uncertainty
2. The fear of ignorance
3. The fear of error

We'll talk about each fear and how to deal with it.

The Fear of Uncertainty: Why You Don't Have to Be Certain to Be Sure

"Are you sure?"

Those three seemingly innocent little words can be real cripplers to your will.

Others may appear to you to be more confident in their decision making than you feel yourself to be. They aren't, you know. You see only their actions. You're not around when worry keeps them awake at night, and you can't see the doubt underneath their actions.

But you're acutely aware of your own uncertainties and fears. That may lead you to believe that others are more decisive than you'll ever be.

It's an illusion. Most of us have doubts, and every reasonably intelligent human being can see at least two sides to every question. The difference is some people are much better able to act. The doers have "the strength of their convictions," regardless of how strong those convictions really are.

How certain do you have to be before you act?

You don't have to be certain at all. You just have to be sure.

See the critical difference? Don't wait to be certain. Just be sure. Sure can be as little as 50.1 percent certain (about the margin that elected John F. Kennedy president).

Make your best judgment and act on it. Frontiersman Davy Crockett said it best: "Be sure you're right, then go ahead."

The Fear of Ignorance: Why You Can Never Know Enough

"If only I had known."

We've all had that feeling. Occasionally, we get the information and insight we needed too late to put it to good use. The result can be frustrating and even enraging, as when you lay out a lot of money for a major purchase and then find out you could have gotten it for considerably less elsewhere. It can also be embarrassing if someone finds out about your costly gaff or if you yourself feel that you should have known better.

The anger and embarrassment can be helpful if they prompt you to act more wisely next time, comparison shopping before you buy, for example. It's always good to learn from a mistake so that you don't make the same mistake again.

But those negative feelings can work against you if they render you unwilling or unable to act the next time you face a major decision. Your fear of looking or feeling like a chump can freeze you.

Before you let that happen, remember that hindsight is often 20/20—or at least a lot clearer than the view you had before you made your decision. You'll almost always get more information after you make a decision, if for no other reason than that the consequences of your actions will teach you.

If you insist on gathering all the information and anticipating all the potential outcomes before you make a decision, you'll never act.

You don't need to know it all.

Let hindsight teach you so you can make better and better decisions, but leave the second-guessing to the critics. You don't have time for such nonsense.

> If you insist on gathering all the information and anticipating all the potential outcomes before you make a decision, you'll never act.

The Fear of Error: Why a "Wrong" Decision Is Better Than No Decision

"Play to win," coaches say, meaning don't play to avoid losing, or you'll be stiff and cautious. But we were all trained to do just the opposite.

We don't learn to read, write, and cipher. We learn to avoid making mistakes while trying to read, write, add, and subtract.

There you are in the "magpie" reading group, working out Dick's and Jane's relationships with Mom and Dad, Spot and Puff. You make a mistake, everybody laughs, and you feel like a fool. Teacher corrects you, and you stumble on, trying not to step on the next land mine.

You do your best on that essay on your summer vacation, and it comes back with the misspellings circled and the sentence fragments tagged.

The only marks on the math exam are the slashes through the wrong answers.

Unfortunately, this perspective often carries over into the world of work, where too often the only feedback you get is negative.

To steal another line from Hamlet, that tends to "make cowards of us all." We waste a lot of time fussing over and postponing decisions because we're afraid of making mistakes—and we pay for action delayed.

The worst decision is no decision. Fight through the fear. Make the call. Take the consequences. Go on to the next call.

Do It Yourself

Remember a few of the major decisions you've made in the last few years. Think about how those decisions played out. Would you call any of those decisions "mistakes"? How would things have worked out had you decided differently?

In a fundamental sense, you really can't make a mistake—unless you don't act at all. No action will ever be all right or all wrong. Your action will carry you on to the next action. Only inaction will leave you standing still.

"Haste makes waste," conventional wisdom tells us. But that isn't necessarily a bad thing. You can clean up the waste. Note that conventional wisdom also advises, "The one who hesitates is lost."

Convinced that you're better off deciding than not deciding? Good. Now here's how to do it quickly and effectively.

Seven Tips for Streetwise Decision Making

1. Stay open to the "third side." It's a pretty pathetic problem that has only two sides.

Most issues have three or four or five sides, approaches, or ways of looking at them. You don't want to ponder possibilities forever, but you do need to get as many options as possible out on the table as quickly as possible. That way you won't keep stumbling over surprises that make you postpone decisions and doubt the decisions you've already made.

2. Cast your nets widely. The car won't go without gasoline, and you can't make a decision without information.

Sometimes you can't make a decision because you just don't know enough yet. You need to consult the experts—and you need to be open about how you define *expert*. Your best source of information may carry a fancy title and a big reputation, or he or she may answer the phones or work on the line. The ones closest to the problem often have the insights you need to solve those problems.

Don't hesitate in seeking input from anyone who can help you make a swift decision.

3. Make a list. Lay out potential actions side by side on a sheet of paper (or flip chart or computer screen or chalkboard or whatever works best for you). Get your hands dirty; neatness doesn't count here. Get the pros and cons out where you can see them. Trying to put them into words will help you clarify your thinking. Often, by the time you finish your list, you'll have your solution.

4. Count the pot. Before you decide to fold your cards or call the bet, be sure you know what's at stake. What are the potential consequences of each action? What's the worst that can happen? What are the odds of it happening?

5. Talk it through. Writing down your thoughts helps you clarify them. So does trying to explain them to somebody else, with the added benefit that you can get some feedback. Talk out your dilemma to someone willing to listen.

6. Sleep on it. We're aiming for speed here. But if possible, do your homework early enough so that you can delay the decision overnight—or over lunch or over a walk down the hall and back, if that's all you can give it. A little time away from the conscious tussle gives your subconscious a chance to play with ideas. Often you'll come up with a connection you wouldn't have gotten otherwise.

Even in the heat of the most pressure-packed decision making, you can almost always buy a little time if you need to. "Let me call you back in five minutes" can give you a chance to collect the thoughts and words you need to make the decision and to express it clearly.

7. Just do it. That shoe company has it right. Get input. Make your list. Then make the call and get on with it.

Don't Just Make the Call—Sell the Call!

You want to find an expert on decision making? How about the folks in the blue coats or the striped shirts who have to make split-second calls in the midst of huge, often enraged, athletes, while hundreds or thousands or millions of critics are watching?

That's right. If you want to find a decision maker, talk to an umpire or referee.

I went to the good folks who run the National Association of Sports Officials. They told me about preparation, about knowing the rules, about being in position to make the call, about hustling even harder than the players do.

Then they added something I'd never thought of.

You can't just make the decision. You have to sell it. Make your "safe" or "out" clear and emphatic so that folks understand the call and your authority to make it.

Does that mean you'll never make a mistake? Of course not. You won't make any fewer than the rest of us mortals—though making

> A little time away from the conscious tussle gives your subconscious a chance to play with ideas. Often you'll come up with a connection you wouldn't have gotten otherwise.

> Take your lumps. The people who work with you already know you're human. They just want to be sure you know it, too.

decisions rapidly and emphatically won't increase and may even decrease the number of errors you do make.

What Do You Do When You Blow the Call?

1. Admit it.
2. Make it right.
3. Get on with it.

Take your lumps. The people who work with you already know you're human. They just want to be sure you know it, too. Do whatever you can to right the wrong. (And yes, that includes apologizing, if need be.) Then get back to work.

In the next chapter, we'll look at ways to keep those inevitable errors to a minimum.

"What got into Frank?"

Decisiveness.

Frank's not really a new man. He's the same old Frank, often uncertain, seldom wholly satisfied with any decision he makes. The difference is Frank has taught himself to go ahead and make decisions anyway, certain or not.

As with most such lessons, he learned by doing.

The first few times were more frightening than Frank will ever admit. But as he saw projects move forward, and as his group finally started meeting its deadlines, he learned that he was able to handle the consequences of his decisions even if he had to alter his course later on.

Frank doesn't just stand there any more. He does something!

Time-Management Tips

1. Don't decide by default.
2. Don't wait to be certain or to know everything before you act.
3. After you make the call, you have to *sell* the call.

Aerobic Exercise for Your Mind

Summary of Part V

1. Learn from your mistakes, but never dwell on them.

2. Don't be afraid to look ignorant. If you don't know, ask.

3. Learn how to find your way around the Internet.

4. Be the master, not the slave, of technology. Learn how to make it work for you and never the other way around.

5. Check the source of all information and check it with a second source.

6. Don't confuse fact and opinion.

7. Revise your writing by the numbers—with a checklist of your common weaknesses and mistakes.

"The hurrieder I go," the great pitcher and philosopher Satchel Paige once said, "the behinder I get."

Here's a streetwise corollary: "the hurrieder you go, the dumber you get."

You're not really dumb, of course. You just act that way when outrageous demands whip you into a mental froth as you stumble from one task to the next. Take time now to regain the use of your smarts. You'll save tons of time in the long run.

If you don't have time to do it right the first time, how will you make time to fix it later? In this section, you'll look at ways to eliminate mistakes. You'll save lots of time that way, and you'll also cut way down on frustration.

You'll also examine three methods for solving problems so that you'll become, if not another Sherlock Holmes, at least a Columbo.

Could computer, fax, and voice mail be doing you more harm than good? You'll take a critical look at the machines in your life to make sure they're really saving—and not eating up—your time.

You'll explore methods for digging out from under the avalanche of information that buries most of us these days and for sifting through that information to separate the helpful from the useless and the downright false.

You'll also learn techniques for expressing your own thoughts quickly and accurately. It won't be poetry, but it will be clear, concise prose, and it won't take you long to create.

Eliminating Mistakes

In this chapter, you'll learn:

- Three ways to minimize mistakes
- How to ask for feedback
- Who will give you honest criticism

Chapter 15

"So, tell me, Sue. How do you think my presentation went?"

"I thought it went very well, Burt."

Burt smiles, nods. He thought so, too.

"Folks really seemed to be tracking," he says.

"Absolutely. They were hanging on every word."

Burt's just missed an excellent chance to learn something—in this case, how to become a better presenter.

He hasn't figured out yet why his coworkers squirm when he asks them for feedback on his performance—and why they seldom tell him anything except exactly what he wants to hear, praise.

That's the problem. Burt doesn't really want feedback. He wants an ego massage. If anyone is foolish enough to offer genuine criticism, he bristles and explains why he did things the way he did—his way—the right way.

Burt's not alone. We all like praise, and nobody wants to be told they made a mistake.

The fact is, Burt did what he always does when he gives a presentation—read straight off his notes, glancing up from time to time, not at his audience, but at a spot on the back wall.

He'll keep right on doing it until somebody tips him off.

Let this motto be your guide: *never make mistreaks.*

A few years back, "Zero Tolerance" became a popular rallying cry to describe policies regarding drugs in school, crime in the streets, and errors on the assembly line. Some disciples of Deming's quality movement preached the necessity of doing it right the first time, every time.

Can you really eliminate all errors?

Short answer: no.

Let me put it this way. I ran each draft of the manuscript for this book (and there were several) through the spell check program on my computer. I also printed out and proofread each page. Some of the chapters appeared in other forms in books and magazines and were thus edited for publication. The material went through several layers of editing at the publishers. Am I ready to swear that you won't find an error? Nope. That doesn't mean I didn't try to make

Streetwise Definition

Typographical error
  "Don't blame me. It was right when I gave it to the printer."

this perfect. It just means I'm human—and so are the editors who helped me get this ready for you.

To paraphrase a bit of bumper sticker wisdom: *mistakes happens*.

Your challenge is to keep them to a minimum and to correct them quickly—without for one second letting fear of failure slow you down or prevent you from acting.

When a publication butchers a name or makes some other blunder, the editor often prints the correction (never as large or as prominent as the original mistake, of course) in a column marked "errata," which means "errors in printing or writing." I ran into one such column under the heading "Erratta." Now I suppose they have to print errata for their erratta?

Three Ways to Learn How to Do It Right the First Time

You can learn to become your own best efficiency expert. After all, you know things about yourself and your work no consultant could ever know. But you'll do most of your best learning while making those mistakes you're trying to get rid of.

1. Learn, don't burn. Accept the inevitability of mistakes. Forgive yourself for making them. And here's the really tough part—encourage others to point your mistakes out to you. The mistakes that are hurting you the most are the ones you aren't aware you're making. You need the help of your coworkers to become fully aware of where you fall short.

How do you get them to tell you? Ask them—and mean it. And don't punish them when they tell you.

When some folks ask you, "How did I do?" you'd better figure out what they're really saying.

Some really want meaningful feedback. Others want affirmation. They're really saying, "Tell me how wonderful I am." If you criticize any aspect of their performance, you quickly find yourself in an argument.

Folks like that never learn.

Under the Microscope

How many is too many?

If Zero Tolerance is unrealistic, what is the magic number? How many errata do you have to tolerate?

All of them.

What's done is done.

Correct the mistake. Learn from it. Don't dwell on it, and don't waste a lot of time assigning blame.

Note, though, that we're talking tolerance. You don't have to like mistakes. And you want to do everything you can to eliminate them.

Don't be one of them. When someone offers criticism, whether you asked for it or not, or when they point out a mistake you've made, don't get defensive, and don't start a debate.

First, say "Thank you."

And mean it.

If you were walking around with your pants unzipped or your slip showing, would you rather have someone tell you, so you could remedy the problem, or go on in blissful ignorance? The person who's caring—and brave—enough to warn you has done you a service.

Same with anyone who offers you constructive feedback of any kind. They're helping you do it better next time, even if that's not the motive behind the comment.

After you've said "thanks," ask questions to get at the specifics. Your goal here is to learn all you can. Don't argue and try to refute the criticism. You have nothing to lose and everything to gain by listening carefully.

You'll evaluate the criticism for yourself later, of course, rejecting what you determine to be inaccurate while learning from the criticism that strikes home.

You can learn from the criticism you receive even if you don't agree with it. Spend a few moments reflecting on why someone might have said what he or she did, and you may gain valuable insights into how people perceive you.

Although others can help you catch and eliminate errors through their criticism, you're still the best teacher you'll ever have. The next two tips will help you teach yourself a lesson.

2. Find the methods in your madness. Even though you didn't mean to make the mistake, you may be able to find meaning in it.

Sigmund Freud taught that there really are no accidents. For Freud, a "slip of the tongue" reflected in some way what your subconscious wanted to express.

You can benefit from paying attention to your "slips" to see if you can determine a pattern.

If you have a hard time remembering someone's name when you get introduced at a social gathering or business meeting, for example, you probably do it every time, not just sometimes.

Caution

The criticism that makes you the maddest has the most to teach you. Don't get angry. Shut up and listen. School is in session.

When you start noting the pattern to your errors, you can start anticipating and eliminating them.

Before that next business meeting or party, for example, you can remind yourself of your weakness for names and concentrate on learning the name the first time you hear it. (Most of us don't remember names because, in our nervous self-consciousness, we don't really hear them.) You can also develop an effective strategy if you forget the name anyway, willing yourself, for example, to say, "Excuse me. I'm terrible with names. Could you give me yours again?" (After we miss the name the first time, most of us feel too embarrassed to ask for it again.)

3. Create an error checklist. Sometimes you may want to focus attention on your errors in a more formal way, by creating a checklist for troubleshooting your own performance, before or after the fact or both.

When I first became a professional writer, for example, I created a checklist for editing my own work. I relied in part on good guides, like *The Elements of Style*, by William Strunk and E. B. White. But I also kept a pad of paper by my typewriter (it was a long time ago!) when I edited my work, noting the sorts of mistakes I kept catching. That way, I could prepare specific guidelines that no book could give me because they were specific to my own writing.

I also created an "idiot list" of the words I always—and I mean always—misspelled or had to look up.

The error checklist helped me catch my mistakes in the revision stage. Even better, it helped stop me from making the mistake the next time around. I was even able to drop words off my idiot list as I mastered them—though I'm always adding new ones, of course.

I was gradually able to wean myself away from the error checklist as I learned from my mistakes.

I've since applied the checklist concept to other areas of my life so that I can review the elements I need to have with me for a presentation, for example, much the same way a pilot has to go through a systems check on the airplane before takeoff. (This is one area where a strict Zero Tolerance for errors seems like a mighty fine policy, don't you think?)

Under the Microscope

Be careful who you ask for criticism.

It may not be fair to ask a loved one or a subordinate, for example, someone who isn't in a position to give you honest feedback.

On the other hand, don't waste your time asking someone whose opinion you don't respect or someone who lacks the requisite knowledge to respond meaningfully.

You need to be careful how you ask, too.

"How'd you like it?" and "How did I do?" are superficial questions inviting superficial and positive responses. The more specific the question, the more potentially helpful the answer.

The best question of all—but sometimes the toughest one to answer—doesn't invite evaluation at all. Instead, ask a content question, reflecting on the meaning rather than the quality of the performance: "What did you get out of all that?"

Again, never argue with the response. ("No! I didn't say that at all!") You're not asking them to recite what you said. You're asking them to tell you what they heard.

When all systems are go, I'm ready for an error-free takeoff.

Our buddy Burt slowly saw the light, coming to understand that he could benefit from constructive criticism.

That wasn't the really tough part, though. The tough part was convincing our colleague that he really wanted to hear the truth.

When Diane finally mustered the courage to suggest that he might want to work on establishing a bit of eye contact during his next presentation, Burt had to fight the temptation to argue. ("Eye contact?! Whattaya know about eye contact? I invented eye contact!") And Diane had to steel herself to keep from flinching.

But that day started Burt on the way to becoming a much more effective presenter. He had himself videotaped and worked hard on eye contact and spontaneity, coming out from behind his notes and actually talking to people. Soon he saw himself become a more forceful presenter.

Diane? Instead of an argument, she got a sincere thank you—and a bouquet of flowers sent to the office.

Time-Management Tips

1. When you make a mistake, learn from it, correct it, and get on with it.
2. Encourage others to point out your errors to you.
3. Find the pattern in your mistakes so you can avoid making them again.

Thinking Your Way to Smart

In this chapter, you'll learn:

■ **Three ways to become an instant expert on any topic**

Like many professionals today, Peg's success as an investments counselor depends on what she knows. She's in part an information processor, digester, and analyzer, functions that figure in more and more professions these days.

To make useful recommendations to her clients, Peg must produce accurate information on a variety of subjects in a hurry.

It's the "in a hurry" part that has her frustrated. She knows her way around a library, to be sure, but who has time for a leisurely browse in the stacks? She finds that she's doing a lot of digging on what she laughingly refers to as "my own time," nights and weekends, to try to keep up with the constant demand for information on everything from property values in Connecticut to the price of tea in China.

She suspects there must be an easier—and faster!—way. She just doesn't have time to figure out what it is.

I truly realized that the "experts" are just folks like you and me the day I found myself appearing on *The Oprah Winfrey Show*.

She was doing a show on how to keep from losing your cool. Among other guests, she had assembled the self-confessed "most impatient drivers in Chicago" (including a policeman!). One of these hypertypes had once nearly killed her own child, she admitted, because she had pulled out of the parking space before the poor kid had gotten himself all the way into the family van.

The program also showcased the woman who gained fame by getting herself arrested at a rock concert in Houston because she refused to wait in line for the ladies' room and used the gents' instead.

I was brought in as an expert on stress management.

How, I wondered as I waited in the "green room" for my turn on stage, had I managed to get myself into a mess like this?

Guest waiting rooms in television studios are always green, by the way. Color experts tell us that green is a calming, soothing color. It wasn't working on me this day!

Several years before, the pressure of job, family, and two book contracts had driven me to explore stress management. I read a ton of stuff and interviewed experts on diet and nutrition, exercise,

> Guest waiting rooms in television studios are always green. Color experts tell us that green is a calming, soothing color. It wasn't working on me this day!

sleep, and time management, turning many of the interviews into magazine articles.

On the strength of those articles, I successfully pitched a book on stress management to a publisher. One of Oprah's assistant producers saw the book, *Slow Down—and Get More Done*, and called me.

And that's how I wound up on *Oprah*, striving mightily to handle the stress of appearing before a live audience and about twenty bazillion folks watching at home.

But even that isn't what told me I had truly become a stress management expert. That happy revelation came as I was standing in line at the supermarket, flipping through one of those scholarly journals in the racks next to the candy and gum. (You know the ones, those "newspapers" that nobody admits to reading but nevertheless have paid circulations in the millions.)

I came across an article on time management, excerpts from a book, actually, written by...me! I had really arrived—somebody ripped off the stuff in one of my books to earn a few bucks.

I figure two more articles in the tabloids, and I will have become not just an expert but the World's Foremost Authority.

And I figure if I can do it, you too can become a World's Foremost Authority, in your spare time, in your own home.

Here's how.

Three Ways to Become an Instant Expert

- The Sherlock Holmes Method
- The Columbo Method
- The George Hesselberg Method

> I figure two more articles in the tabloids, and I will have become not just an expert but the World's Foremost Authority.

Sherlock Holmes Solves the Mystery

For Sir Arthur Conan Doyle's famous sleuth, it really was "elementary, my dear Watson" (a line Holmes never actually uttered in any of the books chronicling his adventures, by the way, just as Humphrey Bogart never said, "Play it again, Sam," in *Casablanca*.)

He would examine a heel print in the dirt, for example, and proceed to reveal not only the height, weight, and gender of the wearer of the boot that had made the print, but also her hometown, IQ, profession, and astrological sign—to dear Watson's (and the reader's) amazement.

Columbo Nails the Murderer

"Excuse me, sir. There's just one thing I don't understand."

With that deadly line, actor Peter Falk's greatest creation, the rumpled, cigar-smoking Lieutenant Columbo of the LAPD, would scratch his head, squint his eyes, and ask the questions that would cause the guilty to trap themselves.

His adversaries invariably underestimated him while wandering into the crafty lieutenant's complex rhetorical traps.

George Hesselberg Gets the Story

My friend George Hesselberg isn't quite as famous as Sherlock Holmes or Columbo, but his approach to finding the information he needs to fill a regular column in a daily newspaper can teach us just as much about becoming expert on any subject.

Hesselberg was driving on the campus of the University of Wisconsin–Madison one day when he noticed workmen on a scaffolding, apparently pulling the ivy off of the venerable Old Science Hall.

How come?

Our intrepid reporter called around until he got his answer. Ivy tendrils were boring into the mortar between the bricks. If allowed to continue, they would eventually turn Old Science Hall into Old Science Rubble. The ivy had to go.

End of story? Not for Hesselberg. He called folks at all the Ivy League schools until he could confirm that ivy was indeed getting scarce at those institutions, too, all in the name of building preservation.

In the course of his investigation, he also learned that the term *Ivy League* didn't have anything to do with ivy! The original federation consisted of just four institutions, which called themselves the IV League. I + V became ivy.

How Holmes, Columbo, and Hesselberg Got So Smart

Holmes reached his seemingly astounding suppositions by paying attention to detail. Invariably, when he explained the basis for his conclusions, he drew on observations in plain sight of the other characters in the story. They didn't notice, but on Holmes, nothing was lost.

Columbo trapped the murderer by asking a series of seemingly stupid questions, apparently belaboring the obvious—earning himself scorn, contempt, and another case solved for the LAPD.

Hesselberg got his story by seeking the source of the information he needed—and seeking and seeking and seeking until he found someone who could answer his questions.

What they did, you can do:

- Pay attention.
- Ask "stupid" questions.
- Seek the source.

What do Sherlock Holmes, Columbo, and George Hesselberg have in common? Curiosity and persistence, qualities all of us can fake even if we don't come by them naturally.

How to Find Out Damn Near Anything in a Hurry

Here are a few of the questions I've bumped up against while writing books about all kinds of things:

- Who first said, "Go West, young man"?
- Where and when was the first traffic light installed in America?
- What was John Wayne's real name?
- Who recorded the song "Mares eat oats and does eat oats"?
- Is Chicago really windier than other cities?
- What kind of fish is a sardine?
- Do fish sleep?
- What's the difference between a pig and a hog?

What do Sherlock Holmes, Columbo, and George Hesselberg have in common? Curiosity and persistence, qualities all of us can fake even if we don't come by them naturally.

- Do identical twins have the same fingerprints? (Which led me to wonder why we even have fingerprints in the first place.)
- Just why are "objects in mirror closer than they appear"?

Dumb questions? Sure, if you know the answers. But if you don't know and need to, they're perfectly good questions and need to be answered in a hurry.

I now begin (and usually end) my searches online. Everything's on the Internet these days—if you can find it, and if you can verify the source of the information.

If you aren't yet online, you need to get there. Plan on spending an hour a day exploring until you're comfortable with the various search engines and information services. Once you pay for your access to the Internet, these sources are free, and many of them are marvelous.

Even if you don't have your hands on a keyboard, you can still "let your fingers do the walking" by picking up the telephone and dialing up an expert. Two great places to start: the reference librarian at the public library and the information/public relations pro at a college or university.

You'll also find that you can almost always call the people who wrote the book on the subject, as well as the people authors cite as experts in their books and articles. You can reach an amazing percentage of such sources through directory assistance. Lots of writers now make it even easier by including their e-mail addresses in their books and articles.

Ready to tackle those ten posers? Just to make it tough, I'll tie the computer behind my back and get an answer from print or an actual human being.

1. Who first said, "Go West, young man"?

    Why bother? Everybody knows the answer to that one, right?—Horace Greeley.

    Wrong.

    That illustrates the danger of going with what "everybody knows." Greeley quoted that line in an editorial, freely giving credit to John L. Soule, who first issued the advice in the *Terre*

Do It Yourself

If you're feeling adventurous, tackle one of the ten preceding questions and try to find an accurate answer. Keep track of false starts and dead ends. Then read on.

Haute Express in 1851. It says so in *Bartlett's Quotations* and the *Home Book of Quotations*, among other sources.

2. Where and when was the first traffic light installed in America?

   Here's just one more great thing about Cleveland!

   The first traffic light blinked at the corner of Euclid Avenue and 105th Street, Cleveland, on August 5, 1914. Read all about it in *Kane's Famous First Facts*.

3. What was John Wayne's real name?

   Again, conventional wisdom is wrong.

   He was born Robert Morrison. His parents rechristened him Marion Mitchell Morrison when he was four. In later years, he insisted that his name was Marion Michael Morrison. You can read why in Donald Shepherd's great bio, *Duke: The Life and Times of John Wayne*.

4. Who recorded the song "Mares eat oats and does eat oats"?

   There's no such song, as I found out when I called the music department at the University of Wisconsin–Madison. It's "Mairzy Doats," recorded by the Merry Macs in 1944, as the friendly fellow on the phone was able to tell me in about twenty seconds.

5. Is Chicago really windier than other cities?

   Nope. The "Windy City" actually ranks sixteenth on the list of America's breeziest, well behind front-runner Great Falls, Montana.

6. What kind of fish is a sardine?

   Any one of a number of species of herring.

7. Do fish sleep?

   With rare exceptions, no.

8. What's the difference between a pig and a hog?

   Up to 180 pounds, it's a pig. Above that, you've got yourself a hog.

9. Do identical twins have the same fingerprints?

   Nope.

   Fingerprints weren't put there to help the police catch criminals, by the way, but for traction.

Streetwise Definition

Expert
   Someone who (a) will talk to you, (b) knows what he or she is talking about, and (c) can talk about it in plain English.

Under the Microscope

It's all out there—but who has time to read it all?

Nobody does. But you have several good choices between reading and skipping.

Get yourself a home study course or enroll in a speed reading course. You won't really learn how to read at 3,000 words a minute—although your basic reading speed will improve over the poky 200–250 wpm you're probably puttering at now. You will learn the supplementary reading skills of skimming and scanning, which will enable you to pick off information and distill the essence of print materials in a hurry.

10. Just why are "objects in mirror closer than they appear"? Because the mirror is convex, to remove the driver's blind spot.

All this wisdom and more lives in books like Barbara Berliner's *The Book of Answers* and David Feldman's *Why Do Clocks Run Clockwise and Other Imponderables*. If you want the Colonel's recipe of eleven "secret spices," you have to go to William Poundstone's *Big Secrets*.

Becoming an instant expert takes some practice and involves systematic search techniques. You'll develop your own favorite sources. Be sure you note these sources well. Most Internet programs have a system for "bookmarking" sites you intend to visit frequently. Keep track of any useful source, including a list of "experts" with their e-mail addresses and phone numbers.

Peg can't figure out how she got along before she got on the Internet. She starts her working day with a fifteen-minute scan of an online news digest that presents on the topics she preselects. She makes regular use of her favorite search engines to find answers to her questions all day long. She's even been able to get firsthand opinion and advice from recognized authorities, all within minutes, with a few follow-up phone calls.

She had no idea how easy it could be to be an expert.

Time-Management Tips

1. Ask stupid questions. Let your ignorance show so you can get the information you need.
2. Invest an hour a day online until you know your way around.
3. Seek out experts and connect with them with an informal phone call.
4. Take a speed reading course or teach yourself how to skim for main ideas and scan for specific details.

Learn How to Manage the Machines

In this chapter, you'll learn:

■ **How to compute the time you spend on technology**

■ **Why technology hasn't saved time the way it was supposed to**

■ **Three tips for taming the technology**

E-mail is eating Renaldo alive—or eating up his work day, anyway.

Dozens of messages greet him the moment he logs on in the morning. Some are important—bringing him useful information or helping him meet his many obligations to clients and colleagues. But others are trivial and even annoying, including the unsolicited advertising messages that have started to seep into the system.

A metallic beep announces each incoming message during the day, disrupting Renaldo's work and demanding attention. Even if he closes the e-mail function on his computer, a small icon pulses in the upper right-hand corner, distracting him.

He's beginning to wonder if technology is all it's cracked up to be. It surely isn't saving him any time. Wasn't that the point?

> The moment Alexander Graham Bell created the telephone, he used it to summon his assistant from the next room.

The moment Alexander Graham Bell created the telephone, he used it to summon his assistant from the next room.

We've been dancing to the telephone's tune ever since.

They're everywhere. Cellular phones have been showing up on the ski slopes of Vail, Colorado. Vending machines in California will sell you a phone. Commercial airlines and rental cars often come equipped with them. Ringing phones and their advance scout, the beeper, have startled audiences at the theater and the opera, occasionally prompting fist fights. The ringing of the phone has become as toxic to some restaurant patrons as secondhand smoke.

Can cellular phone implants at birth be far behind?

The last three area codes in North America have been used up to provide relief for overnumbered regions in Philadelphia, Michigan, and North Carolina.

Although the average charge for cellular phone use has dropped, revenues rose almost 40 percent in 1996, to about $7.8 billion.

We have become a bell-bedeviled nation.

We can speed dial and speed redial. We've got call forwarding, call blocking, and call waiting.

Should you somehow manage to elude an incoming call, despite all this technological wizardry, your voice mail will preserve every word of the message and demand that you listen to it and in some way respond to it the moment you get back in range.

More and more now, your own calls to businesses involve contact with a recorded or a digitally fabricated voice.

> If you wish to receive information about arrivals and departures, press 1.
> If you wish to make reservations, press 2.
> If you wish to talk to a customer service representative, good luck.

I'm not advocating that we toss the technology out the window and go back to tin cans with strings. I love being able to punch in my electric meter reading on my digital phone, and I'm actually learning to use voice mail effectively to screen and organize my calls.

I am advocating that you take a good look at the technology in your life to determine what's helping and what's getting in your way.

We begin, of course, with the money spent on equipment and training, and the time it takes to earn that money. If you're an early adapter, among the first to embrace the new technology, you get a jump on the competition, but you also pay more, make more mistakes, and endure while the manufacturer perfects the process.

But as with so many things in life, it isn't the initial cost so much as the upkeep.

Tallying the True Cost of Technology in Terms of Time

The Time It Takes to Select It

I used to eat at a little diner called "The Red and White." Ruthie handled the grill while Red served up the burgers. The line was always four or five deep behind each of the nine stools, but the regulars found the food and the floor show worth the wait. When your turn at the counter finally came, Red would slap down a sheet of waxed paper and the plastic holder and paper cup for your water and bark out "With or without?"

> I am advocating that you take a good look at the technology in your life to determine what's helping and what's getting in your way

That was the only choice. You took your burger with a thick slab of raw red onion, or you took it without the onion. No menu, no "California burgers," no well done or medium rare. You got it the way Ruthie grilled it, "with or without."

I took mine "with," hunkered down at the counter, enjoyed my burger and coffee, and listened to Red and Ruthie's inspired bickering.

Buying a telephone used to be like that. The telephone was a squatty box with a dial on its sloped face. You could have any color you wanted, so long as you wanted black.

Now we've got choices. Oh, do we have choices! Phones come in every imaginable size and shape, let alone color, and you need a consultant to determine the right package of services and options for your business.

Choice is good. I like choice. But choice takes time.

When you figure the true cost of something like a telephone (or a computer or fax or any other modern wonder), don't just add up the dollars they cost. Count in buying time.

> When you figure the true cost of something like a telephone (or a computer or fax or any other modern wonder), don't just add up the dollars they cost. Count in buying time.

The Time It Takes to Learn How to Use It

By now the user manuals that accompany our new toys have become legendary for their incomprehensibility. Most seem to have been written either by the person who programmed the machine (and who thus has no idea why you can't automatically figure out how to use it) or by someone who has never used it and who has no intention of ever trying to use it. The prose then seems to have been poorly translated from a language having nothing in common with English.

Count your time spent crawling up the slippery slope of the learning curve, along with the time blown making mistakes. (Admit it, now. How many pages of text did you lose into the ether while trying to master your first word processing program?)

The Time It Takes to Get It Fixed

You do in time learn (some of us much faster than others, of course). You and your machine bond and become an efficient team.

Then one horrible morning, you flip the switch, and nothing happens. Or worse, lots of things start happening, all of them bad. Bells ring, error messages blink like the lights of the police car you've just noticed in your rearview mirror, and your beloved program icons blink off like dying stars.

Your partner has gone on strike.

You've got to either fix it yourself or pay someone else to fix it. Count repair time and money into the true cost, too.

Downtime

As you master the technology, you become dependent on it. Who would go back to the old typewriter after learning how to compose and edit text on the computer? (Could you even find a typewriter now, let alone someone to repair it?) So when the computer goes down, word processing and number crunching stop.

Just as you must calculate employee sick time as part of the cost of doing business, you now must figure for the times when the computer is sick, too.

So, along with the sticker price, your checklist for computing the true cost of technology must include:

- Buying time
- Learning time
- Maintenance time
- Downtime

You may not need to compute specific figures for these factors. Simply being aware of them will give you a more realistic picture and, with it, a chance to take better care of your time. But you probably could make fairly accurate estimates if you needed to, since "time" by its very definition is a tangible unit of measurement.

Now you're ready to try to factor in the human elements.

Do It Yourself

Take any of those marvelous machines that surround you in your workplace and figure out how much time you're spending in the four categories we just listed.

Facing Up to the Annoyance Factor

Time was, when I tried to call you on the phone at your place of business, either I got you or I didn't. I got to talk to a human (you or somebody who worked with you) or I got a busy signal. Now I most often wind up in the telephone twilight zone, as your mechanical surrogate invites me to talk to a machine.

Some folks don't like talking to machines. Some feel nervous about having their voices recorded. Some will hang up without leaving a message. Some won't bother to call back. It's hard to calculate the cost of the "tick-off factor," but it's there.

Personally, I'd much rather talk to your machine than get you for a breathless few seconds, only to have you dump me the moment you find out you've got another call coming in.

You're not fooling anybody, you know. I can hear that little thunk on the line. So when you say, "Can you hold on for just a second?" I know to add what you didn't say: "I've got somebody else on the line who may be a hell of a lot more important than you."

How many people have you annoyed this week with call waiting?

> Time was, when I tried to call you on the phone at your place of business, either I got you or I didn't.

Can You Retain "High Touch" in the Age of Technology?

Why would anybody shop at a neighborhood grocery store?

They charge more, they have less selection, and the shelves are so close together you can barely get your body, let alone a cart, down the aisle.

Habit and proximity play a role. But the primary advantage the little guy maintains over the chain store is personal service, the high-touch factor.

The fellow at the cash register greets you by name. He asks after your family, remembers that your daughter has a band recital coming up, forgets that your son is flunking math. He has saved a copy of your favorite magazine for you, and he'll trust you until next time if you come up a few dollars short. If the milk you bought has already gone bad by the time you get it home, he'll replace it for you, no questions asked.

Most of us don't shop at the corner grocery anymore, but we still yearn for a place where "everybody knows your name." Large organizations try to recreate the personal touch of the small business, as when the big bank promises that you'll be a name, not a number, to its tellers.

Some huge corporations have managed to retain the personal touch. Perhaps lured by the folksy, conversational copy in its "magalog," you might telephone Lands' End, the giant direct mail merchandiser based in Dodgeville, Wisconsin. If you do, you'll speak to a friendly, knowledgeable human being, not a machine. If you aren't satisfied with the merchandise you receive, you can return it for any reason—or no reason—even if you've had it monogrammed, for a full refund. Technology and high touch aren't mutually exclusive.

The Paradox of "Impersonal Communication"

But the fact remains, the more gadgets we place between ourselves and our clients, customers, and colleagues, the more impersonal our interactions become.

In one sense, e-mail combines the best of written and oral communication. We can edit messages before we send them, and we can reread and save the messages we receive. At the same time, e-mail communication is almost instantaneous, and we can capture some of the spontaneity and give-and-take of a telephone conversation. I've discovered that I can communicate better with some people by e-mail than by any other medium.

But there's no getting around the fact that e-mail is filtered and can be anonymous. We've introduced "netiquette" to preserve civility online and "emoticons" to communicate mood, but it's still words on a screen. "Flaming" (insulting messages, usually in all caps), "spamming" (a flood of unwanted messages), even stalking occur online, and we've already had our first report of a marriage arranged online gone sadly awry when the "groom" turned out to be a woman.

> The more gadgets we place between ourselves and our clients, customers, and colleagues, the more impersonal our interactions become.

There really is nothing as immediate and effective as face-to-face communication. Although our amazing technology has in one sense brought us closer together in terms of speed and accessibility, it has also driven us apart in terms of actual human contact.

Technology as Waste of Time

We need to look at one more factor on the negative side of the time/technology equation, the most obvious and yet least-talked-about element: online goofing off. Technology in general and the computer in particular have made it much easier to play while appearing to work.

E-mailing with a friend looks the same as writing the quarterly report. Downloading pictures from the *Penthouse* Web site involves the same process as doing product research on the net.

Even well-meaning, conscientious workers who wouldn't think of playing "Tri-Peaks" on company time may be creating occasions to use e-mail and cruise the net, simply because they are enjoyable activities.

What Has Happened to All the Time You've "Saved"?

One of the arguments for quitting smoking—though far from the most compelling in my view—is the financial one: think of all the money you'll save.

Suppose you used to smoke a pack a day, but at the urging of loved ones and your own increasing awareness of the health risks involved, you quit a year ago. At $2 a pack, you will have saved $730.

So, where's the money?

Unless you took that $2 a day, stuck it in a sock, and hid it under the mattress, you don't actually have that $730 now, and you probably can't account for how you spent it.

If you add up all the negatives involved in acquiring technology and still reckon that your technology is in fact saving time for you,

> Technology in general and the computer in particular have made it much easier to play while appearing to work.

then you need to ask yourself one more important question: where is all that time you saved?

Technology was supposed to lead us into the Age of Leisure. (The computer was supposed to create the "paperless office," too. Wrong on both counts.) There are at least three reasons why technology may not actually be saving you time in any useful sense:

1. **The fallacy of increased expectations.** Instead of decreasing the amount of time we take to process a report, the computer may have increased our expectations of how long the report should be, how many graphics it should contain, and how many times it should be edited. If a longer, more heavily edited and lavishly illustrated report is in fact more useful, the company has benefited. But it may simply be a fatter report requiring a great deal more effort to produce.

2. **The last-minute syndrome.** When we knew we'd need at least two days to send a report by surface mail, we set our deadlines accordingly. The advent of overnight mail allowed us to push that deadline back a day. The fax allowed us to wait until the next-to-last minute. E-mail lets us transmit the material as we write it (if we're foolish enough to do so). None of this has saved us any time. It has simply allowed us to put tasks off longer. (Unless we're careful, it will also damage the quality of our written communication.)

3. **The "if you build it they will come" phenomenon.** Main Street used to run right through the middle of town. As traffic increased, we built a bypass to ease congestion. The bypass then got congested, and so we built a bypass for the bypass. You can read some towns' histories in the strata of their bypasses, like looking at layers of rock in the wall of the Grand Canyon. Traffic seems to increase in direct proportion to the number and size of the roads we build to accommodate it.

In the same way, communication may be expanding to fill the channels we've created for it.

> None of this has saved us any time. It has simply allowed us to put tasks off longer.

How to Take Control of the Technology

Bill Henderson has chosen to opt out of the communications revolution.

Henderson is the founder of the Pushcart Press, one of the best independent publishers in America. More recently, he's also the guiding light behind the Lead Pencil Society, a growing group dedicated to the principle that simple ways are best. Henderson's patron saint is Henry David Thoreau, the son of a pencil maker and the author of the famous dictum: "Simplify, simplify."

You don't have to forsake all technology. (I believe that even Henderson still uses modern printing processes to produce his excellent yearly anthology of small-press literature, The Pushcart Prize.) But you do need to make sure that you are using the technology and that it's not the other way around.

To regain control of the gadgets, begin with this simple premise: just because you can doesn't mean you have to.

Through the miracle of modern technology, you can be in constant touch with your associates, and you can grant them twenty-four-hour access to you. But do you really want to? Constant access means constant interruption, and that may not be conducive to efficiency (or sanity).

Three Tips for Making Good Decisions about Technology

1. Get only what you need. During the recent global insanity known as the arms race, the former USSR and the United States stockpiled ever-greater quantities of nuclear armaments, each superpower developing the capacity to wipe out the entire world several times over. This would seem to make no sense unless viewed as a competition. There is no "enough" or "right amount"; we simply need to be sure we have more.

Are you engaged in a technological "RAM race" with the competition? If so, know that you can never win. No matter what you get, someone else will have bigger, better, newer. About the time your

> You don't have to forsake all technology. But you do need to make sure that you are using the technology and that it's not the other way around.

staff becomes proficient on one software, its producer will introduce an upgrade making yours "obsolete."

Assess your needs. Use that assessment to obtain only the equipment and training you need, planning for orderly growth and development.

2. Learn only what you need to know. I know how to drive a car. I know how to put gasoline, oil, and windshield wiper fluid in my car (although my wife is much better at the latter task). I know the phone number and address of a reliable, honest mechanic.

I do not, however, understand how the internal combustion engine works (despite having read several lucid explanations).

I also don't really understand how computers work. To me they are marvelous and magical. I know several word processing programs, can speak Mac and Windows, and can lay out a decent publication in PageMaker. I've learned new skills as I've needed them to do my work.

But I have no intention of mastering programming, just as I'll likely go to my grave still ignorant of that marvelous hunk of machine under the hood of my car.

3. Create communication-free zones. Do you have to answer a ringing phone?

It's nearly impossible for some of us not to, but letting the phone ring may be the first big step in reestablishing control over the technology.

Set reasonable limits for yourself, and clear space of all interruptions. Here are three ways to do it. You'll think of others.

- *Establish a "no communications" hour.* I'm at my best early in the work day. I try to reserve an early-morning hour for writing and thinking, with no phone calls, no e-mail, and no faxes. The "no communications" hour can, of course, be longer or shorter than an hour, can be companywide or confined to certain departments or individuals, can be the same time for everyone or can occur at different times.

> Assess your needs. Use that assessment to obtain only the equipment and training you need, planning for orderly growth and development.

> Our technology has brought us amazing access to information. It has also opened us to a bewildering flood of useless information and misinformation.

- *Bunch your communications*. Return e-mails and phone messages during one or two scheduled periods each day. Make exceptions, if any, only for priority callers.
- *Signal your intentions*. When you leave a message for someone to get back to you, tell him or her when you'd like to be contacted. This allows you some control of incoming communications, and it also helps the caller avoid wasting time calling when you aren't accepting calls.

Our technology has brought us amazing access to information. It has also opened us to a bewildering flood of useless information and misinformation. In the next chapter, we'll look at ways to sift through the data—without spending all day doing it.

Renaldo is now master of his e-mail.

First, he needed a little more technology—software for sorting and labeling incoming messages—to help him sift through the barrage.

He tried "e-mail free" zones during the work day but found the interruptions still too intrusive. So he scheduled two specific times during the day when he would answer his e-mail. His messages became crisper while still doing the job. He also had fewer of them to answer, avoiding some of the back-and-forthing that instant response had created.

Time-Management Tips

1. Figure in the time it takes to buy, learn to use, repair, and replace the machine when deciding whether it will truly help you manage your time.
2. Learn only what you need to know to enable you to do what you want to do.
3. Create technology-free zones in your work day.

Do You Know So Much You Don't Know Anything?

In this chapter, you'll learn:

- **Four truths to help you find your way on the information superhighway**
- **Five ways to test the validity of information from any source**
- **Three ways to stay afloat on the sea of information**
- **Six timesaver sites on the Internet**

Chapter 18

Randall fell into the Internet, and he can't get out!

It's not really quite that dramatic, but almost.

When he first got online access at the travel agency, he survived the initial period of learning and confusion, actually taking to net-surfing like a natural and becoming a much faster, more efficient counselor for his clients.

But a funny thing happened to Randall on his way to the Information Revolution. Somehow, instead of saving time, the net began absorbing it. The answer to one question would lead to another, and soon he was surfing from site to site to site. He joined several list servers and chat rooms, all travel related and thus justifiable as work but all very time consuming.

He realized he was in trouble when he returned from a three-day weekend to find 267 messages waiting for him in his e-mail box.

We live in the Information Age. No matter who you are or where you live, you're now as close as a computer and a telephone line to a virtual sea of numbers, words, and pictures on every possible subject.

You've got access, tons of access.

The Internet has been hailed as the Second Coming of Gutenberg, the great democratizer of knowledge, our salvation from all ignorance.

It has also been demonized as a smut peddler, a substitute for life, a potential addiction, and the final destroyer of the printed page.

It's just a tool, as morally neutral as a blank sheet of paper and a pencil. Like any tool, it can be used for a variety of motives, and it can help you or hurt you, depending on how you use or misuse it.

The good news about the Internet: just about anybody can create his or her very own home page.

The bad news about the Internet: just about everybody has created his or her very own home page.

Good news: everything you could possibly want or need to know is online.

Bad news: tons of stuff you have no possible interest in is also online.

Good news: it's all there.

> The good news about the Internet: just about anybody can create his or her very own home page. The bad news about the Internet: just about everybody has created his or her very own home page.

Bad news: you have to sort through it all, and a lot of the "information" is wrong.

Your challenge is to find the good stuff while avoiding the bad, the irrelevant, the inane, and, most important, the downright wrong. You can get lost out there, and you can waste a ton of time trying to find your way back.

You can also emerge looking like a total idiot. Just ask Pierre Salinger, former press secretary to President John F. Kennedy, who went public with "conclusive proof" that a U.S. Navy missile had shot down TWA Flight 800, "proof" he and about a zillion other Webheads had gotten from the net and that was totally bogus.

The net has already spawned its very own psychological syndrome, information anxiety, defined as "the widening difference between what you think you should understand and what you can understand." If it's all out there, and if access to it is so easy, then shouldn't you know more—and more and more?

Relax. Let's put all this net nonsense in proper perspective.

Four Fundamental Truths about the Internet

1. Most people aren't on it yet. As part of the 1994 Republican Contract with America, House Speaker Newt Gingrich promised a computer in every home rather than a chicken in every pot. Fact is, though, lots of folks still don't have computers, and many of those who do have them use them as electronic toys, not reference libraries.

Only 18 percent of mutual fund shareholders have Internet access, and only 28 percent of those who do have gone online to check mutual fund sites, according to a recent study sponsored by American Century Investments and reported in *The New York Times*.

Mutual fund shareholders are hardly ghetto dwellers, and their ranks undoubtedly include some of the "early adapters" who try out the new technology before the rest of us become convinced. And yet 82 percent of them don't even have access to the net, and 72 percent

> ### Streetwise Definition
>
> *Information superhighway:* "A highway hundreds of lanes wide. Most with pitfalls or potholes. Privately operated bridges and overpasses. No highway patrol. A couple of rent-a-cops on bicycles with broken whistles. Five-hundred-member vigilante posses with nuclear weapons. A minimum of 237 on-ramps at every intersection. No signs. Want to get to Ensenada? Holler out the window at a passing truck to ask directions."
>
> —From the Internet. Source unknown.

of them haven't borrowed somebody else's computer or used the desk terminal at work to check up on their money.

Access will, of course, continue to rise, but predictions of the world Web community are as yet premature.

2. The net won't wipe out other media. New media don't destroy old ones. They cause the old ones to change.

Case in point: the advent of television was supposed to run radio right off the airwaves. All the pundits said so. Radio had been our constant companion, keeping us company (Don McNeil, Arthur Godfrey, Art Linkletter), educating and informing us, and telling us stories, endless stories ("Just Plain" Bill, Helen Trent, Mary Noble, Ma Perkins).

Radio didn't die when television took over as our main source of news and information, our national storyteller, and our "talking night light" (as one wag dubbed it). It changed—from broadcasting to "narrowcasting," with focused formats like easy listening (or "music of our lives"), oldies, hard rock, soft rock, all talk, and all news. Radio has become interactive now. We call Bruce for financial advice, Dr. Joy and Dr. Laura for love advice, Dr. Dean for medical advice. We go to Art for UFO and alien-invasion updates and to Rush for a big swig of conservative philosophy and media bashing.

Radio has survived and thrived by learning to serve different needs.

3. You won't become a net junkie. Heroin is addictive. Nicotine is addictive. Caffeine is addictive. Alcohol is addictive, at least for people who are genetically susceptible to alcoholism.

The net is not addictive. There's no such thing as "net addiction."

It may absorb way too much of your time, especially at first. For some, it may supplement and perhaps even replace face-to-face human contact, as "virtual relationships" become a fact of modern life. For some, it has no doubt become a way to escape "real life" or a means of manifesting inherent compulsiveness.

But so far as we know, it doesn't alter brain chemistry or increase the number of neuro-receivers. "Net withdrawal," to the extent that it exists, is psychological, not physical.

> The net is not addictive. There's no such thing as "net addiction."

4. Information is not wisdom. It's not even knowledge. It's just information.

You need to be the quality control officer.

The net is disorderly at best and total chaos for the beginner (or "newbie" in computer slang). It's awfully hard to find your way.

The computer gives you access to just about everything, but it doesn't synthesize and sift. If you haven't been trained to abstract, synthesize, and summarize, this can be an enormous—and time-consuming—challenge.

And finally, you must distinguish the wheat from the chaff, useful information from nonsense, "true facts" from downright fabrication. If Pierre Salinger couldn't do it, how can you?

Five Ways to Verify Information On— and Off—Line

1. Check the date. I always check the "best if purchased before" date on the carton of milk before putting it into my cart. Information has a shelf life and can spoil, too. Check to see when the site was last updated.

2. Consider the source. Don't unplug your skepticism when you plug into the net. Boot up your bunk detector when you log on. Always ask the fundamental question: "Says who?"

Notoriety is not a substitute for knowledge, and "credibility" does not equal veracity. Even well-known and widely acknowledged sources can be flat-out wrong. (Just ask radio doctor Dean Edell how he feels about venerable newscaster Paul Harvey as a source of medical information.)

3. Track down the ultimate source. By the time you get your information online, it may have passed through many computers, been filtered by many minds. What's the initial source of the information? Pay attention to the citation, the "according to." Sometimes you have to hunt to find it, lost in the linkage garble that tells you where messages came from.

> Notoriety is not a substitute for knowledge, and "credibility" does not equal veracity. Even well-known and widely acknowledged sources can be flat-out wrong.

If you can't find the primary source, ask. If nobody can or will tell you where the stuff came from, be especially suspicious.

This isn't just a problem for online information, of course. "Usually reliable" print sources can be just as wrong. The venerable *Atlanta Journal-Constitution* assured the nation that Richard Jewell was the Olympic Bomber. *The San Jose Mercury News* ran a three-part series linking CIA-backed contras in Nicaragua to crack dealers in Los Angeles. *The Boston Globe*'s Patricia Smith weaved beauti-ful—and fabricated—anecdotes into her columns.

When a book titled *Our Stolen Future*, carrying an introduc-tion from Vice President Al Gore, broke the scoop that "synthetic hormones" in the environment were causing severe declines in sperm counts, media picked up the story of the threat to the human race. Other researchers immediately challenged the conclusions, but they didn't make the front or even the back pages.

4. Separate fact statements from opinion statements. A fact statement can be verified. If someone tells you that it's raining, you can look out the window to determine for yourself if moisture is indeed falling.

A fact statement can be true or false. It may, in fact, not be rain-ing, in which case "it's raining" is a false statement of fact, but it's still a statement of fact because you can prove or disprove it.

A false fact statement may be innocent ("Gee, I really thought it was raining," or "Gosh, it was raining a minute ago") or intended to deceive.

"The weather stinks" is an opinion statement. You can deter-mine the presence or absence of precipitation, but you can't prove that the weather stinks. Some folks love the rain.

Even "it's raining" may be subject to interpretation, of course. One person's rain is another person's drizzle or heavy mist or thick dew. There are few absolutes in this life.

But you can and must separate fact statements from opinion statements and evaluate them accordingly as you sift and winnow your way through the bewildering array of "info-bites" online.

5. Cross-check. "If your mother says she loves you, get a sec-ond source."

This bit of cynical wisdom drives every good reporter to verify fact statements for accuracy by getting a second and perhaps a third source.

If sources conflict, get a tie-breaker, or simply note that you've got conflicting "facts" to deal with and withhold judgment before basing your conclusions on such a shaky foundation.

Three Ways to Avoid Drowning in All This Information

1. Give yourself permission not to know everything about everything. You can now get current weather reports for anywhere on earth, determine the precise distance between most any two towns in America (along with their latitude and longitude and the compass setting to get from one to another), and learn the current state of Hillary Clinton's hair. You *can*. That doesn't mean you *should*. And it certainly doesn't mean you *have to*.

We've heard our government officials spout nonsense about "credible deniability" (a euphemism for "I lied"). Though I reject that notion, I embrace the concept of "permissible ignorance." I don't have to keep track of Elizabeth Taylor's husbands, and neither do you.

Figure out what you really want and need to know. Again, it may be the difference between knowing how to drive and knowing how to build an internal combustion engine. How much is enough?

2. Rip, read, and recycle. Practice skimming for main ideas and scanning for specific information. Learn to read titles, abstracts, summaries, subtitles, captions, boldfaced text, and pull quotes (larger, bold-faced text type, often marked off by lines) to glean main ideas in a hurry. It works for print, and it works on the net, too (although learning how to skim on a screen is a new skill and requires practice).

Don't print it out unless you're sure you need it on paper. If you create a piece of paper now, you're going to have to file it, route it, pitch it, or recycle it later.

3. Create a reading file for airports, buses, and waiting rooms. You don't need to read it right this minute. Print it out and

Do It Yourself

For one day, keep a list of the topics of information you absorb from various media, including online sources. Let the list sit for a day or two, and then go over it, checking those items that you truly want or need to know. Any time wasters here?

put it in your "to-read" folder. This saves you the reading time now and enables you to put waiting time to good use later.

But if you do print it out, don't keep it any longer than you need to. Clutter robs you of the time it takes to move it, clean it, and wade through it to find what you need.

Mark Your Sources and Stick with Them

Addresses on the net tend to be rather long and somewhat complicated, stuff like: http://www.marshallcook.com/~timemanagement/guru/reallysmartguy_online.

You can spend a lot of time just typing in addresses (not to mention the time lost when you misplace a ~ or slant your \ the wrong way, so you have to start all over again).

On my program, when I find a site I like, I can set a bookmark. Next time I want to visit that site, I can simply scroll down my list of bookmarks and click on the one I want. Your program has something similar. Use it.

But be sure to go through your bookmarks regularly to purge the ones you're no longer using, lest your tour through your site list becomes almost as cumbersome and time consuming as typing in addresses.

> Be sure to go through your bookmarks regularly to purge the ones you're no longer using, lest your tour through your site list becomes almost as cumbersome and time consuming as typing in addresses.

Six Great Streetwise Timesaver Sites

1. "My virtual reference desk" includes "virtual facts on file," with dictionaries, a thesaurus, atlases, encyclopedias, a who's who, even genealogical information.
2. "Newslink" plugs you in to breaking news and even allows you to construct your own personal morning newspaper by letting you set up a template of subject areas you want to skim.
3. "Switchboard" is a national electronic telephone directory. If someone has a listed number, you can find them on switchboard. As with most sources, the more you know, the easier it is to find what you want. Try typing in "Smith" and see how many matches you get. But type in "Smith, Jonathan, Dothan, Alabama" and you'll limit your search considerably.

4. Many publications now have an online news service. I like *The New York Times* but also nibble at my old hometown newspaper, *The San Francisco Chronicle*, as well as many others. I must admit, however, that I still prefer the print version, but then, I was raised that way.

5. "Baseball links." OK. I didn't say I stuck to business all the time.

6. Excellent online magazines include *Salon, Slate*, and *Vagabond*. As I write this, all these sources are free once you have access to the Internet. *Slate* was going to start charging for access to its online material but backed off.

The net can open us up to the world without absorbing all of our time if we use it wisely.

Randall calls himself a "recovering netaholic" now.

He wasn't really addicted to the net, but he was spending more and more time on it, time he had to take from family, friends, and less enjoyable but necessary work duties.

He's marked the sites that deliver the information he needs in a hurry and limits his other browsing to a thirty-minute break each day during a slow time. Now his access to information is helping, not hurting, him, and delivering dividends of time at the end of each work day.

> The net can open us up to the world without absorbing all of our time if we use it wisely.

Time-Management Tips

1. Verify the validity of information by tracking it to the ultimate source and by checking with a second source.

2. Separate fact, which you can verify, from opinion, which you can't.

3. Practice permissible ignorance. You don't have to know everything about everything.

4. Create a portable reading file to help you keep current and put waiting time to good use.

Speed Writing

In this chapter, you'll learn:

- ■ Five tips for writing quickly and well
- ■ How to organize your thoughts
- ■ How to edit your own writing effectively—
  if not objectively

Chapter 19

In Jeff MacNally's great comic strip *Shoe*, the boss tells the hapless employee, "We're taking this disagreement to alternative dispute resolution."

Huh?

It's "my way or the highway," the boss explains.

Ah, that we understand.

Dale never wanted to be a writer.

She majored in electrical engineering in college and wound up working as a computer diagnostician and then a LAN administrator for various large corporations. She loves the kind of problem solving her job demands. Her powers of concentration when trying to unravel a systems failure are legendary.

As much as she likes the computer aspects of her job, one confrontation with the blank screen consistently frustrates her—writing the various memos and reports her job requires. She hates doing them, and she knows she doesn't do a very good job on them.

The term may not appear in your job description, but I'll bet you're a professional writer. You may not write books or even annual reports or business plans. But you probably write memos, letters, work orders, directions, equipment orders, job evaluations, responses to job evaluations, resumes, and a lot of other excursions into putting marks on paper or screen so they'll make the sense you intend for a reader.

But unlike folks who carry "writer" as their primary job designation, you do a lot of other things every day. You can't afford to spend a lot of time with writing. You also can't afford the time it takes to do it over and to clear up the confusion and misunderstandings that poor written communication engenders.

Five Tips for Writing It Right—and Fast—the First Time

1. Keep it short and simple. The Ten Commandments require fewer than 300 words, and Abe Lincoln needed only 271 for the Gettysburg Address. You ought to be able to get your thoughts down in a couple of hundred words, too, saving your time and the reader's.

Cut out each and every word that you don't really, really, really need. Don't even say "in order to" if a simple "to" will do.

Make your words easy to read by highlighting the main ideas. You can emphasize an idea by:

- Putting it first
- Using underlining, boldface, or larger type
- Breaking a list out from paragraph form with bullets (as I'm doing now)
- Breaking thoughts into separate sections with subtitles

Be sure to emphasize any action you've taken that affects your coworkers and any response you need from them.

Eschew obfuscation. Keep it simple and clear.

Plain talk is always best. Simple, direct language takes less time to compose and less time to understand. The employment of ponderous polysyllables is pusillanimous. Translation: only a coward hides behind big words.

2. Get off to a flying start. Formal outlines are a waste of time. If you need to organize your thoughts before you write, create a bubble outline. Identify your subject and write it in the center of a sheet of paper. Put down the major points you want to make, without regard to their order or relationship. Attach reminders about data, anecdotes, and examples you'll want to use. Circle the main ideas and number them in the order you want them to appear.

If you need more information, you'll discover that now (rather than halfway through the project). When you're ready to go, you'll know exactly where you're going.

Now engage in a little flash typing. Just let the words fly, without worrying about punctuation, spelling, or sentence structure. The key is to capture the essence of each idea and the flow between ideas.

You'll need to go back and edit, of course, but the time it takes to flash-type a rough (very rough) draft and then edit it will be less—possibly much less—than you would have taken pushing your way along, word by tortured word, trying to create perfection as you go.

On the off chance you don't know how to type fluently, or if you have trouble composing on the keyboard, and if your work life entails significant amounts of writing, you will save yourself incredible amounts of time and frustration by taking the time to learn touch typing and to accustom yourself to composing on the keyboard. It will

Do It Yourself

Take a recent sample of your writing, at least 250 words (one typed page) long. Eliminate every unnecessary word. Change every inflated word ("utilize") to a simple equivalent ("use").

feel unnatural at first, but you'll soon learn how to think with your fingers.

3. Sustain the flow. Take breaks before you need them. Writing is one of the most tiring things you can do while sitting down. Don't wait until you're exhausted. Stretch, take a walk, get some water, and return to the battle.

Don't wait until you're stuck to stop, either for a break or at the end of a day's session. If you do, you'll carry a sense of dread around with you. When you sit down to begin again, you'll have a tough time getting started.

Break knowing exactly how you'll continue. Jot yourself a few notes on the next two or three points you want to make. You'll be ready to start without a warm-up.

4. Finish cleanly. You've said what you needed to say. Now you need to come up with the Big Finish, right?

Wrong.

Trying to come up with an important-sounding conclusion is another waste of time. If the piece of writing is long, reiterate the main idea or recap the main points. If it's short, simply end strongly with your final point.

5. Edit by the numbers. You've written fast and loose—and the writing shows it. You've got some editing to do.

If possible, arrange your work schedule so that you can set the still-steaming writing aside and do something else before you try to revise. That usually means getting the rough draft done far enough ahead of deadline, and that's a matter of good planning.

Do It Yourself

Select several recent samples of your writing, three pages each or longer. Check out the conclusions to each. See if you could cut whole sentences or paragraphs, working back to where your writing really should have ended.

Caution

Leaving a cooling-off period between writing and editing won't allow you to gain "objectivity" about your work. You have time, energy, and ego invested in it, and it will always be yours. But time will enable you to be critical about your "baby."

Don't microedit until you've macrocut. Go through with an ax, chopping out the repetitious, the irrelevant, and the rambling.

Now go over whatever remains, using a checklist of the specific problems you need to look for, misspellings and dangling modifiers, maybe, and also the almost-right word, the soft passive voice construction, the vague reference.

Don't even think about not editing your work carefully before showing it to someone else. You'd save a little time, all right. But you'd spend that time and more writing the second and third memo clarifying the first one, holding the meeting to explain what you really meant, or explaining to the boss why your report caused the client to cancel the contract.

No amount of time or effort will salvage your damaged reputation.

Dale's still no Shakespeare or even Stephen King, but she has trained herself to write clear, concise memos, letters, and reports, simply by organizing her thoughts, writing simply and directly, and letting her work cool off before she edits it. She still can't imagine anybody writing for fun, but she no longer dreads the task at work.

Do It Yourself

Where do you get a checklist for revision? Create one by keeping a pad of paper with you as you edit the next couple of pieces you've written, noting the sorts of mistakes you tend to make.

That's another one of those tasks that take a little bit of time now but save tons of time from now on.

If you want a reference to help you with the editing, keep the *Associated Press Style Book* handy to settle questions such as 6:00 a.m., 6:00 A.M., or 6:00 am, for example. For grammar and structure questions, you can rely on *The Elements of Style*, by Will Strunk and E. B. White.

Time-Management Tips

1. Keep your writing short and simple. Use common words, and don't use too many of them.
2. Take a break from the writing before you run out of things to say.
3. Let it cool before you try to revise it.
4. Develop a checklist of your writing weaknesses to use when you revise your work.

Clutter Control

Summary of Part VI

1. Touch paper just once and get rid of it if you can.

2. Save only what you really need.

3. Catch up to the clutter by spending five minutes of every hour on clutter control, and then put paper on a maintenance diet.

4. Do one thing well at a time with full concentration.

5. Eliminate distractions, including the ones that originate inside your own head.

6. Use SARME—Scout, Ask, Read, Map, Etch—to remember what you read.

7. Use delays. You can rest, plan, or create.

8. Find the specific benefit to you for doing a task.

9. Face your fears and act anyway.

10. Measure your performance against your own needs and goals.

11. Allow yourself to be bad at something the first time you do it.

12. Delegate, trade, or ditch onerous and unnecessary jobs.

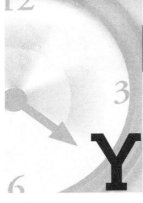

You know you spend a lot of time shuffling through paper, but you may be shocked to find out how much time.

All that paper is costing you precious time—time spent sorting, reading, filing, and tossing, to be sure, but also time moving the paper from one place to another and wading through it, looking for the paper you really need.

You need to fight your way through the clutter.

You can start by cleaning up what's there now. We're not talking about neatness. (My office is anything but.) We are talking about being able to find what you need, when you need it.

You'll also learn how to stem the paper flood at its source, eliminating the stuff before you even see it.

After you take care of the physical clutter, you'll begin to clear out the mental fog, learning to put your mind as well as your work space in order.

You'll encounter five streetwise time-management techniques you might not have thought of before. You'll learn how to:

- Minimize time spent waiting and turn those waiting periods into productive time.
- Eliminate procrastination, saving time and increasing efficiency while decreasing anxiety.
- Tolerate inevitable mistakes even as you minimize them.
- Eliminate jobs you don't want or need to do.
- Actually create time—without stretching the calendar or stopping the clock.

How to Control the Paper Flood

In this chapter, you'll learn:

■ Ten ways to control and eliminate paper

Chapter 20

"I'm a paper pusher."

Reg was shocked to hear those words come out of his mouth when his son Reggie Junior asked him what he did at the office all day. But the more he thought about it later, the more truth he found in the statement.

As a social case worker for the state, his primary job is to counsel clients on their rights and obligations under the new work-not-welfare program. He had gotten into the field because he wanted to make a positive contribution to society and to work directly with people.

But more and more of his time seems to be taken up reading reports and regulation updates, filling out forms, and searching through huge case files for the information he needs.

He hates all the flailing around in paper, and worse, he suspects he's not doing as good a job with and for his clients as he could be because of all the time spent shuffling.

You're spending from 50 to 70 percent of your working time dealing with paper—writing it, reading it, filing it, looking through it for another paper.

The coming of the computer was supposed to usher in the era of the paperless office, but if anything, computers have increased the flow of paper.

If you're ever going to get control of your time—which is to say your life—you're going to have to control the paper flood.

Ten Ways to Reduce, Control, and Eliminate Paper

1. Adopt a constant companion. Keep a notebook with you all the time—in your attaché case, in your desk drawer, in your coat pocket or purse, on your night table. Capture those stray insights and write yourself reminders. This way you won't lose your ideas, and you won't wind up with scraps of paper cluttering your life.

Caution

Be honest with yourself. Do you really need all that stuff out in the open where you can see—and trip over—it? You may simply be worried that you'll lose it or forget to deal with it if you can't keep an eye on it. Careful organization and an accessible file cabinet will take care of that problem and help you clean up your working space, too.

2. Manage your desktop(s). You need a place for everything and everything in its place. That goes for your desktop, and it also applies to the virtual desktop in the computer.

This isn't a matter of being neat. We're talking about getting organized. Your desktop may extend to the floor and every other flat surface not already covered. But as long as you know where everything is and can lay your hands on it without having to wade through the stuff you don't want, you're in good shape.

3. Touch it once. The first time you handle print—from a single-page memo to a 500-page report—decide what to do with it. Then do it. You can:

- Reroute
- Respond
- Read
- Recycle

4. Exercise good sortsmanship. Start by asking a variation on that fundamental question we developed a few chapters back: do I want or need to deal with this? If not, does anybody need to? If so, reroute. If not, recycle.

Do it now. Keep a supply of routing slips, interoffice mail envelopes, and whatever else you need to send the stuff on its way right away. And keep a bucket for recycling within easy reach.

For anything that makes it past this first cut, create a simple system for categorizing every piece of paper you encounter. You don't need anything fancy here. File folders will do fine. You may need no more than three files: DO, READ, and FILE.

5. Make it disappear. There's only one thing better than getting rid of it as soon as you touch it, and that's never having to touch it at all.

Never automatically renew a subscription without balancing the periodical's worth to you with the time it takes to process it. Ask to be taken off mailing lists and routing slips. For a wholesale purge of third-

Do It Yourself

How many times do you pick up the same piece of paper, glance at it, scowl, and toss it back on the desk, promising yourself that you'll deal with it later?

Want to find out?

Every time you handle the paper, slap a sticky dot on it. After a week of dotting, gather up the clutter on your desk and count the dots.

Get the picture?

class mail, write to the Direct Marketing Association, Mail Reference Service, Box 3861, New York, NY 10163-3861, and get off all those lists!

6. RSVP ASAP. If the paper needs only a brief response, do it right now. Create a speed response:

- A personalized Post-it note
- A note written on the bottom of the original letter or memo
- A half-sheet of business letterhead for a short note
- A phone call if appropriate and more efficient

Are you being callous by sending the correspondent's own paper back to him or her? Not at all. Callous is putting off the response or not responding at all. You're being responsive and smart, and you're also saving paper.

7. File it and forget it? Do you really need to keep it?

Most of us never read or even touch three quarters of the stuff we file. Why take the time to file it now and to fumble over it dozens or even hundreds of times in the future? Practice source-point pollution control.

If you do need to hang onto it, put it in the filing folder. Schedule a short filing session once a day (or week or month, depending on the volume of paper you're dealing with) for a time when you're not at your mental peak. (See Chapter 28 on biorhythms for more tips on how to match your energy level and alertness to the task you need to perform.)

8. Strip, clip, and flip. Tear out the material you really need and toss the rest of the publication away. Be especially attentive to lists, tabulations, charts, and graphs that summarize a great deal of material in a small space. Then recycle the rest.

While you're at it, toss out periodicals more than a year old, earlier drafts of written material, old reports that no longer have relevance. Schedule a brief session at the end of each week so the clutter level never gets unmanageable. While you're engaged in this relatively mindless work, you can decompress from a hard week of

Do It Yourself

Grab the first handful of folders in the top drawer of your filing cabinet and go through them. Get rid of every piece of paper you no longer need.

What percentage of the original material is left when you finish?

work, ease your transition into evening and weekend leisure time, and reflect on lessons learned.

9. Shift gears when you read. Reading everything at the same rate and in the same way makes as much sense as driving at the same speed on all roads and under all conditions.

You can skim some materials for main ideas, scan others for specific information, speed-read still others for the essence.

Save the material that requires time and concentration for your peak energy times and for times when you can concentrate without interruption. Reading difficult material requires your best effort, not the last shreds of consciousness at the end of the day.

10. The cop-out compost heap. If you can adhere to the "touch it once" rule at all times, you'll save yourself tons of time. You'll also qualify for the Time Management Hall of Fame.

If that rule's a little too rigid, create another file category, the compost heap.

Can't decide what to do with it? Not sure you should do anything at all? Put it in the compost file and forget it.

Once a week, get out the pitch fork and turn that compost. Some of the stuff will have gotten a bit ripe; you'll want to deal with that right away. But you'll find that a lot of the stuff is now ready to go directly to the recycle bin.

Paper management will soon become a happy habit, one that will save you enormous amounts of time and remove a lot of the frustration from the work day.

In the next chapter, we'll look at a few more specific techniques for cutting through the clutter.

Reg spends more time with people and less with paper now.

He put the time in up front, spending an entire Saturday purging old files and consolidating others. Even that wasn't so bad because he brought his radio and his son, and they made a game out of it, Reg Junior getting to shred all the discards.

The time paid off big time every time he needed to find a regulation, an old form, or a case study. He has a lot less paper to wade through, and his Saturday refresher gave him a good idea of where everything is.

Time-Management Tips

1. Adopt a touch-it-once policy for every piece of paper in your office.
2. Cancel subscriptions and get off mailing lists to eliminate clutter at the source.
3. Clip or copy the part you need and get rid of the rest.

How to Cut Through the Clutter

In this chapter, you'll learn:

- **How to unstack the desk and unpile the floor**
- **Four reasons why you made the mess in the first place**
- **Six ways to reduce the flow of incoming paper**

Chapter 21

Francis has a filthy office.

He's a soil scientist. Dirt is his business. He keeps trays and bottles of soil samples, dozens of them, filling cabinets and closets and spilling out onto his work bench.

He can handle the dirt just fine. It's the rest of the mess that has him fumbling and fuming. He can't find anything on his desk. Some days he has trouble finding the desk. Trying to come up with something as simple as a letterhead envelop can take several minutes—time he could put to much better use playing with dirt.

Are you suffering from stacked desk syndrome or, worse, the dread piled floor phenomenon?

Take a look around your workplace. Do you like what you see?

We're not talking about passing a white glove inspection here, or even about looking presentable when company comes. If your workplace doesn't have to do double duty as reception area, the way it looks has to suit only you.

But the clutter may be causing you to waste precious time picking through paper, searching for that important document, or simply moving piles from one place to another.

Look at it this way: every piece of paper requires you to do something with it, and doing something with paper takes time. The more times you have to shuffle, stack, file, or forage through the same paper, the more that paper costs you in time.

If you can honestly say that clutter isn't a problem for you, that you're just fine with and function efficiently with things just the way they are, here's a time-saving tip for you: skip the rest of this chapter. But, if clutter is a problem, read on.

Here are two solutions that, unfortunately, work only for a few.

Elite Solution 1: Let Somebody Else Do It

Editors deal with more paper than just about anyone else. How do they manage? At large publications, book publishers, and agencies, the top editors have underlings who turn the flood of incoming material into a manageable trickle before it ever reaches the decision maker. Call them associate editors, or editorial assistants, or goalies—whatever you call them, their job is to read through the "slush" of unsolicited material, diverting all but the most promising projects.

Many executives have assistants to open and sort the mail, dealing with anything that doesn't need the boss's attention.

Ronald Reagan trusted his staffers to encapsulate long reports into "mini-memos" of a page or less.

A former chancellor at the university extension in my town had a graduate student read all the educational journals and summarize relevant articles for him.

But most of us don't have such assistants. In fact, many of us are the assistants, dealing with the paper someone above us on the organizational chart doesn't want to waste time on. Elite solution 1 won't work for us.

Elite Solution 2: Train Your Sources to Limit the Incoming Flow

Ecologists now tell us that it's usually easier and more effective to limit the pollution at its source than to try to clean it up later. Many clutter managers have learned the same lesson.

Editors won't look at an entire manuscript. They demand a query letter, one page outlining the project and asking if the editor wants to see more. Perhaps you can train your correspondents to keep it to a page, too.

Then again, perhaps not.

Most of us are going to have to solve the paper problem ourselves. But that's only right, since we usually create the problem for ourselves, too.

Why We Make the Mess in the First Place

"I just don't have time to keep things straightened up," you say?

> Ecologists now tell us that it's usually easier and more effective to limit the pollution at its source than to try to clean it up later. Many clutter managers have learned the same lesson.

Ah, but as you've already seen in so many areas of life, time isn't really the problem. We make time for the things we want or need to do.

So, if you don't think you have time to straighten up, you may simply not be placing a high enough priority on cutting through the chaos. But once you recognize how much time you're actually spending messing with the mess, you'll be ready to move cleanup way up on your priority list.

But there are other, more subtle reasons why we learn to live with our piles instead of restoring order.

1. The nesting instinct. All those piles of stuff may actually be offering you comfort or reassurance, a homey lived-in look, a sense that you belong in this place and the place belongs to you. You may be marking your territory with your messes.

If that's the case, removing the clutter will make you uncomfortable, at least at first. You may feel lost in an environment that suddenly seems bare and unfriendly.

But you can be neat without being monastic. You can keep those talismans, pictures of loved ones, the autographed poster of Jerry Garcia you've treasured since the 1960s, whatever. You just need to make sure that you can get your work done efficiently and find the things you need when you need them.

2. Saver spillover. "You just never know when you might need it."

Is that you, justifying saving that restaurant receipt from the business trip you took to Sheboygan six years ago, or the copy of the annual facilities maintenance report, or the schedule from last year's conference?

If you're an indiscriminate saver, the clutter is a natural although unintended byproduct. You don't want the clutter, but you'll put up with it as the price you have to pay to hold onto everything that has ever crossed your desk.

3. Out of sight, out of mind. You may be afraid that, if you can't see it, you'll lose it. Or perhaps your secret dread is that if you

> Once you recognize how much time you're actually spending messing with the mess, you'll be ready to move cleanup way up on your priority list.

don't keep the project out on your desk, you'll forget to finish it. You're using the clutter as a visual cue.

But all those cues are getting in your way. The folder you really need is covered up, out of sight, lost if not forgotten.

4. The Einstein complex. Thomas Edison had a messy lab. Albert Einstein didn't even wear socks, much less a matching pair. Clutter is a sign of creativity, right?

You may on some level believe that your clutter marks you as an inventive and busy person. And besides, you like the notoriety your mess has earned for you and the good-natured teasing folks give you about it.

Bad news, folks. There isn't any evidence that creativity correlates positively with a messy desk, and truth to tell, sloppy isn't really all that cute. It's just messy. And the mess is costing you time.

If you're ready, then, it's time to cut the clutter. Take the time now, and you'll save the time every hour you're in your newly organized environment.

Small Steps, Big Strides

You can't write a novel, create a five-year plan, or blast the faces of four former presidents out of the stern stone of Mt. Rushmore all at once. You do big projects in small increments, one manageable step at a time. The same goes for conquering the clutter.

It took you a long time to accumulate all that stuff. Short of dousing the stuff with kerosene, tossing a lighted match on it, and running, there's no quick way to divest yourself of it, either.

You're going to do it five minutes at a time.

Take this pledge: for as long as the job takes, you're going to devote five minutes of every work hour to clutter removal. For every hour you're working but not otherwise obligated to attend a meeting or give a presentation, take the final five minutes to attack the mess.

Start with those piles on the desk. Pick up 6 or 7 inches worth and go through, paper by paper, file by file, periodical by periodical.

If you need to do something about, with, or to it, don't do it now. Figure out what you will do and when, and make a note to yourself to do it. Only then are you safe in putting it in the to-do basket.

If you need to keep it, grab a file folder and a marking pen. Create categories that work for you, key words that will enable you to find the material easily later. Make the categories general enough to help you consolidate dozens of singles into just a few composites. A file folder marked "Minutes of the June 3, 1997, board meeting" will serve you only once and is only marginally better than the loose minutes themselves. But a file folder marked "Board minutes, 1997" creates a neat receptacle for many sets of papers.

Do you really need to save those board minutes at all? Keep the recycle basket close at hand. If you don't really need it, never use it, can just as easily get the copy on file in the administrative assistant's office, already have a summary that's just as good and much more convenient—get rid of it.

For the larger, nonpaper items, develop a filing system to match—shelves, the boxes the twenty reams of copy paper came in, those plastic bins on sale in every office supplies store.

When the five minutes are up, go back to your regular tasks, setting a timer if necessary to remind you to take the next anticlutter break in fifty-five minutes.

You may find yourself refreshed and better able to get back to work, feeling psychologically pounds lighter as the pounds of clutter diminish.

> When the desk is under control, go after those file cabinets. Toss out entire folders of material that are no longer relevant.

When the desk is under control, go after those file cabinets. Toss out entire folders of material that are no longer relevant. Go through the keeper files page by page, culling the stuff you don't need. Maybe you don't really need a new file cabinet after all. After a few cleaning sessions, there's plenty of room in the old one! And everything in there is a lot easier to find.

These five-minute clear-out drills may soon become a happy habit, a cleansing break you actually look forward to. You'll gain momentum for the task as you see the mess begin to melt away and an efficient work space emerge.

Ongoing Maintenance

Sadly, a large majority of the people who lose weight on diets gain all the weight back—often with interest. While on that diet, you may totally change your eating habits. But if you go back to old behavior patterns when you attain your target weight, the weight inevitably sneaks back.

Same with work space clutter. Shedding the unwanted pounds of junk is one thing; keeping them off is quite another.

You'll still need to devote a set amount of time each working day to clutter control, perhaps not five minutes an hour anymore, maybe more like fifteen minutes at the end of the day—whatever it takes to make sure the mess doesn't creep back in.

You'll also need to apply good paper management techniques to the incoming paper flow.

Incoming!

Schedule a time each work day to deal with the incoming mail and memos. Be prepared with waste and recycle baskets, calendar, address book, file folders, Post-its, and stick-em dots. Now you're ready for a six-step process to reduce, control, and eliminate:

1. **Toss envelopes immediately.** If you need to save an address, note it in your address book or write it on a Post-it note and stick it to the letter or report.
2. **Note meeting and other appointment times on your calendar.** Then, unless you need the paper for some other reason, get rid of it.
3. **Create the file now.** If you need to save a document (are you sure?) and don't already have a place for it (are you sure of that, too?), create the file for it now, mark it carefully, and put it away.
4. **Schedule it.** If the material is going to require a longer and more thoughtful response, jot yourself a quick note on a Post-it indicating what you want to say and do, and stick the note to the material. Don't toss it on the "to-do later" pile

> Schedule a time each work day to deal with the incoming mail and memos. Be prepared with waste and recycle baskets, calendar, address book, file folders, Post-its, and stick-em dots.

until you've also noted on your schedule exactly when you'll deal with it.

5. **Prune the periodicals.** You may be on the routing list for a lot of periodicals you don't really need to read. But even handling that newsletter, deciding not to read it, and sending it along to the next name on the list require time. Get yourself off those routing lists.

    As we mentioned in the last chapter, learn to skim those periodicals you do need to attend to. If you find something you want to read, clip it from the periodical if it's yours, or make a photocopy if it isn't. Then get rid of the unwanted remainder. Put your clips and copies in a "current reading" folder for that scheduled reading time or for the next time you're stuck waiting in an airport or reception area.

6. **Affix the deadly red dot.** It doesn't have to be a red dot. Any color will do. But whatever color you pick, stick a dot (or star or happy face) on anything you can't file, toss, recycle, or turn around right now.

    Keep those dots handy. The next time you handle the item, stick another dot on it. Do this every time you have to pick it up, even if just to move it out of the way to get at something else. You'll get mighty sick of sticking those dots. And you'll create a vivid visual testimony to the amount of time you spend managing the clutter.

    This will lead you to apply steps 1 through 5 ever more rigorously. It will also prompt you to question yourself every time you feel the impulse to make a photocopy, print out e-mail, clip an article, save a schedule. If you make it, you'll have to manage it.

> Keeping in shape is a lot easier than getting back in shape. Deflect the incoming and manage the day to day so that clutter never again becomes a time-consuming problem.

Keeping in shape is a lot easier than getting back in shape. Deflect the incoming and manage the day to day so that clutter never again becomes a time-consuming problem. Good clutter management will save you enormous amounts of time and spare you needless frustration every working day.

Francis can find the dirt he needs—along with envelopes, paper clips, and everything else—because he made the effort to conquer the clutter. Now he spends that fifteen minutes at the end of each working day putting things right for the next day. And he deflects a great deal of potential mess by never letting the stuff find a roosting spot in his office in the first place.

His office is still full of dirt, but now he's a tidy little soil scientist.

Time-Management Tips

1. Devote five minutes of each working hour to clutter cleanup until you have your office under control.
2. Put your paper on a maintenance diet by performing routine cleanup and reducing the amount of paper that comes in.

Fighting Through the Fog

In this chapter, you'll learn:

- Three sources of mental confusion—and how to combat them
- How to focus on one task at a time
- The three hidden costs of multitasking
- How to identify and remove distractions
- How to remember what you read

Chapter 22

"I'm the poster child for Alzheimer's disease," Dawn tells her friends.

She jokes about her forgetfulness and her seeming inability to remember what she read five minutes ago, but her gathering mental confusion worries her.

In her late thirty's, Dawn works full time as an administrative assistant and comes home to two grade-school-aged children and a husband who puts in even longer hours than she does and needs a detailed map to find his way around the kitchen. As the demands on her time increase, so too does her mental confusion.

She has taught herself not to be too upset by the controlled chaos of a cluttered house, but the mess her mind's in is making her a little frantic.

> Cleaning up stacks of paper is one thing. Cleaning out the mental clutter is quite another.

Cleaning up stacks of paper is one thing. Cleaning out the mental clutter is quite another.

We tend to think of the brain as an internal computer. We file away information and our experiences, both firsthand—the stuff that happens to us—and vicarious—the stuff we read about, see in movies, or otherwise encounter secondhand. When we need the information, we simply bring up the "data" to the screen of the conscious mind in the form of memory.

Except it often doesn't work.

Three Kinds of "Computer Error" That Plague Us All

You've no doubt had many unhappy occasions when you've searched for specific memory—a formula for the math final, a telephone number, the name of someone you met at a party a month (or twenty seconds) before, your wedding anniversary—only to come up empty. It's especially frustrating when the answer seems to be "right on the tip of your tongue," almost but not quite in focus.

You've probably also had the experience of arguing with someone over family history or other shared experience. You have a vivid recollection of last year's Fourth of July celebration, say, but your version of events differs from Uncle Sid's equally vivid recollection. You're both sure you're right, and neither of you is lying.

While you're fishing for the memory you need, you're just as likely to come up with a different flounder—an unbidden memory or fantasy. If the accidental memory serves you, you call it inspiration. If it seems irrelevant, it's a daydream. Either way, you have no idea where the memory came from or why it appeared when it did. It's as if a file opened itself on your computer screen while you were working on something else.

So, either the brain's a lousy computer or it isn't really a computer at all.

We haven't even touched on the strange world of dreams, "memories" of events that never happened, couldn't possibly happen, and might shame you if they did happen. How can "you" have a dream "you" don't understand or don't approve of? Are there two of you?

The fact is, nobody really knows for sure. The most popular recent explanation, left brain/right brain theory, comes up short, as have all previous theories about how the brain really works. We now know a great deal about the physical process—electrical impulses and chemical exchanges, centers of mental activity and areas of specific functioning—but we still haven't really discovered the mind. We don't know where self-consciousness and free will come from.

The mystery frustrates scientists and enthralls mystics. If your goal is to think more efficiently, it needn't bother you a bit. Just as you don't have to know how an internal combustion engine works before you can drive a car, you don't need to understand the brain before you can think effectively.

The Focus Factor: How to Do One Thing at a Time

Watch a child at play, "studying" a bug, or "working" to make a kite. She becomes absorbed in the task or pleasure at hand, her concentration so complete, she really doesn't hear you when you call her in for dinner.

> Just as you don't have to know how an internal combustion engine works before you can drive a car, you don't need to understand the brain before you can think effectively.

As she grows older, her life becomes more complex, and the demands on her time become more intense. She teaches herself to fragment her attention, to do two things at once, to anticipate the next task while working on the current one.

Although this process occurs naturally in most of us, we may help it along by taking time-management classes that teach us to "multitask," fielding a phone inquiry while continuing to type the memo, reading the report while watching television, listening to a book on tape while cooking dinner.

The Hidden Costs of Multitasking

You pay in three important ways when you learn to juggle life's demands by doing several things at once. You lose focus, enthusiasm, and time.

The more hectic life becomes, the more the demands on your time mount, the more you learn to do two, three, and four things at once, the less able you become to concentrate on what you're doing. The absorption that came naturally to you as a kid now becomes elusive; you can't recapture it even if you try.

When you lose your capacity for rapt attention, you also lose the childlike joy you once took in the moment. It's much harder to enjoy anything you aren't fully mentally invested in.

Even if that doesn't bother you, the third price tag of multitasking should: when you try to save time by doing more than one thing at once, you wind up wasting your precious time.

Three Reasons Why Multitasking Wastes Time

- You don't do either thing well.
- You have to do things twice.
- You exhaust yourself physically and mentally, reducing your efficiency and the amount of time and energy you can apply to a task.

If you're serious about using time efficiently, you need to relearn the child's art of doing one thing at a time. You need to start now, and you need to work at it every day.

In the two previous chapters, we tackled the physical clutter you were tripping over as you tried to get things done. Now we'll look at two more subtle forms of mess—what you hear or don't hear and what you see or don't see—that may be fragmenting your concentration. Improvements here can allow you to make your workplace support your work.

Noise Pollution as Environmental Hazard

The whir of the copy machine, the beep of the fax, the chink-kachunk of the vending machine, the hum of the air conditioner, the babble from the break room provide the soundtrack of daily office life. If such noises are consistent and predictable, you've probably simply become accustomed to them, and they don't create a distraction.

But some of us are most sensitive to such murmurings than are others. And most of us are likely to be disrupted by the occasional jackhammering of street repairs outside the office window or the clanging of workers pounding on the air ducts in the basement. If noise is a distraction, you have three options: no noise, white noise, or your noise.

1. No noise. You may be able to stop the annoyance at the source. Your officemate may not even know he hums while he reads his e-mail, for example.

If you can't remove the noise, you may be able to remove yourself from the noise. Cellular phones and laptop computers may afford you the ability to escape.

Your third option may be to simply shut the noise out with ear plugs.

2. "White" noise. Rather than seeking silence, you may be able to use a neutral noise to cover the annoying ones. The steady murmur of that motel room air conditioner may have saved you from a sleepless night by masking the occasional door slamming down the

> If you can't remove the noise, you may be able to remove yourself from the noise. Cellular phones and laptop computers may afford you the ability to escape.

hall or the noisy goodbye from the parking lot. You can use any sound that doesn't itself distract you by calling attention to itself. Many find commercially produced nature noises (babbling brook, mountain stream, breaking waves) perfect for this use.

3. Your noise. One person's noise is another person's symphony.

Some of us keep classical music on the radio in the background as we work. Some listen to "oldies" or heavy metal or the all-polka-all-day station. Others keep the murmur of talk radio as a constant companion throughout the day. Some crave silence.

There's no one right way for all. The proper sound environment for you is the one that doesn't intrude on your concentration and that in fact keeps your subconscious mind happily occupied so that it doesn't kidnap conscious thought and run away with it into daydream.

If you share your workplace, and you and your officemate(s) don't agree on what a sound environment should be, avoid dueling portable radios. The cacophony you produce won't serve either or any of you. Seek a compromise, an option that isn't anybody's first choice but that works for all. If that isn't possible, use simple technologies (portable radio with ear plugs) to create individual sound spaces.

Sights for Sore Eyes in the Workplace: The Good, the Bland, and the Ugly

Sights can be as distracting as sounds.

Ugly will irritate. Beauty will entice. They are equally distracting. Only the visually neutral will leave you alone to do your work.

Arrange your workplace to create a bland background while you perform work requiring concentration. Bland for you may be a blank wall or a Picasso print. You be the judge of that. Just be sure you create a sight line that supports your need to focus.

The color of that blank wall may affect you. Green is traditionally calming. Blue is also restful. But color stereotypes are no more universally true than any other kind. If green or blue doesn't soothe you, select a color that does.

Caution

If you can really concentrate with Rush Limbaugh or Dr. Laura railing in the background, then try to arrange your workplace so that he or she can keep you company. But be honest with yourself, and make sure you aren't paying more attention to Rush than to that rush order.

Even lighting may work for or against you. First, make sure you have enough light. Dim lighting is like low-grade static, forcing you to work harder to focus. Fluorescent lighting creates glare, especially on glossy paper. Natural light from the window may give you "screen squint." If you're left-handed, and your source of light comes over your left shoulder, you're casting shadows on the page ahead of where you're writing. These are subtle distractions, but they can add up, and they're usually easy to fix.

Anything that moves invites attention. Keep the aquarium and the bird cage out of your line of sight, and don't face an open doorway when you need to concentrate.

Last year I moved into a sixth-floor office with a view of Madison's lovely Lake Mendota. The lone computer outlet is on the wall by the window, but I set up my workstation so that I'd be facing the blank wall instead of the lake. That way I look at the screen while I type.

I sit at my desk, with my back to the window, when I read. But when the phone rings, I allow myself to stand facing the window while I talk.

By restricting my access to that pretty lake view, I increase my concentration and ability to focus on my work. I use the view as a reward when the telephone forces me to take a break from reading, writing, or thinking. My nice view works for me, not against me.

Such strategies can help you bring your external environment under control. We'll now move to the internal environment of your mind. You'll find that, as your powers of concentration improve, the external annoyances we just dealt with will have less power to disrupt you.

Do It Yourself

Take an inventory of the sights and sounds in your workplace. Is your environment working for or against you? Draw up a list of the specific changes you can make to improve this setting. Then do it.

How to Do One Thing at Once

Even if you could somehow seal yourself off in a noiseless, visually neutral environment while you work (sensory deprivation chamber? padded cell?), you still wouldn't be free of distractions. In fact, the mental noise would become all the louder—as it does late at night when you have trouble falling asleep after an especially taxing day.

Internal "noise" can be every bit as irritating as—and a good deal harder to handle than—the external kinds.

Most of the internal distractions fall into one of three categories:

- Daydreams or fantasies
- Worries or preoccupations
- Inspirations or breakthroughs

The first type is pleasant, the second often painful, the third helpful, but all are harmful to concentration.

Here are three techniques to help you maintain your focus and control the internal buzz.

1. Acknowledge your distraction. Don't ignore the mental chatter or pretend it isn't there. That will only make it more insistent. Acknowledge the random thought. Then use the appropriate strategy, depending on the variety of distraction:

- Daydream or fantasy: smile and reschedule. More about this in step 3.
- Worry or preoccupation: remind yourself of the action you plan to take and when you intend to take it, and send it packing. Step 2 covers this.
- Inspiration or breakthrough: capture the flash with a quick note to yourself for later.

2. Use your list. Earlier we were talking about using your to-do list rather than letting the to-do list "use" you to run your life. One of the best uses for that list is as an aid to concentration. Put your plan of work in tangible form so that you can chart your progress. When you find yourself worrying about item six when you should be completing item three, let the list pull you back on track by assuring you that you'll get to each item in its turn. Because you know the list won't let you forget the task later, you're free to forget about it now.

3. Schedule your daydream. Your list creates a productivity schedule for you. But as noted earlier, you should also schedule rest,

> Don't ignore the mental chatter or pretend it isn't there. That will only make it more insistent.

rewards, and minivacations into each work day. During those two- to five-minute rests, call forth that distracting daydream and fully indulge it. You'll emerge refreshed and energized, and your daydream will have lost its ability to waylay you.

How to Remember What You Read

If you're a baseball fan, you don't need to apply any special technique to reading the sports pages during baseball season. You'll read rapidly, with perfect comprehension and uncanny recall. (My wife has at times been annoyed with me for remembering Sandy Koufax's lifetime earned run average while forgetting the names of relatives and friends.)

You need help with concentration and retention only when the material you must read holds no inherent appeal or apparent relevance to you.

For years, I've taught a simple five-step process called SARME to students from high school through postgraduate school. The comment I get most often is, "I wish I'd learned this years ago." With this method, you'll concentrate on what you're reading, organize the material according to its relevance to you, and remember the important points as long as you need to.

Here's how SARME works, or rather, how you work SARME:

Scout. Anticipate the scope and depth of the material. Skim through, reading headlines, summaries, subheads, tabulated lists, and other key points. Read the conclusion, if any. Read captions for any illustrative material, if any.

Ask. Based on your quick scouting mission, jot down a few relevant questions you expect the material to answer for you.

Read. With these questions in mind, read the material at a comfortable speed. Don't consciously slow down, thinking this will help you understand and remember better. In fact, the contrary is true.

> You need help with concentration and retention only when the material you must read holds no inherent appeal or apparent relevance to you.

> Most of your forgetting takes place within those first two hours. If you reinforce the information right away, you strengthen your recall tremendously.

If it's a long report, article, or textbook chapter, break the long work into sections for this and the next step.

Map. Quickly note the key information from the piece. Don't simply underline or highlight the text. Jot notes in your own words. Be sure to answer the questions you posed initially, if they still seem relevant to you.

Etch. Review your notes within two hours of reading the material. Most of your forgetting takes place within those first two hours. If you reinforce the information right away, you strengthen your recall tremendously. Think of specific applications of the material to your life and work. Create images when possible since they are much easier to enter into long-term memory.

Dawn still wouldn't call herself a model of tranquillity, but since she started applying the principle of doing one thing at a time, the mental vapors have started disappearing like midmorning fog. She still forgets things, of course. She figures that's natural when you run at full speed most of the day. But she is again able to concentrate on the task at hand, and when she reads or hears something important, she's able to make sure it stays with her. She has the sense that she is going a lot slower, and yet, she seems to get everything done and still have a little breathing room.

Time-Management Tips

1. Do one thing at a time with full concentration.
2. Identify and eliminate or mask distracting noises.
3. Do the same with distracting visual stimuli.
4. Acknowledge the mental distraction and then refocus on the task at hand.
5. Schedule daydreams.
6. Use SARME—Scout, Ask, Read, Map, Etch—to remember what you read.

Turn Downtime into Your Most Productive Time

In this chapter, you'll learn:

- Three reasons why you have to wait
- How to turn the wait into a rest or into a productive session

Chapter 23

Dennis feels the meter running every time someone or something keeps him waiting.

He's a real "time is money" kind of guy. He schedules his time precisely and creates routes for his sales calls that take advantage of every possible shortcut and eliminate any doubling back.

He prides himself on being on time for every appointment.

Maybe that's why he has so little tolerance for people who aren't on time. Dennis can't stand to be kept waiting, and unfortunately, he's not very good at hiding that fact. He knows his poorly concealed anger might be costing him sales, and he suspects that his impatience while waiting may be causing his frequent headaches.

If only everyone else would read a good time-management book and figure out how to stick to a schedule!

When you were a kid, I'll bet you spent a lot of time waiting and wishing. I know I did.

Mondays, I'd start waiting and wishing for Fridays. About the time I got to school each day, I'd start waiting and wishing for recess, and then lunch, and then the magic hour of 3:00, time to go home. I can't imagine how much time I spent staring at time, in the form of those clunky old school clocks that went "click-thunk" each time the big hand struggled another minute forward. (Was it my imagination, or did the "click-thunks" get louder for the final two or three minutes of each hour?)

The more I looked, the slower that minute hand moved. So I'd play the waiting game, trying to make myself wait fifteen minutes between clock checks. I rarely made it that long.

Along about Halloween, I started waiting and wishing for Christmas. After Christmas, there was still New Year's Day, a wonderful occasion for a kid who got to go to the Tournament of Roses Parade almost every year. But January 2, I started waiting and wishing for baseball season, and once baseball season finally arrived, the wait for summer vacation became all but intolerable.

Ah, but after a few weeks of the endless, unstructured days of summer, I sometimes caught myself feeling twinges of something that just might have been boredom. So I'd start wishing and waiting for our family's annual two-week trek to some mountain lake. After that I could look forward to my late-summer birthday.

Then the cycle of waiting and wishing started all over again.

Why Don't Adults Get Bored?

Boredom isn't a lack of things to do. It's a lack of anything you want to do. Boredom is equal parts restlessness (exhausted people don't get bored; they fall asleep) and lack-of-want-to, complete indifference or aversion to any of the possible activities you might do next.

So, how come we never seem to get bored now?

We still get restless, although less frequently and intensely as we mature (read "become more frequently exhausted"). And we certainly continue to suffer from lackawanna (more or less frequently and intensely in inverse proportion to how much we genuinely enjoy our work and family life). But always we suffer, too, from too much to do and too little time to do it. We push on to the next task, damn the lackawanna, full speed ahead.

Also, as we get older, we become aware of the dwindling number of days left to us. Even the Mondays in February become more precious in that context, and we don't want to wish any of our time away looking forward to another time.

What would you give for one of those endless Christmas Eve days of your youth, when time seemed to crawl and the hours refused to pass?

Fact is, you still have them, probably several little Christmas Eve days each working day. It's called waiting.

We wait for the coffee to perk, wait for the bus to come, wait for somebody to unjam the copy machine, wait for the client to respond to our voice mail message, wait for our luncheon date, wait in traffic, wait at the doctor's office or the Quicky Lube (which can never be quite Quicky enough). Time passes slowly at these times, not because you're anticipating the joy of good surprises under the Christmas tree, but because you need to be elsewhere, doing other things.

Most of us hate waiting. The more crowded your to-do list or day planner and the more impatient you tend to be, the more difficult the

Do It Yourself

Make a list of your waits. Include any wait long enough to annoy you.

Keep this list in front of you and add to it as you read the rest of this chapter. Use it to create specific streetwise strategies for turning these frustrating times into good times.

Relative status and power often dictate how long folks will wait for one another. Students wait for professors, secretaries for bosses, laborers for superintendents, and not the other way around.

wait will seem. We've reacted by trying to speed up our activity and eliminate the spaces between activities so we can cram more of them into a day. But this can actually work against us—increasing the pressure and thus the frustration when, despite our best planning, something makes us wait anyway.

One Bad Way to Do Away with Waiting

Folks who are always late never have to wait. They make everybody else wait. That's one solution to the problem of waiting. It's a very bad solution.

Relative status and power often dictate how long folks will wait for one another. Students wait for professors, secretaries for bosses, laborers for superintendents, and not the other way around.

The other determinant is dependency. You may not afford your plumber many status points, but you'll wait for him or her indefinitely as you keep swapping an empty bucket for a full one under the oozing water pipe.

How long are people required to wait for you? How long are they willing? What will they think of you while they wait?

I suspect that keeping people waiting isn't really your style anyway. Folks who seek help with time management are generally the ones being kept late by others. You get to places on time, and you expect others to do the same. That's one reason why for you waiting is inevitable.

I've suggested that you build time cushions into your daily life. But when you allow more travel time than you might need under perfect circumstances and, by some miracle, circumstances actually turn out to be perfect, you'll get there early. That means even more waiting.

One Pretty Good Way to Eliminate Some of the Waiting

Folks who keep you waiting tend to do so chronically. You can eliminate some of the waiting in your life by eliminating some of those people.

Stand me up once, shame on you. Stand me up twice, shame on me. I don't make a second appointment with the person who blew off the first one.

You don't always have a choice. One of the chronic wait-creators in your life might be your boss, your spouse, or your kid. You can try to convert these folks into the cult of punctuality, but you'll most likely fail. That's another reason why you'll have to wait sometimes.

How to Make the Wait Matter Less

You know certain activities will involve waiting. As much as you can, engage in those activities at times when waiting won't make as big a difference.

But few doctors schedule appointments for 6:00 (A.M. or P.M.) or Saturday afternoons. You have to take what you can get, including the cancellation at the dentist right in the middle of the day. You'll always have to do some waiting.

Three Inescapable Facts of Modern Life That Make Waiting Inevitable

1. There are too many of us in the same place.
2. We're all trying to get someplace else.
3. We get in each other's way doing it.

No matter which line you pick at the market or the bank, the line you pick will move the slowest, right? (When my wife and I run errands together, we hedge our bets by standing in separate lines. We even make a friendly competition out of it to see whose line "wins.")

You'll always wind up behind the person with twenty-six items in the "12 Items or Less" line. That person will wait until those twenty-six items have been scanned and totaled before beginning to think about paying. And then he or she will drag out a change purse and pay in pennies, 4,284 of them.

What can you do?

> No matter which line you pick at the market or the bank, the line you pick will move the slowest, right?

You can rant and bellow. You can make snide comments under your breath. You can dump your groceries on the ground and walk away. You can switch to another line—and wind up behind someone who wants a refund on a quart of ice cream purchased at another store, in another decade.

Or you can take that lemon and squeeze until you get lemonade.

How to Escape the Wait: Three Steps That Will Make You More Productive and Less Rushed

Step 1. Accept the wait as inevitable. Waiting is destructive for two reasons. First, if you haven't allowed sufficient time for waiting, the wait will destroy your schedule and cause you to be late for other appointments and to fail to complete necessary tasks. You can defuse this time bomb, lowering the stakes in the waiting game, by refusing to overpack your schedule. That way, the wait can't hurt you as much.

Waiting can be even more destructive because of what it does to your insides. Oh, how you seethe as you idle in traffic or jiggle and fidget in the waiting room. That seething can trigger a corrosive stress reaction, harming you physically as well as emotionally.

> You may not be able to eliminate the wait, but you can minimize the damage it can do to you by accepting what you can't change.

You may not be able to eliminate the wait, but you can minimize the damage it can do to you by accepting what you can't change. Stop blaming the fates (or the jerk who kept you waiting). Stop festering about where you should be and what you should be doing. Be where you are, doing what you're doing.

Step 2. Rename the wait. You speed through the day, pushing your body and mind beyond fatigue, putting off needed rest. You won't allow yourself to stop—

- Until you get home and can finally kick off your shoes and put your feet up
- Until the kids are fed and bathed and storied and put to bed
- Until the weekend
- Until the vacation
- Until retirement

Some of those "untils" never come, of course. Sometimes, when they do, they come too late to help because you've already been pushed past the point where you can relax.

Meanwhile, you may have rushed and squirmed and fretted your way through four or five potential rest periods a day.

Rename the wait. Call it a rest instead.

Oh, what a difference. Waits are cold frustrations. Rests are warm comforts.

Could you really feel warm and embraced stuck in the middle of traffic? Probably not right away. Such a major change in mindset takes some working at and some getting used to. But it can be done. I know because I've done it—not right away, and not every time, but often enough that I now realize the anger and frustration aren't inevitable results of waiting.

Step 3. Use the wait. You're running late, racing the green turn arrow to the intersection. But the bozo in front of you is poking along, blissfully unaware of your need to make that signal. The bozo, of course, makes the light while causing you to miss it.

You can scream and fume, spiking your blood pressure while adrenaline oozes out your ears. Or you can proclaim a rest and take one of your minivacations for deep breathing or mental roaming.

Too unproductive for you? Spend forty-five seconds visualizing a perfect golf swing or tennis stroke. There's evidence that positive visualization can improve performance.

> Conduct a mental dialogue with someone you've always wanted to talk to.
> Brainstorm solutions to a problem.
> Plan a week's worth of dinner menus.

You'll wait a lot longer than forty-five seconds at the doctor's office. So come prepared. Bring that book you've been trying to find time to read, or the crossword puzzle you'll never allow yourself the time for later.

> Tend to your knitting.
> Write a haiku.

Rename the wait. Call it a rest instead. Oh, what a difference. Waits are cold frustrations. Rests are warm comforts.

Read one of those moldy magazines that seem to survive only in historical societies and waiting rooms. Pick something you wouldn't usually read. For me, that might be *Cosmopolitan*, *Modern Maturity*, or *Highlights for Children*. I tend to catch up on *People* that way, too. You'll gain a new perspective on life and learn things you never would have known. And that way it won't make any difference that the magazine is old; it's all new to you anyway.

Results of Turning the Wait into a Rest

You'll be better rested and more relaxed (and better read). You'll be more efficient and effective. Who knows? You might write some great haiku. And you'll get to where you were going at exactly the same time you would have anyway.

Dennis had no success converting the rest of the world to his cult of punctuality. So he learned to turn the waits into productive times to catch up on his paperwork and study new product specs.

It took some doing. The "natural" anger reaction took a while to fade. But now Dennis can greet his tardy clients with a sincere smile.

He also built a little more flex time into his supertight scheduling so that being kept waiting doesn't destroy his whole day.

Dennis has slowed down—just a bit—and finds that he actually gets more done. He's also closing on a higher percentage of his sales calls.

Time-Management Tip

1. Use the inevitable delays to rest, plan, or indulge your imagination.

Put Off the Urge to Put It Off

In this chapter, you'll learn:

- Five reasons why you procrastinate—and
- Five ways to stop

Chapter 24

"Never put off until tomorrow what you can put off until next week."

Sure, Don can joke about his chronic procrastination. For a while he even wore one of those little round "toit" buttons (to show that he had finally "gotten a round toit"). But he knows his tendency to put tasks off isn't really funny.

He winds up skating awfully close to the edge of a lot of deadlines, and a few times he's fallen through and been late on important jobs.

Don hasn't consciously totaled up the lost time and increased stress his procrastination is costing him, but he sure knows well the feeling of panic he gets when the deadline approaches and the hated task looms large.

He's ready to trade in his "round toit" for a way to wipe out his work avoidance.

The national association of procrastinators met recently in Houston, Texas, for their annual gathering. I wonder how many of them were late? I was going to check, but I never got around to it.

Like all of our other human failings, procrastination makes great subject matter for jokes. But real-life procrastination is no laughing matter.

No time-management technique will do you a whit of good if you still allow yourself to postpone the difficult or the unpleasant. The job doesn't get any easier while you wait. Quite the contrary, your sense of dread will build, making it increasingly difficult to bring yourself to the task.

Your delay will probably complicate matters. You'll then have to deal with the complications, often before you can even get at the original job.

Thus, procrastination costs time while creating unnecessary stress.

So, if it's so awful, how come so many of us do it? Why are there some jobs we just never seem to "get around to," no matter the consequences of our evasion?

> No time-management technique will do you a whit of good if you still allow yourself to postpone the difficult or the unpleasant.

Five Reasons Why We Procrastinate and Five Ways to Stop Putting It Off

Reason 1: You Haven't Really Committed to Doing the Job

When I teach a workshop for would-be and beginning authors, I often start by asking why they want to write a book. Such an extended project demands a huge commitment of time, energy, and emotion, after all. Most of the answers I get fall into one of three categories.

The first reason, simply stated, is that the writer feels good while writing (or, conversely, feels wretched when not writing). Writing seems to be almost an addiction or a compulsion, although a relatively harmless one.

The second set of reasons basically cluster around the notion of communication and storytelling: "I have something to say, and a book seems to be the best way to say it," or "I've got a story I want or need to tell." I've even heard folks say that the story seems to be using them to get itself told.

The third set of reasons stems from the notion, sadly mistaken, that authors become rich and famous with relatively little effort. Many of the folks in this group don't want to write a book; they want to have written a book so that they can reap the supposed rewards.

Most of the folks in the first category and many in the second actually go on to write that book. Few in the third group ever do.

Occasionally, I get a reason that doesn't fall into any of these categories.

"My English teacher back in good old P.S. 134 said I'd make a good writer," one might say, or "Folks in my book group think my life story would be inspirational."

Assuming that they aren't being coy, that they don't really mean "I think I'd make a great writer," or "I think my life story would be inspirational," my response to this sort of reason borders on Mom's old admonition: "If somebody told you to jump off a cliff, would you do it?"

> My response to this sort of reason borders on Mom's old admonition: "If somebody told you to jump off a cliff, would you do it?"

The key here is the source of the motivation. We generally don't need to prioritize or otherwise force or trick ourselves into performing actions that are internally motivated. But the more the motivation comes from the English teacher or the book club or the mate or the boss or any other external source, the less likely we are to do it.

Know anybody who got into the family bakery business, or became a lawyer, or joined the Marines because somebody expected or demanded it? If so, you probably know an unhappy baker or lawyer or Marine.

You may chronically put off an activity because you aren't really sold on doing it at all. Reasons include:

- You don't think it's your job.
- You think it's somebody else's job.
- The job's a waste of time.

If that's the case, you need to answer two fundamental questions:

- What's in it for me if I do it?
- What will happen to me if I don't?

The first question may redirect and increase your motivation. You're no longer doing it because someone said you ought to. You're doing it to impress a boss, help a friend, make money, or get to a task you really enjoy.

The second question is the negative version of the first. Your motivation may become avoidance of something unpleasant, like a lousy job evaluation, an angry or alienated spouse, or a disappointed child.

If you can find no internal motivation—no benefit for doing the job and no penalty for not doing it—you may well decide not to do it at all.

Even if you can see a benefit to doing the job, you may still decide that the costs in time and energy (and the other things you aren't doing) outweigh the benefits. In that case you can:

Do It Yourself

Think of a recent job you tackled even though you didn't want to. What was the source of your resistance to the task? What motivated you to do it despite this resistance? What can you learn from this experience to apply to future jobs?

1. Do what you have to do to get out of the job. This is not the same thing as simply putting it off. This is a definitive decision not to do it and to accept the consequences, if any. In the long run, that sort of decision costs less, in time and stress, than does the passive resistance of procrastination.
2. Do it anyway—but for your own reasons.

Reason 2: You're Afraid of the Job

This is a hard thing for many of us to admit—to ourselves let alone to someone else. But it may be what's keeping you from doing a job you need or want to accomplish. If you can identify your reluctance as fear and track it to its source, you can deal with the fear and get on with the job. Here are three of the most common varieties of performance anxiety:

> If you can identify your reluctance as fear and track it to its source, you can deal with the fear and get on with the job.

1. **Fear of failure.** Consider the student who never studies and flunks out. He can always tell himself, "If I had studied, I would have passed the stupid course." But what if he had studied—and still failed?

    For most of us, "won't" is a lot easier to deal with than "can't." If you don't try it, you don't have to confront the possibility that you can't do it.
2. **Fear of success.** On the other hand, if you do pass the course, folks will expect you to do it again, or to go out and get a job, or to apply what you've learned. If you never try, you'll never have to face the consequences of success, either.
3. **Fear of finishing.** "If I pass the course, I'll graduate. If I graduate, I'll…"

    You'll what? If you don't pass the course, you'll never have to find out what happens next. If you never write the novel, you'll never have to know whether a publisher would have accepted it. If you don't finish basic training, you'll never have to know whether you could have really hacked it in the military.

Do It Yourself

Bring to mind a task that caused you anxiety and perhaps even fear when you thought about it. What was the outcome? Did your fear prevent you from taking on the task? Were you able to use the fear as energy to get the job done?

Identify the fear. Give it a name and confront it. Imagine the consequences of your actions or nonactions as objectively as you can. Would naming and claiming your fear have changed the outcome?

Use this technique the next time you confront the resistance of fear. The fear won't go away. But if the goal is worth pursuing, you'll be able to act despite the fear.

Sometimes the not knowing seems more acceptable than the possible consequences of finding out for sure. But how sad to let such fears prevent you from ever trying.

Reason 3: You Don't Place a High Enough Priority on the Activity

You're sold on the idea that somebody ought to do the task. You'll even agree, if pressed, that you're the person to do it. You may even want to do it.

You just don't want or need to do it enough, and you always want or need to do something else more.

Thus, the task—cleaning the leaves out of the rain gutters in autumn, say—keeps getting bumped down the list, below other, more pressing jobs. You've got to go grocery shopping first because you won't have anything to eat if you don't. You've got to mow the lawn first because it will look awful if you don't. (And nobody can see the leaves in the rain gutters, after all.)

This sort of procrastination problem may eventually work itself out. As the other tasks get done, those leafy gutters work their way up the list. Or the problem may take on a higher priority after the first hard rain of the season.

Establishing priorities is subjective, especially when dealing with activities that are neither urgent nor particularly important relative to other activities. Take a look at the job that just isn't getting done and see if you can redefine it in terms of the ultimate benefit you'll receive for doing it.

First time through, this definition may be negative:

"If I don't clean out the rain gutters, I'll get a flood in the garden the first time it rains hard."

Positive motivations tend to be much stronger. Recast it in the positive form:

"If I clean out the rain gutters, I'll protect my garden from flooding."

Look for the ancillary benefits of getting the task done:

- "I'll finally stop worrying about it."
- "I'll get some nice exercise out in the sunshine."
- "I can listen to a ball game on the radio while I work."

Are these considerations enough to move the task up the list? If so, get at it! But if not, you must either resign yourself to living with the consequences of your nonaction or find a way to get the job done without actually having to do it. You could hire the neighbor kid, thus trading money for time, for example. Or you could add "It won't cost anything if I do it myself" to your list of ancillary benefits, perhaps tipping the balance in favor of doing it.

Reason 4: You Don't Know Enough to Do the Task

When I get "writer's block," it's often my subconscious mind's helpful way of suggesting that I don't really know what the hell I'm talking about.

This is true for other sorts of motivational blocks as well. You may simply not know enough to do the job right. You haven't consciously recognized or admitted this to yourself, but you know it deep down, and this knowledge is manifesting itself in strong aversion.

Gather the information you need. If all else fails, read the directions (a desperate last resort for many of us). Then plunge into the task.

> ### Caution
>
> Learn to discern between the legitimate need to gather information and a stalling mechanism whereby reading the book or going to talk to the guy at the hardware store is simply a way to put off confronting the job. If your problem is good old lackawanna rather than lack of information, you'll need a different strategy.

Reason 5: You Just Plain Don't Wanna!

On a preference scale of 1 to 10, giving Rover his flea bath rates a minus 2.

It isn't merely unpleasant. It isn't just disgusting. It's downright dangerous. Rover does not like his flea bath. Last time you tried this little experiment in torture, you wound up scratched, Rover was traumatized, and the bathroom looked like a tidal wave had hit it.

The fleas are back. Rover is scratching. If you don't do something—and fast—you'll have fleas all over the house.

You've got two choices, and you don't need a book on time management to tell you what they are:

- Gut it out.
- Farm it out.

Get on the old raincoat, put a tarp down around the tub, and pop Rover into the suds. Or make an appointment with your friendly neighborhood dog groomer.

Identify the reason for the procrastination. Confront your attitudes and fears. Weigh the consequences.

Then deal with it!

Don's still not Mr. On Time Every Time, but he's getting there.

He did the tough work—assessing his reasons for putting tasks off and taking conscious steps to overcome his procrastination.

He found out something that surprised him. He wasn't actually so afraid or even anxious about the tasks he was putting off. For Don, procrastination was primarily a pattern. He put things off because he had always put things off. Tottering on the brink of deadline disaster was a bad habit.

Like all habits, this one was tough for Don to break. He finds himself backsliding into old evil ways at times. But now that he's become conscious of the habit, he's able to overcome it most of the time.

He's doing better work, getting it done on time, and worrying a lot less about it.

Time-Management Tips

1. Redirect your motivation, away from the external source and toward the benefit to you. Look for positive, personal motives.
2. Confront your fears and learn how to act in spite of them.

Perfecting Perfectionism

In this chapter, you'll learn:

- How perfectionism defeats you
- How to overcome perfectionist tendencies

Barbara never took up smoking because she was afraid she'd look stupid until she learned how to do it right.

That was one of the few times in her life that her perfectionism actually helped her.

Her motto might well be, "Anything worth doing is worth doing perfectly." A lofty sentiment, but in practice, it makes it hard for Barbara to start anything, paralyzed as she is by the certainty that her efforts will fall short of the ideal.

Start-ups are agony for Barbara. As a freelance graphic designer working out of a home studio, the time she wastes staring at a blank computer screen directly costs her money. When she isn't filling that screen, she isn't earning.

When she finally does get something laid out, she spends what she knows to be an unreasonable amount of time "tweaking," making almost endless minor adjustments, trying somehow to get what she has created to conform to her vague notion of the ideal.

Barbara needs to learn to be less than perfect.

The Myth of Perfectionism

Of all my "favorite" Gary Larson *Far Side* cartoons, my favorite favorite involves a dog, the dog's master, a lawn mower, and the myth of perfectionism.

Picture the scene. The dog has just finished mowing the lawn, as evidenced by a wavy swath of mown grass and a push mower standing at the end of the swath. The dog has made a botch of the job and is getting chewed out by its irate master, who is pointing an accusing finger and shouting "Bad dog! No biscuit! Bad dog!"

Maybe the mow job isn't perfect. But the angry master is missing a fundamental point—*his dog mowed the lawn!* Not even Lassie or Rin Tin Tin ever mowed a lawn. Doesn't that dog deserve a biscuit, for the heroic effort and for the partial, if imperfect, achievement?

You're both the dog and the master. Life asks you to do the seemingly impossible several times a day, and like the good, willing soul you are, you do your best—often performing feats of high-level creative problem solving just getting the kids to day care and yourself to

> But the angry master is missing a fundamental point—*his dog mowed the lawn!* Not even Lassie or Rin Tin Tin ever mowed a lawn.

work. And like the mean master, you then berate yourself for not having done a good enough job of it because the kids' socks didn't match and you didn't remember to bring the overheads for the meeting.

Time to cut yourself some slack. If you do, you'll do more and better work, and you'll need less time to do it. Far from helping spur peak efficiency, your perfectionism is dragging you down by costing you precious time and psychic energy.

Read on to discover why.

How the Bad Dog/No Biscuit Mentality Defeats You

All or nothing often gets you nothing.

If you have a hard time settling for anything less than perfection, you're much less likely to attempt a project in the first place. The penalty for failure is just too great, and failure is almost assured if you insist on measuring your performance against the ideal.

For a writer, we might call it the "Shakespeare syndrome." Here's how it prevents you from doing the work you need to do:

Strike one: Shakespeare was the best writer who ever lived.
Strike two: I'll never be able to write as well as Shakespeare did.
Strike three and out: Therefore, it's useless to even try to write.

What's wrong with this picture?

You could argue that the first two strikes are logically true. Shakespeare may or may not have been the best writer who ever lived (whatever such a silly statement might mean), but you can always find somebody who does what you do better than you do it on some scale of value.

And even if you spent your life trying to imitate that person's style as well as his or her achievements, you'd probably never become the same as (never mind "as good as") that ideal—especially since you manufactured your hero's perfection in your own mind to start with.

Do It Yourself

Call to mind the last time you finished a project. It doesn't have to have been as difficult as a dog mowing a lawn, but think of something that challenged you.

How did you react to your achievement?

- Did you pick it apart, looking for flaws?
- Did you worry about how others would judge it?
- Did you immediately plunge into the next project without giving much thought to the completed work?
- Did you allow yourself at least a moment or two to feel good about finishing the job?

If you're like most of us, you probably did some picking and some worrying—if you allowed yourself time to reflect on the job at all. But chances are you didn't give yourself even a mental "biscuit," the reward of taking pride and pleasure in your work.

So why doesn't that lead us to the inevitable conclusion that it's best never to even try?

Because the world doesn't need another Shakespeare. We've still got the work of the original. What the world needs is your best work, done your way, be it writing or crafting or selling or bossing or digging a ditch.

Your best. Not "perfect" (whatever that means).

Why Imperfect Doesn't Mean Sloppy

In Chapter 15, you spent considerable time working to eliminate errors in your performance. Am I now telling you that errors don't matter and that it's only the effort that counts?

Not at all. "Less than perfect" doesn't mean "bad" or "sloppy." Your goal should always be to do the best you can, given your abilities, knowledge and experience, the time and resources available to you, and the level of quality needed in the particular situation.

If you're a perfectionist, your best will never seem perfect to you. You must come to see that your best is plenty good enough and quite possibly as good as most anyone could have done in the same circumstances.

> If you're a perfectionist, your best will never seem perfect to you. You must come to see that your best is plenty good enough.

Comparisons Are Odious

The key phrase in that last statement is "as good as."

We're always making comparisons. We even argue about them. Babe Ruth was a better hitter than Hank Aaron (or vice versa). Joyce Carol Oates is a better writer than Stephen King. New York deli bagels are better than any other bagels in the world. We're either Ford people or Chevy people, Sears people or Penneys people. We're brand loyal, and we can give you reasons why "our" brand is better than "your" brand.

Consciously or unconsciously, we also tend to compare our performances and even our characteristics with those of others or with some statistical norm or ideal. Are you tall enough? Do you weigh what you should? Do you have sex as often as you're supposed to? There's always a magazine article to tell you how you measure up.

Such comparisons are, as my father often told me, "odious." You don't exist in relationship to the norm. You are what you are, more even than the sum of your abilities, traits, and characteristics. When you use comparisons, either to diminish yourself ("I could never be as good as...") or to pump yourself up ("I'm better than..."), you really haven't said anything meaningful about yourself.

The Fallacy of Instant Judgment

Even if your comparative judgments were meaningful, you're the last person in the universe to be able to make them accurately.

When you become absorbed in a project, you lose all objectivity. You can't judge it as an observer would. Even if you aren't especially emotionally invested, your ego is involved, and the product is "yours." This is true whether you're writing a love sonnet or catalog copy for plumbing fixtures, whether you're trying to convince someone to buy your brand of peanut butter or to embrace your religion.

When you finish a job, you may feel elated, dejected, remorseful, relieved, or even some combination of all these. But the feelings derive from doing and completing the work, not from the quality of that work. The fact is, you can't judge that quality. You're much too close to it. That's why a "cooling off" period between conception and judgment is so important. Even then, you won't be able to be objective about your work (it will always be your baby), but you should be able to be critical of it and able to improve it.

The Fallacy of the Classic

Emotional involvement is just one reason why you can't accurately judge the quality of the work you just completed. Another reason stems from the very fact of that work's newness.

Again let's consider our friend Will Shakespeare and all of his wondrous works. Shakespeare's plays and sonnets are rightfully held up as classics and force fed to you in school (probably way before you're ready to appreciate them, but that's another matter). You

> When you finish a job, you may feel elated, dejected, remorseful, relieved, or even some combination of all these. But the feelings derive from doing and completing the work, not from the quality of that work.

learn that these and the other ideals presented to you in your textbooks and anthologies are great (whether you like them or not).

But you never get to see Shakespeare's first drafts. You don't read his crossouts and the stuff he balled up and threw in the wastebasket. (Yeah! Shakespeare had to have a wastebasket.)

Nobody taught you from the "not-so-classics" or the "pretty good," either. You saw only the ideals, the best, the stuff that survived the critics and the test of time.

It's not just literature. You were taught math and science the same way, as classic truths sprung from the minds of geniuses. You didn't share the failures, the process, the long journey toward discovery. Unless you study the history of a discipline, you don't get to see how often those "truths" become displaced by newer "truths." (The world is round and revolves around the sun.)

When you try to write something or work through a problem, you have only the classic to compare it to. That's like holding up a newborn baby, in all of her red, wrinkled, squalling humanity, and asking her why she doesn't have a PhD or a high-paying job.

> You never get to see Shakespeare's first drafts. You don't read his crossouts and the stuff he balled up and threw in the wastebasket. (Yeah! Shakespeare had to have a wastebasket.)

The Fallacy of the Ideal Form

One more mental trick keeps you from being able to judge your work fairly.

When you begin any project, you have some notion in your mind of what it's supposed to be when it's done. As long as it stays in your mind, it can remain vague and fuzzy, and you can get away with thinking of it as perfect. As long as it isn't anything specific, it can be anything.

But the moment you give it specific shape and substance, it becomes just this and no other, and all those vague possibilities you held in your mind disappear. So, of course, the real is never as good as the ideal.

That doesn't make the creation in any sense bad or deficient. It just makes the creator remorseful for having "failed" to achieve the unattainable ideal.

Why Practice May Never Make Perfect

You will never attain that ideal form because it's an illusion that can exist only in your mind and not out in the real world.

But you can and will get better and better at what you do.

Practice doesn't make perfect, but it does make better. As you gain experience, learn from previous efforts, gather feedback, and compare the results you got with the results you wanted, you'll make changes in the way you do your work. You'll make many of these changes consciously, and some of them will be major. You'll also make many changes unconsciously, and some of them may be too small to even detect easily.

Caution

If you're not careful, practice can make putrid—or at least reinforce mediocrity.

If by practicing you simply mean doing the same thing again and again in the same way, you may be reinforcing bad habits and inefficient techniques. You need to be open to criticism and to possibilities for change if your experience is to teach and change you.

How You Can Free Yourself from Perfectionism

"Anything worth doing is worth doing badly."

That's not how the saw goes, of course. But there's as much wisdom in this fractured adage as in the original.

You must grant yourself the courage to be rotten.

You must declare a moratorium on the whole notion of a "mistake."

You must allow yourself to take chances and try out possibilities.

If you don't, you'll never be any better at the task than you are right now. And you may not even allow yourself to take on new tasks, for fear that you won't be perfect or good enough or as good as someone else.

Do it now. Judge it later. If the doing gets tangled up in the judging too soon, judgment strangles performance every time. It's easier to criticize than to create, and most of us have had more practice at it.

Like any other change in attitude, your evolution from cautious critic to dynamic producer will take time. You'll backslide into your perfectionist ways often. Be gentle with yourself, and you'll find that you've freed yourself to be more productive and efficient than in your wildest perfectionist dreams.

Barbara doesn't fuss herself into productive paralysis anymore. This motto now hangs above her workstation:

Anything Worth Doing Is Worth Doing Rotten

right next to this one:

Don't Tolerate Mistreats

Gradually, she's learning to withhold judgment of her work as she creates it, and she never tries to revise until the work cools off. She still gets "creator's remorse," but she doesn't act on it. She finds that her feelings when she finishes a project have almost nothing to do with the quality of the work when she goes back to revise it later.

She also finds that she's doing more and better work than ever, with time left over to take up a new hobby.

But she still has no plans to take up smoking!

Time-Management Tips

1. Don't judge your performance against irrelevant, unrealistic, or unreasonable standards. Measure performance against your own needs and goals.
2. Practice can make you better—but not if you simply repeat bad techniques.
3. Take chances. Allow yourself to be rotten when you try something new.

Get Rid of the Tasks You Don't Want or Need to Do

In this chapter, you'll learn:

■ How to get rid of:

  Unnecessary work

  Busywork

  Work you do to avoid the real work

  Work someone else should be doing

Chapter 26

"If you want it done, dump it on Gladys's desk. Good old Gladys will do it."

Every workplace should have a Gladys. Folks like good old Gladys make great delegators out of the rest of us.

But her tendency to take on the world's problems is making a wreck out of good old Gladys. She's working longer and harder than ever. All that extra effort isn't even showing up on her performance evaluations because she's letting other peoples' work get in the way of her own. (After all, folks are always in a big hurry to have it done, and Gladys doesn't want to disappoint anyone.)

Gladys is sinking in a quagmire of her own making. She just can't say no. She needs to figure out why not.

Much of time management seeks to help you do things faster and do more than one thing at once so that you can fit more doing into the same limited amount of time. But no time-management plan can work without attention to the tasks themselves.

Here's where the famous admonition to "work smarter, not harder" comes into play.

Spend just a little time today questioning some of the tasks you do every day, and you can save tons of time every day from now on.

> Spend just a little time today questioning some of the tasks you do every day, and you can save tons of time every day from now on.

How to Eliminate Unnecessary Steps

"I'm so busy doing the dance," a worker laments, "I haven't got time to learn the steps."

Let's free up some time by eliminating some of those steps, the ones that aren't getting you anywhere.

Get Rid of the Cobweb Catacombs

When I first came to work with the University of Wisconsin Extension, I discovered that every adult education program we offered generated an enormous amount of paperwork, starting with the financial planning form, by which we set the fee for the program, and the instructional form, which gave each program its tracking number. Then came the forms to order mailing labels and brochure duplicating from state printing. The process built through a series of confirmation forms that would have done a NASA countdown proud: six-month confirmation, two-month confirmation, six-week confirmation, two-week confirmation, along with the audiovisual request form, the food and beverage break form, the...well, you get the idea.

It soon became clear to me that some of these forms served no useful purpose to me or to the people planning and teaching the programs. This occurred to me because I'm the one who had to pay attention to all those forms (which were "urgent" and needed "immediate attention").

It took me a little longer to determine that some of the forms didn't do anybody any good at the conference center or the finance office or the printer, either. We were just doing the forms because we had always done the forms. And we had always done them in triplicate.

For some reason nobody could explain to me, we needed not just one, not two, but three copies of each form. One went in my files. One went in the department administrator's files. And one went into a file I took to calling the cobweb catacombs.

I decided that if the department administrator had one in her files, and her files were always open to me, and her office was a mere few steps down the hall from mine, then I didn't really need to have a copy in my files. And nobody seemed to need the copy in the cobweb catacombs. So couldn't we maybe just make one copy?

Those of you enmeshed in the web of a bureaucracy, any bureaucracy, know that it's never that simple. Some folks get extremely threatened by the notion that we might not need to have all that nice paper backing us up.

I did succeed in getting rid of a couple of the forms, and I did eliminate the cobweb catacombs—small victories in the war on wasted time.

Are a couple of unnecessary forms and an extra step in filing really worth the fight it takes to get rid of them? Depends on how many people you have to fight and how hard you have to fight them. But you do have the power to stem some of your daily work flood. You don't need status or tenure if you have common sense and the voice of reason on your side. Couch your proposal in terms of the

> You do have the power to stem some of your daily work flood. You don't need status or tenure if you have common sense and the voice of reason on your side.

good of the organization, to achieve the goals you and your boss share, and you have a chance to succeed.

It's worth the fight. It's worth questioning the need for any process that requires your time and attention. Get rid of it now and you draw the benefits every day from now on.

Two More Forms of Unnecessary Work: Busywork and Work Avoidance Work

When I worked as a construction laborer during summers to put myself through college, I soon discovered that the hardest days were the ones when there was no work. I had to look busy or catch hell from the superintendent. That meant inventing tasks that made me look as though I were doing something constructive without getting in the way of anybody who had real work to do.

I swept sidewalks, pushing the dirt up to one end of the walk, then turning around and pushing it back down to the other. The supe didn't have to try to invent something for me to do, and I was within shouting range when he did have a job for me.

I've been in a lot of office settings where bosses created busywork for subordinates rather than having to face the prospect of figuring out something real for them to do (or to endure watching them play computer solitaire).

But I've also caught myself creating busywork for myself because it makes me feel productive. (Those old construction laboring habits die hard.) Also, doing something simple but unnecessary may be a lot easier than actually planning what I ought to be doing next.

> When you take a hard look at the things you do, don't just look to eliminate tasks that others ask or require you to do. Get rid of the self-generated busywork, too.

When you take a hard look at the things you do, don't just look to eliminate tasks that others ask or require you to do. Get rid of the self-generated busywork, too.

I've also caught myself doing low-priority or unnecessary jobs to avoid doing the harder task I really need to be doing. For me, almost anything is easier than budget planning. It's amazing what I'll do to avoid it. As long as I'm doing something, I'm just "too busy" to get to the onerous stuff.

In many offices today, the most pervasive form of work avoidance work is "surfing" the net. Web casting certainly keeps you busy, you're undoubtedly learning something (although its application to the workplace may be tenuous), and once you learn to find your way around you start having a wonderful time.

But that seductive screen gobbles time in huge gulps. And while you're "busy" surfing, other work is waiting—work that may put you under severe time pressure later.

Not all net surfing is work avoidance, of course (just as not all sidewalk sweeping is done merely to look busy). But the surfer knows how to determine the usefulness of the ride.

When you catch yourself doing work avoidance work, redirect your time and energy.

The "Not-to-Do" List and the "Let-Others-Do-It" List

We do a lot of what we do today because we did it yesterday, and the day before. We're accustomed to doing it, perhaps even in the habit of doing it, and doing it is actually easier than not doing it.

You may need to create a "not-to-do" list to remind you of the tasks you've decided to eliminate from your routine. This may seem silly, but that doesn't necessarily mean it's a bad idea. See if the list helps you; just don't let anybody else see it.

Which leads us to those tasks that should be done—but not by you.

Make a list of those tasks that you now perform but you feel should be done by someone else. Reasons for putting tasks on this list include:

- You lack the authority to do it right.
- You lack the skill, information, or tools to do it right.
- If you do it, other tasks with higher priorities don't get done.

This list does not, unfortunately, include:

- "I don't want to."

Do It Yourself

Take a hard look at the work you do. See if you can find any tasks that are unnecessary because they:

- Exist simply to keep you looking or feeling busy
- Enable you to put off other, more important work
- Duplicate other tasks and don't need doing again
- Don't really need doing even once

You've started your "hit list," tasks you'll be able to eliminate to free up time for the real work.

Do It Yourself

Add to your hit list those tasks that other people really ought to be doing. If possible, also note the people who ought to be doing them.

- "I don't like to."
- "It's not in my job description" (although this point might become the subject of a future planning discussion with your supervisor).

Delegating, Swapping, and Letting Go

Once you determine that someone else should be doing a job you're now performing, you have three options for getting someone else to do it.

1. Delegating. A lot of folks are fortunate enough to have someone else to answer the phone for them, thus absorbing the interruptions and screening callers. Some folks have other folks to open and sort their mail for them, too, and make the coffee, and fill out all those stupid forms and a lot of other less-than-glamorous tasks.

Time-management books always suggest that we save time by delegating such jobs to others. (This doesn't actually "save" any time. It simply shifts the time from one person to another.)

Unfortunately, this option is open only to bosses. If you have no one to boss, you have to answer your own phone and open your own mail. This time-management book is for you, too, so let's explore two other options.

2. Swapping. One program assistant loves to file and fill out forms but dreads answering the telephone. Another program assistant, working in the same office, hates the paperwork but loves answering the phone.

Not surprisingly, the first assistant doesn't do a very good job with callers, whereas the second is invariably courteous, cheerful, and helpful.

Neither assistant has the authority to delegate work to the other. But they might be able to arrange a trade, with their supervisor's approval, of course.

3. Letting Go. Some folks don't let anyone else open their mail or answer their telephone because they won't rather than because they can't.

This may stem from a lack of trust in the subordinate—a bad situation for a variety of reasons. But the inability to let go may not have anything to do with anybody else. Some folks just have a terrible time delegating. Even if they do assign a task to someone else, they find themselves "supervising" so much that they spend as much or more time on it—and alienate the coworker in the process.

When you hand a job off to someone else, don't tie a string to it. Make sure your coworkers know what they're supposed to accomplish, and then let them accomplish it their way. If they don't get the desired results in the allotted time, work on these specific outcomes. But keep your hands off the work in progress.

That way you really save the time, and your coworker doesn't have to put up with your fussing.

Do It Now, Do It Later, or Do It Never

Does it need a meeting, or will a memo do? Does it need a memo, or will a phone call do? Does it need a phone call? Does it need doing at all?

"Because we've always done it" is a rotten reason to do anything.

Keep a stack of Post-it notes handy. As you plan and direct your work flow, get used to the idea of using three rather than merely two categories: do it now, do it later, and do it never.

Deciding to do it never isn't the same as simply not doing it. If you toss it back on the pile and push it to the back of your mind, it will continue to clutter your physical and mental space, and it will need dealing with again and again. Make the decision not to do it—and tell anybody whose work is affected by your decision.

If it won't take long, and it doesn't interrupt something important, do it now. If it doesn't carry a high degree of urgency or if you have a task with a higher level of urgency needing your attention, do it later.

Don't let the medium of communication affect your decision. My e-mail announces its arrival with beeps and pulsating icons. The paper mail just sits on the desk. Even if I've turned my e-mail off, I get the blinking icon in the upper right-hand corner of the screen.

> When you hand a job off to someone else, don't tie a string to it. Make sure your coworkers know what they're supposed to accomplish, and then let them accomplish it their way.

If you decide to do it later, note when you'll do it and what, specifically, you're going to do. If you don't, your attempts at organizing may degenerate into evasion instead.

But that doesn't make the e-mail message more important than the paper message.

A ringing phone creates a heightened sense of urgency in many of us, but that shouldn't automatically give the caller a higher priority than the person sitting across the table.

If you decide to do it later, note when you'll do it and what, specifically, you're going to do. If you don't, your attempts at organizing may degenerate into evasion instead.

Peeling Off the Layers of Perfection: The "Good Enough" Tenet of Time Management

You've decided to do it now. As we noted in the last chapter, you should also decide how well you need to do it. If it has to be perfect before you'll let it go, you've got a big time-management problem.

I'm not advocating shoddy work or irresponsible performance. But I suspect that isn't really an issue here. Sloppy, irresponsible people don't read time-management books. Conscientious people do. But the line between conscientious and perfectionist can be hard to find, and perfectionists have a tough time finishing anything.

The computer can make the problem worse. Because we can edit so easily, because we can always surf for more information, because we can run one more set of data at the push of a button, we may raise our quality expectations until we reach such lofty (and utterly ridiculous) pinnacles of perfectionism as "zero tolerance for error."

How good is good enough? Who's going to see it? What are they going to do with it?

The meeting minutes that will be filed and forgotten need to be factually accurate and written in clear English; they don't need to be rendered in rhyming couplets.

The agenda for an informal meeting of department heads calls for a lower level of sophistication and polish than does the final draft of the annual report for the stockholders.

Working figures for the preliminary budget meeting don't need to be carried out to ten places past the decimal point. To the nearest thousand dollars is probably close enough, and more precise calculations are in fact a waste of time since the numbers will all be changed later.

"Simplify, simplify," Thoreau advised us. You can't flee to Walden Pond, but you can eliminate unnecessary tasks, delegate or swap others, and give each task an appropriate level of attention.

By managing your tasks, you'll be expanding the amount of time available to you.

When Gladys finally sought the reason behind her tendency to do everybody else's work for them, she didn't like the answer she found.

She had become the company "fixer," she realized, because she was deeply insecure about her job status. Deep down, she figured she was buying respect, perhaps even admiration, and becoming indispensable to others.

Once she saw her motive clearly, she also saw how futile her efforts were. Useful, yes? But respected and admired? Not "good old Gladys," everybody's gopher.

When she realized that her own job performance was suffering, she started finding the courage to say no, politely, firmly, consistently.

> "Simplify, simplify," Thoreau advised us. You can't flee to Walden Pond, but you can eliminate unnecessary tasks, delegate or swap others, and give each task an appropriate level of attention.

Time-Management Tips

1. Create a list of jobs that don't need doing and jobs that someone else ought to be doing.
2. Delegate or trade onerous jobs when you can—making sure you really let the old jobs go.

The Secret of Making Time

In this chapter, you'll learn:

- The substitute method for making time
- The physics of time-management choices

Chapter 27

Jimmy feels like a jerk.

Jimmy Junior just asked him to play catch with him in the back yard. Jimmy's been putting in long hours at the office all week. It's finally Saturday, and the sun is shining. He's been promising JJ all week that they'd have some fun Saturday.

But now Jimmy's paying bills, and then he has to mow the lawn and trim the hedges. Then it's time to get dressed to go out to dinner.

"Not now, son," he hears himself say. "I'm too busy."

He sees the look of disappointment on his son's face, and it makes his heart ache. And it isn't just guilt he's feeling. He'd really love to be playing catch instead of struggling with family finances.

But the work has got to be done. Jill has enough of her own to do.

How can he find time for a game of catch with his boy?

"How do you find the time?"

Do folks ask you that? Take it as a compliment. It means the speaker can't figure out how you manage to do all the things you do.

Beware. It also probably means the speaker is about to ask you to do something else.

> Research now validates
> what conventional wisdom
> has always known: "If you
> want something done, ask a
> busy person."

Research now validates what conventional wisdom has always known: "If you want something done, ask a busy person." For the past twenty-five years, University of Maryland Professor John Robinson has studied how Americans spend their time. He figured he'd reach a lot of either/or conclusions: folks either read books or watch television, for example. Instead, he found a split between folks who do a lot of things and folks who don't seem to do much of anything.

The world isn't so much divided into folks who either go to the opera or work on their cars, Robinson concludes. Some folks go to the opera and work on their cars, whereas others mainly take up space and convert oxygen into carbon dioxide full time.

So, where do those doers find the time? More important, where will you find the time to do all the things you want and need to do?

You won't. You'll never find time, and nobody will give it to you. You must make time.

"I just don't have the time," we say when confronted with something we don't really want to do. "I'm too busy."

It's not true. You do have time. You've been given the same twenty-four hours a day every other creature has. You're not too busy. You've chosen to do something else. You want or need to do something else more than the choice confronting you now.

If you can discipline yourself to remove "too busy" from your vocabulary and consciously make choices instead, you will have learned to make time where it didn't seem to exist before.

All the information in this book is designed to help you make time in one of two ways:

1. You can make time by increasing your energy and mental focus, thus accomplishing your tasks in less time. You can do this by:

- Taking frequent minivacations throughout the day (Chapter 7)
- Heeding your natural biorhythms (Chapter 28)
- Getting proper rest (Chapter 29), nutrition, and exercise (Chapter 31)
- Combating stress and worry (Chapters 30 and 32)

2. You can make time by organizing your tasks more efficiently. Efforts in this category include:

- Creating and properly using a to-do list and other scheduling devices (Chapter 5)
- Reducing or eliminating start-up time on difficult projects (Chapter 6)
- Separating the important from the merely urgent (Chapter 9)
- Heeding the 80/20 principle of time management (Chapter 10)
- Following your own agenda instead of someone else's (Chapters 11, 13, 14)
- Taming the technology (Chapter 17) and combating information overload (Chapters 18 and 19)
- Controlling the clutter (Chapters 20 and 21)
- Turning downtime into productive time (Chapter 23)

Do It Yourself

Bring to mind a recent instance when you found yourself torn between two activities, both good things for you to be doing. What did you choose? On what basis did you make your choice? How did you feel about the choice afterwards? Were you later able to accomplish the task you had to skip?

Hang onto this example. You'll need it in a few minutes.

The first approach assumes that you can do more activities in the same amount of time. The second approach, the one we're focusing on now, posits that you can make smart choices so that you're doing the right activities with your time.

The Substitution Method of Making Time

Take "I'm too busy" off the table. Instead, examine all of your options and decide what you truly want and need to be doing. See beyond the limited choice of the moment.

Suppose, for example, you find yourself in a classic work/family squeeze play. You should take your family to the park for a picnic—and the fact is, you really want to. But clanging phones and last-minute meetings kept you from getting your presentation ready for Monday. Your choice seems to be family picnic versus presentation prep.

You can argue this one with yourself for the rest of the day—neither going on the picnic nor shaping up your presentation—and still not reach a decision that will satisfy you. It isn't just family versus work, of course. You work to earn the money that supports the family and makes nice things like picnics possible.

You're stuck in the classic lose/lose. Whichever you choose, you hurt.

In hindsight, streetwise time management throughout the week would have eliminated the problem. Had you tamed the telephone and the e-mail, stuck to your agenda, eliminated a few of those "urgent but not important" tasks, and conquered your procrastination, for example, you probably could have gotten the presentation ready before you left the office Friday—and without staying as late as you wound up doing anyway. You'll do better next time.

But that leaves you stuck this time. What to do?

Widen your options. You can put the choice in perspective, and you can create a way to get both activities done with time and energy to spare.

You can, in short, make time. Here's how.

Take "I'm too busy" off the table. Instead, examine all of your options and decide what you truly want and need to be doing.

What other activities do you have planned or are you likely to engage in between now and the time for your presentation Monday at 10:00 A.M.? You know, for example, that you'll be sleeping approximately thirteen hours (six and a half hours each Saturday and Sunday night). Instead of *picnic versus presentation*, you could substitute *presentation versus sleep* and determine to stay up all night Sunday to prepare.

You could also fall on your face in the middle of your presentation. Although in the last fifteen years, many of us have traded about ninety minutes of sleep per night for more work and other activities—without ever planning to do so, of course—it's probably not a great idea, for reasons we'll discuss in Chapter 29.

But it's important that you put all the options on the table without automatically eliminating anything. That way, you can make a truly informed and purposeful choice. How about:

> *Picnic versus church?*
> *Picnic versus read the Sunday newspaper?*
> *Picnic versus clean out the garage?*
> *Picnic versus cruise the Internet?*

Examine enough such choices, and you'll find a swap you're willing and even eager to make. That way, you can have your family picnic and your presentation prep while sacrificing something of lesser importance and time sensitivity.

Do It Yourself

Now rethink that tough choice you brought to mind a few minutes ago. Instead of limiting yourself to the two choices, expand your options to include other activities you might be able to substitute.

In hindsight (which is always, as we know, 20/20), can you find a way out of your seeming time trap that would have allowed you to accomplish both activities while sacrificing something less important to you?

What's done is done, but rethinking the choice now will help you make a better choice next time.

The Addition/Subtraction Theory

For every action, there is an equal and opposite reaction.

Remember that from your physics class? If you try to step from an untethered rowboat onto the dock, you'll probably wind up in the water. The forward thrust of your body pushes the boat back—and right out from under you.

The key to making time lies in understanding the "physics" of choices: if you say yes to one choice, you must say no to another.

When you decide to "fit" a new activity into your day, you should at the same time decide what you won't be doing. For the equation to balance, the time exchange must be roughly equal—an hour of "no" for every hour of "yes."

If you don't heed this law of time management, it will still apply to you—just as the rowboat will still fly out from under you if you don't pay attention to the appropriate law of physics. You just won't be in control of the tradeoff. If you leave time choices to chance, or who yells at you the loudest, or how much you can get done before you collapse of exhaustion, I can predict the two elements of your life that will suffer: (1) your health and (2) your relationships.

By default, you'll steal from the two most important areas of your life, skipping sleep and exercise, for example, or spending little time talking with the people who mean the most to you.

The choices are yours. You always get to choose. Be mindful. Choose well. You really can make time for everything you want and need to do in life.

Let's give poor Jimmy another chance—an instant replay when Jimmy Junior approaches his dad, ball in one hand, glove in the other, and a hopeful look on his face.

As you'll recall, Jimmy Junior wants to play catch, but Dad's paying bills, with yardwork on deck. Although he hates to disappoint his son—and himself—he can't find the time. He's just too busy.

But when he removes "too busy" from his vocabulary, if he stops trying to "find time" or waiting for someone to leave a package of time on his doorstep, he can figure out how to make time for a game of catch on a Saturday afternoon.

Could those bills wait until tomorrow? (After all, they won't go out in the mail until Monday anyway.) How about the yardwork? (The neighbors probably won't call out the county maintenance crew if his lawn gets one day shaggier.) If he puts one of the tasks off until Sunday, what will he give up on Sunday to compensate?

Using the addition/subtraction theory, watch how his choice shifts. Instead of limiting himself to:

Play catch with son versus mow the lawn
Jimmy adds

> When you decide to "fit" a new activity into your day, you should at the same time decide what you won't be doing.

Mow the lawn Sunday versus watch golf on the tube.
Now he sees his choice as
Play catch with son versus watch golf on tube
Good dad that he is, Jimmy plays catch with Jimmy Junior—and counts the seasons until JJ is old enough to help him with the yard-work, so they can both watch golf together.

Time-Management Tips

1. You'll never find time. You must make time.
2. You make time by swapping one activity for another.
3. Before deciding on a trade, list all your choices.

Sound Mind/ Sound Body

Summary of Part VII

1. **Eat, sleep, and exercise at about the same times every day. It may sound boring, but it sure is healthy.**

2. **Do the hard jobs when you're most alert.**

3. **Caffeine, nicotine, and alcohol may be keeping you awake.**

4. **Sleeping pills aren't the solution.**

5. **Don't waste time and effort trying to eliminate all the stressors. Tame the stress inside you.**

6. **If it's worth doing, do one thing at a time. If it isn't, put it in the "to-hell-with-it" basket.**

7. **Eat a low-fat, high-fiber diet.**

You've spent the first six sections of this book getting charged up and moving rapidly and efficiently through life.

Now you need to slow down a bit.

If you truly want to become a streetwise time manager, creating more time for the things you want and need to do, you must learn to minimize the stressors in your life and to handle stress effectively.

That involves learning how to listen to your internal biorhythms so that you can live in time with those rhythms as much as life allows.

You'll examine the quantity and the quality of your sleep, discovering how much sleep you really need and how to make sure you get it.

You'll discover the specific sources of stress in your life and learn how to reduce that stress and the hurt it can inflict on you. You'll also learn to cope effectively and effortlessly with the stress you can't avoid.

Finally, you'll explore elements of diet and exercise that can give you more energy naturally.

The more energy you have, the more time you'll be able to create in your life.

Keep Time to Your Own (Bio)rhythms

In this chapter, you'll learn:

- How to chart your biorhythms
- Five ways to honor your body's natural rhythms
- When—and how much—you should eat

Chapter 28

Carla figures she zones out at staff meetings because that's what staff meetings are for.

Struggling to stay awake at her desk after lunch also seems natural enough. Since she skips breakfast, she usually has a fairly large lunch, and besides, she always feels drowsy in the early afternoon.

But as "natural" as these waking naps seem to Carla, she knows they aren't doing her performance reviews any good. And truth to tell, she worries about it a bit. She's only twenty-seven, after all, and in good shape. She shouldn't be so tired just when she needs to be alert.

It's one of life's little ironies: by the time you get old enough to stay up as late as you want to, you start having trouble staying awake through the evening news.

Just about every kid who ever lived has fought to stay up past bedtime. You, too? If so, the more tired you became, the harder you no doubt fought the inevitable.

"But, Mom," you probably wailed with your last waking breath, "I'm not sleepy!"

You might as well have gone peacefully. You've spent the rest of your life living by the clock rather than by your inclinations.

> In the "time before time," people lived by the natural rhythms of the day and the season.

In the "time before time," people lived by the natural rhythms of the day and the season. They got up when the sun rose, worked and played in the daylight, and went to sleep when the sun went down again.

But ever since Thomas Alva Edison finally found a filament that would get hot enough to glow without burning up, we've been able to defy the cycle of the sun, keeping ourselves up past our "bedtimes" with artificial light.

We awaken to the clangor of the alarm clock, yanking ourselves out of sleep rather than allowing ourselves to drift naturally up through the layers of sleep into waking. We hurtle out of bed and into the day's obligations, becoming estranged from our own dreams.

We eat by the clock, too, at "meal time," when it fits the schedule, or not at all. We combine work with food, to the detriment of digestion, with the "power breakfast" and the "working lunch" and the "business dinner."

If we become tired at the "wrong" time, like in the middle of the afternoon staff meeting, we fight off fatigue with caffeine or sugar or both, overriding our need for rest.

And we pay for it.

What Would You Do If You Could Do Whatever You Wanted to?

Most of us have developed a daily cycle involving one long block of from six to nine hours of sleep and two or three meals, the largest coming at dinnertime.

You've trained your body to a cycle through repetition and reinforcement, but your body may show its displeasure by being groggy and sleep-ridden at get-up time, queasy at dinnertime, wakeful at bedtime. You may simply struggle through these discomforts, or you may take drugs to help you rise, eat, and sleep at the "right" times.

Ever wonder what you'd do if you let yourself do whatever felt right? What if you had no obligations or appointments, a true vacation? You could get up when you wanted, eat when you wanted, nap if you wanted, stay up all night if you wanted.

You probably wouldn't do much too differently for the first few days. Our learned patterns become quite entrenched. But after a few days, as you begin at last to relax and ease into a new way of life, what would you ease into? What if you let the body, rather than the schedule, drive your day?

Scientists have wondered about such things. One experiment involved putting folks into an environment free of all obligations, free of all clocks and watches, even free of sunrise and sunset. Subjects had no schedules to follow and no clues to when they "should" sleep and wake and eat.

Here's what they taught us by their reactions:

1. When left to our own devices, we will establish a fairly consistent pattern.
2. That pattern varies with the individual. One schedule does not fit all. What's "natural" varies from person to person. There is no one "right" way to pattern the day.

> Ever wonder what you'd do if you let yourself do whatever felt right? What if you had no obligations or appointments, a true vacation?

3. We like to graze. Rather than taking our nourishment in two or three major infusions, called "meals," we tend to eat smaller amounts several times a "day."
4. Sleep, too, comes in shorter segments. Rather than one large block of sleeping and one larger block of waking in every twenty-four-hour cycle, people sleep for shorter periods, more often.
5. The cycle isn't twenty-four hours long. Folks have their own built-in "day," and most of these natural cycles are a bit longer than twenty-four hours.
6. During each cycle, we have regular ups and downs. As any-one who has semislumbered through a meeting or movie well knows, not all states of wakefulness are created equal. Sometimes we're a lot more awake than at other times.

Attentiveness tends to undulate between peaks and troughs, and folks seem to hit two peaks and two troughs during each daily cycle.

So, what can you do about it?

This kind of information can be as frustrating as it is fascinating. Such findings seem to indicate that we're all living "wrong," in defiance of our own natural rhythms. Not much from this "natural" cycle seems applicable to the world of work and family and to the pattern set by clocks and calendars.

Perhaps that's why so many of us live in ignorance of something so fundamental to our lives, our own natural energy levels.

Let's take a second look. Perhaps you can make some adjustments, even while having to adhere to the basic outlines of the twenty-four-hour day and the five-day work cycle. Here are a few ways you can acknowledge, honor, and accommodate our natural rhythms.

Why Our Values Are Often in Conflict

Your body has an inherent natural rhythm. To the extent that you can, you must rediscover your rhythms and live by them. Relearn how to listen to your body and recognize when you're tired or hungry or angry or restless, rather than override these feelings because they're "improper" or simply inconvenient.

We've all picked up opinions about diet and sleep, based on experience and inclination, study, folklore, and social pressure. Sometimes these four sources agree: you love apples, science says apples are good for you, and folklore teaches, "An apple a day keeps the doctor away." And aside from the scare over pesticides, society seems to approve of apple eating. The only real drawback seems to be that Adam and Eve business.

Often, though, the four influences are in conflict. "Eat your spinach," your mama and Popeye the Sailor told you. Scientists agree that spinach is wonderful stuff. But society has singled out spinach as the very symbol of something that's good for you but is really yucky, and, truth be told, you really don't like spinach unless you mix it with at least equal parts sour cream.

Conversely, chocolate has gotten a bad rap (perhaps largely unjustly) for years, but lots of folks love to eat it, and some may even experience something like "chocolate addiction."

Smoking provides a more complex and troubling example. Most smokers start young, and peer pressure often plays a big part in getting started. Most beginning smokers react violently and negatively to their first few smoking experiences. From coughing to throwing up, the body does its best to repel the invasion of a foreign substance into the system.

If we persevere, though, the body learns to handle, then to enjoy, and finally to crave the smoke as we develop an addiction to nicotine. I've heard this addiction described by someone who should know as more powerful and harder to break than the physical dependency on heroin—powerful enough to keep people smoking even after they've developed emphysema or lost a lung to cancer.

Now science has established the causal link between smoking and these killer diseases to the satisfaction of most everyone except tobacco company executives. Twenty-five years ago, the surgeon general slapped a warning on every pack of cigarettes.

Society has sent a mixed message. Ads for cigarettes originally touted the product as a health aid, and athletes lent credence to this claim with their endorsements. As information from the medical community began to refute these notions, the appeal shifted to the cigarette as refreshment ("Take a puff. It's springtime"), social prop,

> "Eat your spinach," your mama and Popeye the Sailor told you.

status symbol, and image enhancer. Marlboro didn't sell as a "woman's" cigarette with a red filter. As soon as they shed the red filter and started putting cowboys into the ads, sales took off.

Most of our movie heroes smoked, and after a hiatus, many are now smoking again (including an angel, portrayed by John Travolta).

Smoking in public was for men—or fallen women—only. Then women gained "equality." ("You've come a long way, baby.") When the medical evidence against "secondhand" or "passive" smoke began to become pervasive and persuasive, many municipalities banned smoking in restaurants and public offices, and legal efforts to prevent sales of cigarettes to children intensified.

But already the pendulum is swinging back, and the backlash for "smokers' rights" is being felt.

What have you decided about smoking? If you're a smoker or a recent ex-smoker, how many times a day do you have to decide? Have you decided that you don't really have a choice at all?

It's not as simple as just "doing what comes naturally." We initially repel the smoke but become hooked on it later.

It's not easy to know what's "approved" or "appropriate." Society says, among other things, that smoking is cool and that it will kill you.

But a combination of the body's initial reaction to smoking and a dispassionate review of the evidence on smoking and health can tell us what's right for us—even if we don't always do it.

Given the difficulties in knowing what's "right" and the inevitable clash between what our natural rhythms tell us and what socially enforced patterns dictate, you still might be able to alter your living pattern so that you're living more in harmony with your internal "music." Here are a few possibilities.

Five Ways to Honor Bodily Rhythms

1. Establish a regular pattern. Many of us live by at least two different patterns: the work week pattern and the weekend pattern. We may reward ourselves with a late Friday and Saturday night, get up a lot later on Saturday and Sunday, and eat more and different things at different times.

> Given the difficulties in knowing what's "right," you still might be able to alter your living pattern so that you're living more in harmony with your internal "music."

Huge swings in pattern create constant disruption and the need for continuous readjustment. As we'll see in the next chapter on sleep, shift workers suffer the most from this sort of disruption. Bringing the weekend and the weekday a little closer together may help you find and adhere to your true rhythm.

2. Eat when you're hungry, not when it's time. Many of us have learned not to trust ourselves to eat naturally. We may have so thoroughly trampled our own natural sense of hunger and satiation, we're not even sure when we're truly hungry or when we've eaten enough. But short of suffering from an eating disorder, we can recapture—and trust—a more natural sense, an internal sense, of when we want and need to eat.

3. Take your nourishment in smaller portions. Grazing, noshing, snacking—whatever you call it, most of us do it, and feel guilty about it. But research indicates that grazing is a healthier way to eat than packing it all in once, twice, or three times a day. Insulin-dependent diabetics learn to eat several small "meals" a day. Some of the rest of us should try it, too.

4. Nap. We'll explore the subject of sleep in greater detail in the next chapter. For now, suffice it to say that fifteen minutes of sleep or rest when you really need it is much more beneficial than the hours of "catch-up" sleep you get—or try to get—later.

5. Schedule by the "rhythm method." Honor thy peaks and thy valleys.

One of the ways the human race seems to divide itself is the great morning person/evening person dichotomy. Some of us naturally wake up early and alert. Others do not. Some of us hit our creative and productive stride about 10 at night and work well far into the morning—or about the time the morning people are getting up.

Most of us, whether morning person or evening person, have to produce by the clock. Though both of us report to work at 9:00 A.M., the morning person is already hitting a midday trough, whereas the evening person hasn't yet become fully conscious. The system serves no one but the timekeeper.

Some escape by working at home or by seeking a vocation that more accurately reflects their inner rhythms. (Could a morning person

Streetwise Definition

Marriage
That institution by which a morning person and a night owl pledge to try to live together in biorhythmic chaos until death do them part.

become a jazz musician? Could an evening person find happiness as a morning drive-time radio personality?)

Most of the rest of us learn to adjust to the clock rhythm, but we all pay for it.

You need to discover your own rhythms and then accommodate them as much as possible.

When you can't control the schedule (the big staff meeting invariably arrives just as your energy leaves), compensate ahead of time with a little extra deep-breathing, a longer minivacation, maybe a brisk walk. Compensate, too, by being aware of the source of your reactions. (The boss's proposal may not really be as stupid as it seems; you're tired and grouchy, after all.)

First learning and then honoring your internal rhythms is one more way you can live a more productive, happier, and healthier life.

Carla tracked her biorhythms for two weeks and found out what she already knew—she is definitely not a morning person. She has to really struggle to get up and get to work on time, hits an energy surge about midmorning, and then goes into the dumper about 1:30—even, she notes, if she doesn't have an especially large lunch that day.

She's learning to honor those rhythms as much as possible by scheduling the tough mental activities for her peak times of alertness. She's also flattening out the ups and downs a bit by regulating her habits. She even manages a bit of breakfast at her desk now.

There's nothing she can do to reschedule those 1:00 P.M. staff meetings, but she's learned to gather strength and energy ahead of time by eating a light lunch and taking a brisk walk before the meetings.

She feels better, she's doing a better job at work, and she even finds she has more energy when she gets home.

Do It Yourself

You can use that mood log you create by tracking your energy level patterns. Schedule the tasks that require creative thought and clear decision making for your peak times. Leave the relatively no-brainer tasks for the troughs. (You may even be able to sneak in a nap here, but more on that in the next chapter.)

Time-Management Tips

1. Establish a regular pattern for eating, sleeping, and exercising.
2. Schedule difficult tasks for your biorhythmic peaks. Save the easier stuff for the troughs.

How to Get the Sleep You Need

In this chapter, you'll learn:

- How much sleep you really need
- Six steps to help you get that sleep
- Four common sleep disorders
- The role of nicotine, caffeine, and alcohol in sleep
- How to keep a sleep log
- When to seek a doctor's help to sleep

Chapter 29

Brenda worries about a lot of things, but she never had to worry about something as simple and natural as sleep—until a few weeks ago, anyway.

She always went right to sleep—"As soon as my head hit the pillow," she'd say—and slept soundly until the alarm clock summoned her to get up and go to work. She stayed up later Friday and Saturday nights, of course, but she could sleep in weekend mornings to make up for it.

But recently she's been having trouble falling asleep. Her mind races, and she keeps thinking about all the things she has to do the next day. She's been under an unusual amount of pressure at work, true, but that's never bothered her this way before.

She really hates the tossing and turning. She's tried counting sheep, pretending she's floating on a cloud, putting on soft music, and nothing has helped. Although she's wary of taking any kind of drugs, she's thinking of getting one of those over-the-counter sleeping tablets.

You've probably never fallen asleep while giving a presentation to a large group of people—a horror brought on by a disorder known as narcolepsy.

But I'll bet you've nodded off while listening to one. I'll bet you've snoozed your way through more than one television program, school band concert, or movie, too.

You may have been reacting to an especially long, hard day. You may have been bored. But you may also be chronically sleep deprived. Should you be concerned? It depends on what else you've been sleeping through. If you fall asleep every time you sit in one place longer than ten minutes, you may have a problem.

If you catch yourself snapping awake just as your car is drifting across the center line and into oncoming traffic, you've definitely got a problem, a big problem, one that endangers you and everybody else on the road.

I'll bet you've snoozed your way through more than one television program, school band concert, or movie, too.

Are You Getting Enough Sleep?

How much is "enough"?

Your mother probably told you that you should get your eight hours every night, and Mom's wisdom stood up for decades. But in the 1950s, doctors began suggesting that we could and should get by on less sleep. One prominent article in *The Saturday Evening Post* suggested that only sluggards and dummies waste their time sleeping eight hours a night.

About that time, the scientific study of sleep began (which makes it an extremely young science). We didn't even learn about a phenomenon known as REM (rapid eye movement) sleep, the stage of sleep during which dreaming occurs, until about fifty years ago (a discovery that derived, by the way, from the observation that a dog's eyes move behind closed eyelids when it dreams its doggie dreams).

Sleep deprivation experiments (which must rank fairly high on the sadism scale) have clearly established that we need to sleep. Bad things happen when you keep folks awake for days at a time. But even here, the conclusions are murky because some of the same bad things happen if you let folks sleep but deprive them of their dreams (another feat of cruelty accomplished by rousing sleepers every time they slip into the REM cycle but allowing them otherwise to get their "normal" sleep). After a few days of dreamless sleep, folks start having the dreams, or delusions, while they're awake, displaying the symptoms of schizophrenia. (In case you're getting worried—you do dream, although you might not remember your dreams.)

But we don't know why we dream. For that matter, we don't even know for sure why we need to sleep at all. There have been lots of theories, but research has failed to prove any of them out. One compellingly logical notion, for example, posits that we sleep so that our poor hyperactive brains can cool off. But now we know that the brain is actually more active while we sleep. Different centers light up, true, but the brain certainly isn't resting.

On the all-important question of how much sleep we need, experts are divided. Some side with Mom, suggesting that most of us do indeed need between seven and nine hours of sleep a night, with Mom's eight a reasonable average. But others suggest that "normal"

> Sleep deprivation experiments (which must rank fairly high on the sadism scale) have clearly established that we need to sleep.

sleep varies widely with the individual. Thomas Edison is often cited as an example of a highly creative and productive individual who thrived on three or four hours of sleep a night (although revisionist biographers have suggested that Edison took a lot of naps, and some even suggest that his alleged nocturnal habits are folklore).

So, we don't know for sure why we do it, and we don't agree on how much of it we need. What do we know about sleep?

The Five Stages of Sleep

"Early to bed and early to rise," Ben Franklin admonished us, would make us "healthy, wealthy, and wise," attributing a practical benefit if not moral superiority to getting an early start. But there is probably no "normal" sleep pattern or "right" time for waking up and going to bed. Folks have very different "natural" cycles; some are simply more alert late at night and have a terrible time trying to fight their way out of deep sleep when the alarm clock rips the morning.

Getting up at dawn may do the early bird a lot of good, but it's not so good for the worm.

Sleep itself is not a single, clearly defined condition. Sleep is actually a series of five stages of progressively deeper sleep, including the REM/dream stage. Most people will cycle through the five stages three or four times during an eight-hour sleep. The dream stages tend to get progressively longer during the night, and dreams sometimes continue from episode to episode.

Lots of books purport to interpret your dreams for you, but no one has satisfactorily explained how you can have a dream that you can't understand. (The right side of the brain shows its murky, symbolic films, without subtitles, to the literal-minded left side of the brain.)

Some claim to be able to see future events in their dreams, and most of us certainly revisit—and often reshape—the past in dreams. Others claim to be able to teach you the techniques for lucid dreaming (conscious awareness of the dream state and the ability to change the "plot line").

The Things That Go Wrong in the Night

1. Insomnia is by far the most well-known and common disorder preventing you from getting your sleep, so common, in fact, that most of us suffer from it at one time or another.

   As the name suggests, sleep onset insomnia involves difficulty falling asleep, whereas terminal insomnia (which sounds a lot worse than it is) manifests in waking up too early and being unable to get back to sleep.

   Temporary insomnia often accompanies the presence of unusually high stress, and generally the insomnia eases when the source of the stress ceases.

   Doctors advise simply riding out temporary bouts of sleeplessness. If you can't fall asleep or get back to sleep in a reasonable amount of time ("reasonable," of course, depending on the individual), don't fight it. Get up and do something else (but not something stimulating) until you feel drowsy. Then try again.

   Force yourself to get up at your normal time, even if you've been awake for long periods of time during the night. If you adjust your wake-up time to try to compensate for the lost sleep, you'll prolong the insomnia. The condition will pass, and the short-term loss of sleep won't really hurt you.

   If the insomnia is prolonged or even chronic, get to a sleep disorder clinic (which are sprouting like bagel stores across the country, a sign of our stressed-out times).

   Recent research at these clinics suggests, by the way, that some "chronic insomniacs" actually get a lot more sleep than they think they're getting. Some even sleep a "normal" seven or eight hours but still report having been sleepless for most of the night.

2. During episodes of sleep apnea, the sleeper stops breathing for a few seconds. Many people experience mild sleep apnea every night with no apparent ill effects. However, some sufferers have several prolonged sessions each night, often waking themselves—and their partners—with a sudden gasp. Sufferers from severe bouts of sleep apnea will feel fatigued

> Temporary insomnia often accompanies the presence of unusually high stress, and generally the insomnia eases when the source of the stress ceases.

and logy, even after a "full night's sleep," and may find themselves nodding off at inappropriate times during the day.

If you or your sleeping partner is concerned that you may have sleep apnea, you can monitor your sleep in your own bed with an apparatus that registers oxygen levels. The monitor involves nothing more invasive than a Band-Aid-like device on the tip of a finger. You may then "graduate" to a night of monitoring at a sleep disorders clinic to confirm the diagnosis.

3. Most of us also get the start reflex now and again, most often just as we fall asleep. Many report dreaming that they're falling, and when they tense, they "start" themselves awake.

Again, a little is normal, but a lot is trouble. Rare individuals get the start reflex dozens of times a night, robbing them of sleep.

4. Folks suffering from literal dream disorder actually act out their dreams. Most of us don't keep twitching and starting and otherwise thrashing around during the night because a little switch at the top of the spine prevents us from acting out our dreams. But in rare instances, the little switch doesn't work.

Dream that you're about to catch a pass and glide into the end zone, and you may leap and run into the bedroom wall—or even out the door and down the stairs!

You don't want this disorder to go untreated, in yourself or your roommate.

What Should You Do about Sleeping?

Most of us will never suffer from apnea, excessive start reflex, or literal dream disorder, and our bouts of insomnia will be short term and self-curing. But experts now suggest that most of us aren't getting enough sleep. One report asserts that 33 percent of the American population is chronically sleep deprived. Short term, this makes us cranky and less efficient. It may be a hidden factor in many

Experts now suggest that most of us aren't getting enough sleep. One report asserts that 33 percent of the American population is chronically sleep deprived.

traffic accidents. We don't know the long-term consequences because we haven't been studying sleep long enough.

Six Steps for Getting a Good Night's Sleep

If you encounter sleeplessness in the form of onset or terminal insomnia or both, you may be able to treat yourself with one or more of these remedies.

1. Avoid nicotine, caffeine, and alcohol. Nicotine is a powerful stimulant. It's also addicting, and it carries harmful tars and other impurities linked to lung cancer and other life-threatening diseases. You're clearly better off without it. If you can't quit, at least try to avoid smoking within a few hours of bedtime.

Caffeine is also a powerful and pervasive stimulant, present in coffee and cola, of course, but also in chocolate, tea, aspirin, and lots of other less obvious sources. Caffeine remains in your system for four hours after you ingest it so that after-dinner coffee at eight may be hurting your sleep at midnight.

Alcohol is certainly not a stimulant. In fact, it's a powerful depressant. It just doesn't feel that way because the first thing it depresses is our inhibition. But it still belongs on the short list of sleep disrupters. That shot at bedtime may help ease you into sleep, but alcohol blocks your descent into deep and restful sleep.

2. Take sleeping pills short term or not at all. Sleeping pills and tranquilizers may help you fall asleep and may in the short term help you get through stress-induced insomnia. But these drugs have some serious drawbacks:

- They don't work for everyone and even have the opposite effect on some, causing prolonged wakefulness.
- They, too, block descent into deep sleep.
- You may build a tolerance, requiring larger doses to achieve the same effect.
- You can also become addicted to them.

> Caffeine remains in your system for four hours after you ingest it so that after-dinner coffee at eight may be hurting your sleep at midnight.

- Worst case, you may wind up needing sleeping pills to sleep and stimulants to wake up, taking higher and higher doses of each in an extremely dangerous cycle.

3. Keep regular meal times. Try to eat at approximately the same times each day, and avoid eating too close to bedtime. Digestion is a very active process and may interfere with your attempts to relax and fall asleep.

Nutritionists chime in with the advice that we'll process and use nutrients most efficiently by eating the big meal in the morning and then tapering off during the day and by eating several small meals rather than two or three large ones. However you refuel, regular habits will benefit healthy sleep.

4. Stick to regular bed and rising times. A regular sleep schedule—getting up and going to bed at approximately the same time each day—will help combat insomnia.

That means seven days a week. If you tend to follow one schedule during the work week but depart from it drastically for weekends, you may well have trouble falling asleep Sunday night and even more trouble dragging yourself out of bed Monday morning.

Folks who work split shifts have an incredibly high incidence of insomnia. The constant disruption is just too hard for most of us to adjust to.

5. Exercise regularly. People who work out regularly report deeper, more satisfying sleep than their more sedentary brothers and sisters. Exercising on a regular schedule and not within three or four hours of bedtime is best for most of us.

All this regularity may seem downright boring. But if you're having trouble sleeping, some adjustments here may enable you to solve the problem without drugs or other therapies.

Whatever you do about steps 1 through 5, experts agree...

6. Don't worry about it. There's nothing worse than lying awake thinking about how awful it is that you're not sleeping, how much you need that sleep, how bad you'll feel tomorrow if you don't get to sleep.

Do It Yourself

You may have already started your sleep log, a description of your sleeping habits and the factors that affect your sleep. You can also create a prescriptive sleep list—those actions you'll take to ensure deeper, most restful sleep. Consider the times you now go to bed and get up; your use of alcohol, nicotine, and caffeine; and your eating and exercise habits. List any changes you'd like to make in these areas.

If you decide to try to change your sleep pattern, give yourself at least three weeks before you begin to judge whether or not the change is effective for you. It takes at least that long to begin to change your pattern.

That is, of course, exactly what most of us do when we can't sleep.

The occasional sleepless night is a natural reaction to life's stresses; almost all of us will have our share along the way. If you can't sleep, examine your life for unusual sources of stress that may be causing the problem. If a specific problem or challenge is stealing your sleep, try the techniques we'll discuss in the next chapter to diffuse your anxiety.

If grief is causing your stress, know that both grief and stress will abate with time, and with them your sleeplessness. Again, your reaction is perfectly natural.

If Sleeplessness Persists...

If you're concerned that a chronic lack of sleep may be robbing you of efficiency and alertness, hurting your relationships, perhaps even endangering your long-term wellness, first get a clear idea of how much and when you're actually sleeping by keeping a sleep log for two weeks.

Now you're ready for a chat with a sleep disorders expert. He or she may have some immediate suggestions for you or may suggest an overnight stay at the clinic for a thorough monitoring of your sleep.

> If grief is causing your stress, know that both grief and stress will abate with time, and with them your sleeplessness. Again, your reaction is perfectly natural.

Is It a Problem or Just a Pattern?

Are you sleeping "right"? Is your pattern "normal," even if it doesn't fit the schedule Ben Franklin laid out in *Poor Richard's Almanac*?

For years, a good friend and colleague of mine went to bed at 10:30 each night, awoke between 2:00 and 3:00 in the morning, read for about an hour, and slept again until 5:45. He was getting about six hours and fifteen minutes of sleep each night, and he certainly wasn't following any prescribed pattern.

He was also alert, healthy, and full of energy, a high achiever and a keen observer of life. He may not have been "normal," but he certainly seemed to be thriving on his "abnormal" sleep pattern.

My own predilection for getting up between 5:00 and 6:00 A.M. strikes many as perverse, and I used to worry about it. But it seems to be natural for me. I don't use an alarm clock, and I always had a terrible time trying to "reward myself" by sleeping late on weekends. Those early morning hours are productive for me, and I truly love watching the sky lighten before the dawn. I've stopped worrying about it. My sleep pattern doesn't seem to be doing any harm.

How about you? Got a problem? Only you can say. If you decide that you do, this chapter has given you the tools for understanding the problem, making some life changes, or perhaps getting some help.

Brenda didn't buy those sleeping pills.

Instead, she decided that work stress and the breakup of a long-term relationship a few weeks before accounted for her temporary insomnia.

Brenda went to bed at her usual time each night. If she couldn't fall asleep within twenty minutes, she got up and read until she felt drowsy. She was usually able to fall asleep after that, but some nights, she even had a second session with a not-too-exciting novel.

She made herself get up at her usual time each morning, even if she missed sleep, and she tried to keep about the same sleeping hours over the weekend, too.

After eight days of this routine, she woke up and realized she'd had no trouble falling asleep the night before. Her temporary bout of insomnia was over, and she had learned the techniques she'd need to handle the inevitable next bout.

Time-Management Tips

1. If you have trouble sleeping, caffeine, nicotine, or alcohol may be part of the problem.
2. Don't rely on sleeping pills for long-term relief from insomnia.
3. Keep regular times to eat, sleep, and exercise.

Learn How to Declare a Truce in the War on Stress

In this chapter, you'll learn:

- **What stress really is**
- **Why you encounter stress every day**
- **How stress hurts you**
- **How to achieve "eustress"**
- **Ten ways to reduce your stress level**

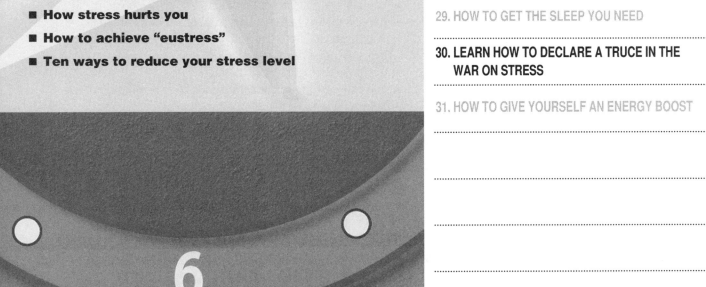

Chapter 30

Marlene can't even relax right any more.

She careens from one task to another during hectic days full of office work and work at home and the hassles of getting from one to the other. She fights down a panicky feeling all day long.

But it's what's happening to her when the day's done that really has her concerned. When those rare chances to relax and unwind finally present themselves, she can't do it. She stays tense and worried, too far gone into her stress to be able to let it go for a few minutes of life-restoring rest.

She's beginning to think the only thing that can save her would be running away to a deserted island.

"You know you're too stressed if you wonder if brewing is really a necessary step for the consumption of coffee."

That's part of a puckish self-examination that circulated on the Internet recently. "You know you're too stressed," the test continued, if:

- You can achieve a "runner's high" by sitting up.
- The sun is too loud.
- You begin to explore the possibility of setting up an intravenous drip solution of espresso.
- You believe that, if you think hard enough, you can fly.
- Antacid tablets become your sole source of nutrition.
- You begin to talk to yourself, then disagree about the subject, get into a nasty row about it, lose, and refuse to speak to yourself for the rest of the night.
- You find no humor in *wasting your time* reading silly "you know you're too stressed if..." lists.

Such satire never hits home unless it holds at least a kernel of truth.

Two social scientists named Holmes and Rahe created a more serious scale for measuring stress back in 1967. The Holmes–Rahe Social Readjustment Rating Scale assigned stress points to life situations. If you tallied 300 points or more on the scale within the last year, you were presumed to be at increased risk of illness or depression. Some of the events, with their point values, were:

> "You know you're too stressed," if: You can achieve a "runner's high" by sitting up.

- Death of a spouse (99)
- Divorce (91)
- Getting fired (83)
- Marital separation (72)
- Jail term (72)
- Personal injury or illness (68)
- Death of a close friend (68)
- Sex difficulties (53)
- Trouble with boss (45)
- Trouble with in-laws (43)

No big surprises here—but some serious omissions, according to sociologist Georgia Witkin. In 1991, she added new elements to the stress scale to more accurately reflect modern life in general and the evolving role of women specifically. Witkin's scale includes:

- Raising a disabled child (97)
- Single parenting (96)
- Depression (89)
- Abortion (89)
- Child's illness (87)
- Infertility (87)
- Crime victimization (84)
- Parenting parents (81)
- Raising teenagers (80)
- Chemical dependency (80)
- Son or daughter returning home (61)
- Commuting (57)

Great deal, huh? Stress depresses you, and then depression increases your stress.

Perhaps the only major surprise here is that "raising teenagers" rates only an 80. (800 seems more accurate, at least on the bad days.)

How about you? Can you tally 300 points or more, based on life events of the past twelve months? If you can, can it really make you sick?

Do It Yourself

List the major sources of stress in your life just now. Don't worry about assigning points or numbers to these stressors, but do rank them in order of their effect on you. Hold on to this list as you read on.

The Parable of the Mice in the Refrigerator

Hans Selye is the founder of modern stress research. In one of his most famous experiments, he introduced mice to a stressful environment (in this case, the inside of a refrigerator) to see how they'd react. Invariably, they went through three distinct stages. First, they fell into a funk, hunkering down to gut out a particularly long winter. (I went through a similar reaction during my first winter in Wisconsin.) But when the winter persisted, the mice went into a productive and cooperative frenzy, making nests and otherwise adapting their environment to make it more hospitable. (That's me, too, learning to put up storm windows and dressing in layers.)

Stage three really got Selye's attention and deserves ours. Almost without exception, the mice dropped dead. The cold wasn't lethal, but something about living under extreme stress for prolonged periods of time apparently was.

Subsequent researchers like Christopher Coe have made the connection. Coe separates baby monkeys from their mothers and measures the effect of this trauma on their white blood cell count. Take the monkeys from their mamas, and the white blood cell count plummets, thus depressing the immune system and leaving the monkeys vulnerable to all sorts of diseases. Reunite them, and the blood count rises.

> Take the monkeys from their mamas, and the white blood cell count plummets, thus depressing the immune system and leaving the monkeys vulnerable to all sorts of diseases.

The Good Stuff Is Also Stressful

Another look at the Holmes–Rahe stress scale begins to bring the problem of stress into even sharper focus. Other items on the scale include:

- Marriage (85)
- Pregnancy (78)
- Retirement (68)
- Christmas (56)
- Addition of new family member (51)
- Vacation (43)

Wait a minute! Aren't these supposed to be the *good* things of life, the events we work toward and wait for?

They are, but they're also stressful, making huge demands of time and energy and requiring major adjustments.

Take Christmas. (Henny Youngman fans will no doubt add "Please.") All those preparations, the staggering expectations, the relentless requirement that you be happy! Most of us simply add this huge load to our everyday cares and responsibilities; life and work go on, Christmas or no. And just on the off chance that things don't go perfectly, you can add feelings of guilt, inadequacy, and remorse to the list of burdens.

Happy holidays!

But what about vacation—that oasis of rest and relief we struggle toward all year long?

You take on additional roles as travel agent, tour guide, recreation director, and master sergeant in charge of logistics. You exhaust yourself preparing for the trip while also trying to catch up and get ahead on your regular work. You leave familiar routines and surroundings behind for the unknown. So you're already hitting the top of the stress scale even before the first flat tire, missed plane connection, or botched motel reservation.

Are we there yet?

The Bozo Factor

The world is full of bozos, and you're one of them. Don't be offended. I'm another one. We can't help it. We just keep getting in each other's way.

Put us into cars and we become particularly caustic. The guy who cuts you off in traffic stresses you. When you honk your horn at the offender, you stress the driver next to you.

Holidays, with their own sets of stressors, compound the highway insanity. "Driving probably will become even wilder now that Christmas (in P. G. Wodehouse's words) has us by the throat," George Will noted in a call for civility in *The Washington Post*.

Do It Yourself

Take that list of stressors you've been working on and add the good things in your life that are also creating stress.

"Holidays and homicide go together like eggnog and nutmeg, so 'tis the season to study the wildness in the streets."

Relationships—or lack of relationships—inherently cause stress. Divorce is stressful (91 on the scale), but so are marriage (85), marital reconciliation (57), remarriage (worth 89 big ones on Witkin's revised scale), and—are you ready for this?—something Witkin calls "singlehood" (77).

Son or daughter leaves home and you get 41 nicks to the parental psyche. But according to Witkin, you get 61 points if your little darling moves back in.

You can't win. Enter into a relationship with another human being, get out of one, or avoid relationships all together—you open yourself to increased stress no matter what you do or don't do.

Add in all the everyday things that people do to bother you, things like:

- Cutting you off in traffic
- Emptying their car ashtrays in the parking lot
- Cutting in line at the market
- Trying to buy more than twelve items in the twelve-items-or-less line
- Talking loudly during the movie
- Chewing with their mouths open
  and on and on.

Stress Happens

One more plunge into the stress scale to pick up another insight into stress:

- Change of financial status (61)
- Spouse begins or ends work (58)
- Change of line of work (51)
- Change in residence (47)
- Change in number of arguments with spouse (46)

- Change in eating habits (29)
- Change in sleeping habits (27)
- Change in recreation (26)

Lose your job or get evicted from your apartment? Highly stressful. But so is winning the lottery or moving into your dream home. The one constant here is change—regardless of the nature of the change. All change is stressful.

Which means, of course, that living is inherently stressful. Stress is inevitable.

You can't even buy your way out of stress. Psychologist Ed Diener's recent study indicates that higher personal incomes often bring their own set of stresses.

Little wonder, then, that a recent *U.S. News & World Report* cover story announced, "Stressed Out? You've got lots of company. But there are ways to fight back."

Being Blessedly Stressed

You can't avoid stress. But you don't really want to.

Selye and researchers who followed him have learned that the total absence of stress is no better for you than too much stress. To remove all stress from your life, you would have to remove all relationships and all challenge. That probably explains why retirement rates so high on the stress scale. Yes, you shed the responsibilities and deadlines, but you also lose definition, purpose, a reason to get out of bed in the morning.

Selye coined the term *eustress* to signify the ideal compromise—not too little, not too much, but just the right amount of stress in your life.

Your goal, then, should be to live in eustress as much as possible and to take especially good care of yourself during those inevitable times when you must exceed your safe stress limits.

But you may not be able to engage in safe stress by "fighting back," as that *U.S. News & World Report* headline suggests you do.

> **Streetwise Definition**
>
> *Eustress*
> The ideal level of stress in an individual's life. That level varies from individual to individual.

Three Great Lies of Our Age

We've declared war on stress. Time management is one of the weapons in our arsenal. Our battle cries include:

> You can do more with less.
> Work smarter not harder.
> A leaner work force is a more efficient work force (thus the terms *downsizing* and *rightsizing*).

You can put these bromides on the list of "great lies of our time" (right alongside "The check is in the mail," "I'll still respect you in the morning," and "I'm not selling anything. This is an educational survey").

You can't do more with less. You can only do more with more. If you're working more, you're doing something else (like sleeping and playing) less.

Anyone who advises you to work smarter not harder is telling you to produce more. He or she doesn't care if you have to work smarter and harder to do it.

A leaner work force means somebody has to take on the work that somebody else was doing. If you've still got your job, that somebody is you.

Fight, manage, plan—do whatever you can to try to squeeze more work into the same limited minutes in the day—at your own risk. You're probably incurring still more stress.

So, if stress is an inevitable byproduct of living, and if modern life puts us under ever greater stress, how can you possibly avoid taking on too much of it?

You probably can't, but you can manage the stress by understanding its nature.

The Fundamental Truth about Stress

Stress isn't "out there" someplace, in the evil boss or the colicky kid or the traffic jam. Those are the stressors that trigger the stress.

> You can't do more with less. You can only do more with more.

Stress is inside you, your psychological responses to life's challenges.

Do what you can to mitigate the stressors, yes, but there's a lot you can't do anything about. You can do a great deal to modulate and modify your internal reactions, thus eliminating much of the stress if not the stressors.

You can learn to cope with life as it is—without letting it kill you.

You Have to Incur Stress to Lose Stress

Before you begin your strategic retreat from the stress wars, one final visit to the stress scale, where, nestled between "Trouble with boss (45)" and "Trouble with in-laws (43)" we find:

- Revision of personal habits (44)

That's right. Any attempt to modify your stress response is itself stressful. So you'll need to know that you'll feel increased pressure, not relief, when you begin to retrain some of your responses to stressors. Don't get discouraged. This is normal and short-lived. You'll get through it, and the benefits will be more than worth the effort.

One Size Does Not Fit All

I'm going to suggest some strategies for reducing your stress level. You'll need to modify, adapt, add to, and subtract from these suggestions depending on your specific responses to potential stressors.

Your stress response is different from anyone else's—one more element that makes you uniquely you. We have different tolerances for pain, different energy levels, different susceptibilities to and pre-dispositions for various diseases—and different tolerances for stress. When folks like Witkin, Holmes, and Rahe assign points to various stressors, they are at best predicting the response in the "average" person—that strange being who makes $21,914 a year, has 1.782 children, and doesn't, in fact, exist.

Streetwise Definitions

Stressor
   A source of irritation, anxiety, or conflict in your life.

Stress
   Your internal reaction to the stressor.

Pay attention to what stresses you and then do your best to compensate.

You also have a unique perception of what is and isn't stressful. A round of golf on a Saturday morning may be relaxing for one and a frustrating endurance test for another. It doesn't depend on how good you are at golf so much as on how much you care how good you are. One person's party is another person's trial. Pay attention to what stresses you and then do your best to compensate.

Ten Ways You Can Reduce Your Stress Level

1. Acknowledge and honor your feelings. Some feelings seem unacceptable or even dangerous. Perhaps you've learned that it's not OK to be angry at your parents, to think less than respectful thoughts about your minister, or to lust after your best friend's spouse. You can deny such feelings, but you can't stop feeling them, and the process of denial takes psychic energy and creates stress. Feel what you feel. Then figure out how you should act—or not act—on those feelings.

2. Find safe ways to express your feelings. Present your case to your supervisor, even if you don't think doing so will change that supervisor's decision. You'll have acknowledged and validated your feeling by giving it substance. (And your supervisor might even surprise you.)

Expressing feelings doesn't always help decrease stress, however. Rather than venting your anger, screaming at another driver in a traffic jam will actually increase the anger and your internal responses to it. You end up more, not less, stressed. In that case, you're a lot better off trying the next suggestion.

3. Unplug. You don't have to blow up every time someone lights your fuse. You can snuff out the fuse instead. How? Mom had it right; it really can be as simple as counting to 10. When you feel the anger flare, don't tell yourself you're not really angry (because it isn't "nice" to get angry). Don't rant, either. Take a deep breath and count (or laugh or spout nonsense or sing or whatever works for you).

But if you do that, you'll be letting that lousy driver ahead of you get away unpunished, right? Yeah, you will. But will screaming at him really punish him or teach him a lesson? You know it won't, and that knowledge will only frustrate you more.

Remember, too, that he's not trying to stress you out. He's not paying any attention to you at all; that's what's so annoying! He's just trying to get someplace in a hurry, just as you are.

And finally, remember that you're probably being somebody else's stressor, too. When I asked a workshop full of folks to list things other people do that annoy them, one person mentioned the bozo who crunches the ice in his soft drink at the movies. As I added the comment to our list, I silently vowed never to crunch the ice in my soft drink at the movies again.

If all that doesn't help you maintain your perspective, ask yourself this: is it worth making myself sick over? All that churning inside really can help make you sick. And you're letting it happen to you. Do you really think "teaching" that "lesson" is worth it?

Don't get mad. Don't get even. Just get on with it.

4. Fix it. Getting annoyed at the sight of a mound of cigarette butts in the parking lot ranks high on a lot of folks' lists of annoyances. A lady in one of my recent workshops had a wonderful solution. She carries a "butt removal kit"—plastic sack, whisk broom, and pan. When she comes upon a tobacco dump, she simply removes it. Instead of getting angry and frustrated, she has accomplished something tangible to make her environment a little better.

5. Create quiet time alone—every day. This can be nothing more than those minivacations we talked about earlier. But you may need more—a half hour to read or listen to music or do nothing at all.

You may need it, but you may not feel comfortable taking it. We spend so much time surrounded by other people and by almost constant noise, silence and isolation can be intimidating. Don't be frightened of your own good company. Alone with your thoughts, you'll get to know yourself again.

6. Plan your escape routes. When you check into a motel or hotel, do you immediately figure out how you'll get out in case of

> Remember you're probably being somebody else's stressor, too.

fire? You'll probably never find yourself in a motel fire, but if you do, your simple precaution might save your life.

Fire can break out in everyday life, too. Figure out how you'll escape when it does.

"When the going gets tough," Dwight Eisenhower once assured us, "the tough get going." This can mean, although I'm sure Ike didn't intend this interpretation, that if the going gets unbearable, you might need to get going—out the back door for a break before reentering the fray.

Will you find the courage to say, "Can we take a five-minute break here?" If you do, I guarantee others will silently thank you for it.

7. Wallow in successes and pleasures. I'm almost finished writing this long chapter in a book that's important to me. I plan to reward myself with a good, warm lunch. I intend to enjoy every bite. I'll probably tell myself what a great guy I am to have finished this chapter.

Don't just check your accomplishments off the list. Acknowledge them—and the talent, energy, and determination they required. Don't just shovel in fuel. Enjoy the pleasure of the food.

8. Give less than 100 percent. Giving 100 percent isn't even good enough anymore. With inflation, athletes must now give 110 percent. But nobody really has "110 percent" to give. You have limited time, limited energy, limited resources. You can't solve every problem, meet every crisis, rise to every occasion.

Some challenges don't deserve 100 percent. Save something for later.

9. Create a third basket. New tasks go into the "in basket." Finished work goes in the "out basket."

And some tasks should go in the "to-hell-with-it basket."

10. Do one thing at a time. One of the truly pernicious lessons of modern time management involves multitasking, doing more than one thing at a time.

But we dilute the effectiveness of our work and rob the joy from our pleasures when we engage in multitasking.

> Giving 100 percent isn't even good enough anymore. With inflation, athletes must now give 110 percent. But nobody really has "110 percent" to give.

We also show a fundamental lack of respect for others if we keep typing while on the phone or hide behind the newspaper when a loved one is trying to talk to us.

Talking on a car phone while driving can endanger more than a relationship. That sort of reckless multitasking can endanger lives—yours and others.

Watch kids at play. They are so focused, so rapt, they truly don't hear us when we call them. You had that power of concentration once. You can cultivate it now, giving full attention to everything you do. Don't try to spin ten plates on ten poles. Spin one plate really well.

Marlene's life is still full of stressors, but she hasn't had to run away to a deserted island to reduce her level of stress.

Now that she has come to understand that stress is what happens inside her and that she can control that stress even when she can't do much about the causes of that stress, she's making it through the day in much better shape. That means she can actually relax, kick her shoes off, and wiggle her toes without the stress ruining her rest.

She still thinks about that island retreat, but now she has the energy to begin dreaming of being able to take a relaxing vacation rather than a total escape from life.

Do It Yourself

Take your list of personal stressors and our list of ten ways to combat stress. Make a new list—those specific things you can do to reduce the stress in your life. Examine those times during the day when you're multitasking and see if you wouldn't be better off shedding the "multi" and just "tasking," one task at a time. List items that can go in your "to-hell-with-it" basket. Figure out your escape routes for especially stressful times. This kind of anticipation now can save you from a great deal of stress later.

Time-Management Tips

1. All change is stressful. Compensate for any disruption to your pattern.
2. You can't change all of life's stressors, but you can control the stress reaction in you.
3. Unplug your anger.
4. Create quiet time every day.
5. Acknowledge and enjoy your accomplishments.
6. Do one thing at a time.
7. Create a "to-hell-with-it" basket.

How to Give Yourself an Energy Boost

In this chapter, you'll learn:

- The real effects of sugar and caffeine on your body and mind
- Three guidelines for a healthy diet
- Suggestions for getting regular exercise
- Your ideal weight and how to maintain it
- Why it's so hard to lose weight by cutting calories alone
- Three steps to a successful exercise program
- The ideal time to exercise
- The right kind of exercise for you

Chapter 31

"I'm too young to feel this old."

That's Marge Becker speaking, and what she's saying would surprise her friends.

Marge is a slender, energetic superwoman in her early forties. She balances the demands of being wife to Reg, mother to Jessica and Angela, and a successful decorator and freelance color consultant. She's one of those doers, constantly on the go, about whom other people say, "I don't know how she does it."

Lately, Marge has been wondering the same thing.

More and more, now, she finds herself yawning by midmorning. She feels groggy after lunch, and she's too exhausted after the work is finally done to enjoy those blessed free moments.

Marge watches her diet and tries to get enough sleep. A physical exam ruled out illness. She just can't seem to muster the extra energy she's been able to rely on all of her life.

She wonders if she must accustom herself to a gradual decline into old age.

I can't promise that regular exercise and a diet high in oat bran will enable you to live forever or fight off all illness. I can't even pretend that anything I say here won't be contradicted by some new "scientific" study tomorrow. (After all, the "experts" used to tell us to eat a hearty breakfast of eggs and bacon.) But the suggestions about diet and exercise in this chapter can do a lot to help you maintain a high level of energy throughout your busy day.

> The suggestions about diet and exercise in this chapter can do a lot to help you maintain a high level of energy throughout your busy day.

The Not-So-Awful Truth about Sugar and Caffeine

When you start to sag in the middle of the day, do you reach for a donut and a cup of coffee to pick you up again?

I'm not a member of the sugar police, and I guzzle more than my fair share of diet cola—the high octane kind, not decaf. But I am going to suggest that you need to be streetsmart about what you eat and drink.

How to Give Yourself an Energy Boost

For a while there, studies seemed to implicate caffeine as a possible cause of everything from cancer to coronaries. (But not cavities. Sugar was the culprit there.) But lately, about the worst thing anybody seems to be able to say about caffeine is that we become physically addicted to it—as most anyone who has tried to quit cold turkey can attest.

Sugar has pretty well wriggled off the hook, too. At just 17 calories per level teaspoon (as the Sugar Advisory Board keeps reminding us), it really won't induce instant obesity, and if you remember to brush your teeth after you eat a candy bar, the sugar won't even rot your teeth.

Caffeine and sugar act as stimulants, increasing energy, alertness, and a general sense of well-being. What's so bad about that coffee and donut as a midday pickup? Not a lot, but do consider these three potential side effects:

1. **Empty calories can replace useful ones.** Sugar and caffeine provide an energy surge, but there's no real nutrition in them. If you eat a lot of donuts instead of "real food," you won't get the fuel you need to maintain good health.
2. **After the boost comes the crash.** The sugar high and the caffeine buzz do n't just wear off. They may drop you faster than they picked you up. You may be deepening that natural biorhythmic trough we talked about in Chapter 28.
3. **You aren't addressing the real problem.** When your body tells you that it's tired, what you really ought to do is give it a rest. If you're using sugar and caffeine to push yourself harder than is good for you, you'll eventually hurt yourself physically and psychologically.

Three Guidelines for a Healthy Diet

1. **Don't eat more than you can use.** You store fat when you take in more calories than you need to maintain your level of activity. That's fine if you're planning to hibernate, but otherwise, the extra weight really won't do you much good. Find

Caution

You may be taking in more sugar and caffeine than you think.

Take a look at that list of ingredients on a "healthy" granola bar, for example. The manufacturers have to list the ingredients in order, most prevalent ingredient first. So if "sugar" is first or second, that bar may not be so healthy after all.

Also, sugar may actually make the list three or four times, as brown sugar, glucose, dextrose, and coconut oil, for example.

You know that coffee and colas carry a lot of caffeine, but did you know that tea, aspirin, and chocolate do, too.

If you need to regulate your intake, start by becoming aware of the sources of sugar and caffeine in your diet.

the level of intake that lets you maintain a good weight and a high energy level.

2. **Eat plenty of fiber.** My wife Ellen calls it "the tree bark and prunes diet." Doctors recommend a diet high in fruits, vegetables, and grains to help you avoid cancer, heart disease, arthritis pain, and scores of other ills. Oat bran really is good for you.

3. **Reduce the percentage of fat in your diet.** Thanks to product labeling laws, you can know how much fat the food you eat contains. By substituting the low- or nonfat version for the "regular," nonfat milk for whole milk, nonfat yogurt for sour cream, ground turkey for ground beef, broiled or baked fish for the same fish fried, you can cut the amount of fat you consume dramatically.

Will the nonfat yogurt taste as good as sour cream? Oh, please! But you can get used to it. I find I even prefer "blue milk" to the regular stuff now.

Shake It Up Baby: Why You Need to Get Moving

We got you well rested in Chapter 29. Now you're going to get up out of that chair and get your body moving.

Movement creates energy.

Not too many years ago, most of us made our livings through the literal sweat of our brows—working the land or performing some other form of physical labor. Now many of us ride the computer range or in other ways earn our daily bread while sitting down.

If your routine doesn't naturally include exercise, you need to incorporate natural exercise into your routine. You'll feel better in at least five ways.

1. You'll feel better physically. When you first start exercising, you may actually feel pretty rotten. Muscles that haven't moved since you were playing capture the flag as a kid don't respond well to a sudden reawakening. But if you start slowly and stick with it, the pain will subside, and you'll begin feeling more alert and alive.

2. You'll feel better mentally. You exercise more than just your muscles. Every time you forsake the couch for a workout, you release nature's own feel-good chemicals, called endorphins.

You'll also send yourself some wonderful messages about your own worth. When you exercise, you tell yourself you're worth the effort. Your sense of well-being and confidence will increase, and that in turn will help motivate you for your next workout.

The connection between exercise and improved mental outlook is well established. Most of the therapies used to treat clinical depression include exercise, and it can help a simple case of the blues, too.

3. You'll have more energy. Inactivity breeds more inactivity. That workout you skipped yesterday makes it that much easier to skip today's, too. But once you fight your way free of the gravitational pull of the couch, you'll find that movement also feeds on itself.

As long as you don't overdo it, exercise will actually boost your energy levels. You may feel tired right after your workout, but you'll soon feel a surge of power and alertness that will carry you through the day.

4. You'll sleep better. As we discussed in Chapter 29.

5. You'll more easily attain and maintain your ideal weight.
How much are you actually supposed to weigh? It's hard to tell. Society's perception of the beautiful female form, for example, changes over time. Compare a painting by Rubens, who liked his nudes zaftig, to a fashion layout featuring some of today's stick models. Insurance tables keep adjusting the "ideal" weight up or down, depending on the reams of statistics on health and longevity they analyze.

You should get to and keep at that weight that lets you live an active, energetic, healthy life. If you feel you should lose weight, dieting alone is a brutally hard way to do it. As you decrease the calories you take in, you should also increase the calories you burn up. Exercise helps you burn calories faster. Your metabolism stays high for several hours after a workout. That means the furnace continues to burn more fuel even when you're back on the couch.

Do It Yourself

If you want to make some changes in your diet, first keep a log of everything you eat for a week. You may get some surprises.

Some of us eat more than we think, the noshing between meals actually adding up to two or three more "meals."

Some of us get a lot more fat than we're aware of, as it sneaks in wearing the innocent disguise of the skin on the chicken or that little pat of butter in the baked potato.

When you have your consumption list for the week, go through looking for calories you'll eliminate and low- or nonfat foods you'll substitute for the regular versions. You'll create a regimen for a relatively painless, commonsense approach to eating streetsmart.

Caution

If you diet without exercising, your body tends to burn muscle tissue instead of fat. You may lose weight while actually hurting your overall physical condition.

Also, if you diet too severely, your body thinks you're starving and lowers your metabolism to compensate, making it harder and harder to burn calories. If you don't exercise, your body will actually fight your efforts to lose weight.

Three Steps to a Successful Exercise Program

You say you're ready to start working out. But how should you begin? Carefully.

If it's been a while since you've broken a serious sweat, get a physical exam to make sure all systems are in proper working order.

Then follow this three-step plan.

Step 1. Commit for the long term. You aren't getting in shape for some short-term goal like playing on the company softball team or fitting into last year's swim gear. You're committing to a new and better way of living. You'll do it one day at a time. "Getting there" isn't half the fun. It's all "getting," and there's no "there."

If you have to stop exercising for a while for any reason, don't give up. Simply start in again, dropping back to a level that provides a satisfying workout without hurting you.

Step 2. Don't overdo. "No pain, no gain" is a myth, probably spawned by the people who make liniment. Slow and steady definitely wins this race. You might begin with nothing more than some slow stretches and a walk around the block. Your body will tell you if it's being overtaxed. Build gradually.

Any exercise is better than no exercise. Doing a little is better than doing none.

Step 3. Do it regularly. Don't leave your exercise program open to debate. If you do, you'll lose that debate more often than you win. Schedule a regular time, and then just do it.

What Kind of Exercise Is Right for You?

You've got lots of choices.

You can jog, walk, or swim, row or bike, take up martial arts, or find dozens of other ways to exercise your options. You can spend a lot of money on equipment and clothing, or you can put on an old sweatshirt and sneakers and just get moving. You can read books and keep logs, or you can just let your body guide you.

The right kind of exercise for you is the exercise you'll stick with for the long haul. If you hate it, you'll stop doing it. Find activities you can enjoy. Anything that sets your body into sustained motion and elevates your heart rate will help you. Skating, skiing, shooting hoops, playing a set of tennis, and walking the dog all qualify.

Some need the discipline of a scheduled time and place and a leader to put them through the paces. Others thrive on solitary refinement.

Some do only one thing. Others vary their activities.

Look for ways to build exercise into your life. Ride a stationary bike while you watch the evening news. Turn your daily mini-vacation into a brisk walk. Explore possibilities for biking or walking to work. Barring that, park farther from the office, and take the stairs instead of the elevator. With a little creative effort, you can get plenty of exercise every day without spending much time at it.

Exercise takes time. So does reading the ingredient lists on the foods you buy. But both are important parts of streetwise time management. Attention to diet and commitment to regular exercise pay off in increased energy levels, better stamina, and a general sense of well-being. You'll wind up saving time by investing a bit of that time in these crucial areas.

Marge Becker has decided she isn't so old after all.

She's still in high gear all day long, with Reg, the kids, the job, and the freelance business all making demands on her time.

But now that she swims laps at the Y three mornings a week and takes a vigorous walk the other four mornings, she finds that she gets an energy surge about the time the mental fog used to roll in.

She's working more efficiently. She even has time left over at the end of the day. It seems like magic—spend thirty minutes at the beginning of the day and you gain an hour at the end of the day—but that's exactly what has happened for Marge.

Under the Microscope

When's the best time to exercise?

Some evidence now indicates that morning is the ideal exercise time because exercising first thing in the day:

- Removes any worry about fitting it in later
- Burns a maximum amount of fat after an all-night fast
- Increases metabolism and thus energy through prime working hours

But the best time for you to exercise is the time when you'll do it regularly. The only potentially bad time to exercise may be within a few hours of bedtime, as we indicated in Chapter 29.

Do It Yourself

Take another look at that daily routine of yours. Search for opportunities to build exercise naturally into that routine.

If you need to make thirty minutes a day for exercise, apply the addition/subtraction theory. What will you give up to make time for exercise?

After four months of regular exercise, she wonders how she ever tried to survive without it.

Time-Management Tips

1. Eat a low-fat, high-fiber diet.
2. Make natural exercise a part of your daily routine.
3. Commit to fitness for the long term.
4. Find the right kind of exercise for you—something you'll stick with.
5. Exercise doesn't have to hurt to work.

Check Out Your Attitude

Summary of Part VIII

1. To tame your anxieties, you first have to name them.

2. Make a plan. Do something right away. Decide to do something later. Or decide there's nothing you can do.

3. Your own anger undermines you. Choose never to be angry—and then work to put your decision into practice.

4. Among other techniques, deep breathing, positive visualization, and laughter help eliminate anger.

5. Let your creativity interrupt you.

6. Schedule creativity sessions.

7. Note your core values and translate them into specific actions.

8. Schedule time to do those activities that support your values.

Worry steals your time and energy while undermining your sense of well-being. It gives you nothing in return. It's past time to get rid of worry.

No matter how "natural" it feels, worry isn't inevitable. You learned to worry, and you can learn to stop worrying. You'll learn how in this section.

Anger isn't an inevitable response to life, either. You can actually learn to diffuse your own anger. You don't have to express it or stifle it. You can just skip it!

Anxiety and anger rob you of your ability to think creatively. When you rush from task to task, desperately scratching items off the to-do list, you lose touch with your own insights and inspirations. Learn how to pay attention to those "ah-ha!" moments again.

Learn, too, how to schedule your creativity. Yes, you can actually make an appointment to have ideas, lots of ideas, more and better ideas than you thought you could ever have.

Streetwise time management means knowing what you're doing. It also means knowing why you're doing it. Finally, you'll step outside the daily race to articulate and affirm your core values, the reasons why you're really living. Time spent here will be the best time, and it will help you make sense out of everything else you do.

Stop Letting Worry Rob You of Time and Energy

In this chapter, you'll learn:

- The three causes of worry
- Ten ways to get rid of worries
- Five specific kinds of worry
- Five ways to deal with them
- How to know if you have an anxiety disorder
- What to do if you do

Chapter 32

Ira's a worrier, always has been and figures he always will be.

He blames his mother, who fretted and fussed over him and questioned his every decision with the words, "Are you sure?"

The adult Ira's never sure about anything. He worries about the decisions he has to make, and he worries about the ones he already made.

His best worry times are late at night, when he knows he should be sleeping. So he worries a lot about all the sleep he's losing.

Time for Ira to stop worrying before he worries himself into serious illness. But don't tell him that—he'll only worry more.

Is there any help for poor Ira?

Worried about managing your time well? You're wasting your time.

Worry steals your time and energy. It disrupts your rest, damages your ability to make decisions, and robs you of the pleasure and satisfaction you should get from work and play.

When you worry, you aren't planning, working, or solving problems. Worrying never resolves anything.

Worry ignores the present to fixate on a future that never arrives.

Worrying is like paying interest on a debt. You have nothing to show for it, you still have to pay back the principal, and you have no money left for the things you need. Substitute energy and time for money and you understand what worry really costs you.

You learned to worry, and you can learn to stop. You can replace worry with action.

> Worrying is like paying interest on a debt. You have nothing to show for it, you still have to pay back the principal, and you have no money left for the things you need.

Three Causes of Worry

1. **A decision you must make:** a big one ("Should I stick with the security of a regular paycheck or start my own business?") or a small one ("Should I order the double cheeseburger with fries or the salad with low-cal dressing?")
2. **An action you must perform:** like giving a business presentation or attending a social gathering
3. **An event outside your control:** like global warming or fighting in northern Ireland

Although the worries in the third category tend to be much larger in scope, they are also less immediate and therefore take up less of the worrier's psychic energy than do more immediate concerns, like the question of what to have for lunch.

Whatever you're worried about, you must realize that worry doesn't help.

Ten Ways to Get Rid of Your Worries

1. Don't resist or deny the worry. That only sends it underground, where it will fester and grow. It will return, stronger than ever, to attack you when you're most vulnerable. Face your fear. As you stop fearing the fear, it may begin to subside. If so, worry has already done its worst.

2. Name it as you claim it. Sometimes worry comes disguised as the formless furies, vague dread or anxiety that can shake you out of a sound sleep and leave you wide awake until daybreak. Or it may take on a specific but false aspect. You may think you're worried about the coming congressional election or the sorry shape your public schools are in—important concerns, to be sure—when you're really worried about a mole on your neck that suddenly changed shape and turned red.

Give it a name. Write the worry down as specifically as you can. Now you can begin to deal with it effectively.

3. Consider the consequences. Worry doesn't exist apart from you. Like stress, it's a reaction that takes place inside you. Since you created it, you can rechannel or diffuse it.

Ask: "What's the worst that could happen to me?"

If you eat that cheeseburger and fries, you'll consume about a week's allotment of fat, along with an enormous number of calories. This will not do you any good, and as a regular habit, it might shorten your life. On the other hand, the one meal will not kill you—and it will taste very good.

Perhaps you're worried about that presentation you're scheduled to give in two days. What, specifically, lurks under that general

---

Do It Yourself

This quick exercise will help you measure the true worth of worry:

1. Write down something you were worried about when you were a child.

2. Write down something you were worried about in high school.

3. Write down something you were worried about a year ago.

Now ask yourself these three questions about each worry:

1. Am I still worried about this?

2. How was the situation resolved?

3. Did worry help in any way to resolve the situation?

I'm willing to bet that in each case worry did little or nothing to help. Specific action may have resolved the situation, the passage of time may have eased or erased it, or you may have simply learned to live with it.

What are you worried about right now?

performance anxiety? Perhaps you're worried that you might make a mistake and, if you do, somebody might laugh at you.

Ask: "Could I live with that?"

You might not like it, surely, but you could certainly live with it. Now ask: "What are the odds?"

Have you been in similar circumstances? If so, how did things go then? Did you make a mistake? If so, did anybody laugh?

4. Push the worry to the max. They won't just laugh at you. The laughter will turn to jeers. They'll start throwing things at you! They'll chase you from the room and out of the building! You'll lose your job, your spouse will leave you, and you'll wind up at the homeless shelter.

Naw. That isn't really going to happen.

Now, stop worrying, which accomplishes nothing, and prepare thoroughly for that presentation.

5. Figure out what, if any, action you will take. You've got three choices:

- You can do something now.
- You can do something later.
- You can do nothing.

Play with possibilities. You could eat the cheeseburger and fries now and fast for the rest of the month. You could compromise—single cheeseburger, with tomatoes and onions, no fries. You could eat the salad and steal bites of your friend's burger.

Actions you might take regarding the business presentation include:

- Hitting the Internet to gather data
- Practicing in front of a sympathetic audience
- Faking a sore throat and going home "sick"
- Asking someone to make the presentation for you

You may decide to do nothing because you feel that nothing you can do will help the situation or because the costs of any action you might take outweigh the potential benefits. Deciding to do nothing is quite different from failing or refusing to decide at all. If you examine the situation and decide there's nothing you can do, you'll remove the ambiguity and thus relieve a great deal of anxiety. If you evade the decision, you'll go right on worrying.

Perhaps you're worrying about a decision you can't make yet. If you're losing sleep over tomorrow's decision, tell yourself, "I don't have to decide that now." Repeat as often as you need to.

Now tell yourself, "Whatever I decide will be fine." Tell yourself often enough and you'll begin to believe it, not because you've brainwashed yourself but because your intuition will recognize the truth of the statement. Whatever you decide really will be fine because you'll act on it and, having acted, move on to whatever comes next.

6. Follow through. If you've decided on immediate action, do it!

If you've decided to do something later, write down what you're going to do and when you're going to do it. Be specific: date, time, and place. Then be sure to keep that appointment. Otherwise, you'll soon learn to disregard anything you write down to do later.

If you've decided to do nothing, let it go.

7. Abide by your decision. Make each decision once. If you decide to eat the cheeseburger, enjoy the cheeseburger. If you decide on the salad, dive in. If you decide not to eat at all, savor the virtuousness of your hunger. Whatever you do, do it wholeheartedly. Resist second-guessing yourself.

Just because you've decided on future action or on no action doesn't mean the worry will go away. If it resurfaces in your conscious mind, send it packing, reminding yourself, "I've already decided that." Do this as many times as necessary.

8. Realize you are not alone in your anxiety. You know your inner demons well, but you never see the demons others bear. You see only the composed masks we all wear in public. That fact may lead you to assume that others aren't worried. It isn't true. People worry; they just don't show it to you. Athletes call it "putting on your game face." We all do it to get along.

Caution

This may not be easy. You probably have a long pattern of worrying, perhaps going back into early childhood. And you're probably receiving some benefit from all that worry. If nothing else, worry may be serving as a substitute for action or as a means of avoiding confrontations or evading decisions. Your worries may give you a sense of engagement with life, and you might feel quite lost for a while without those familiar worries. Work your way through this discomfort. You'll emerge with time and energy for doing instead of worrying.

Other folks probably don't see your fears, either. They probably figure you're cool and calm—unless you choose to tell them otherwise.

I realized the truth of this observation when I spoke at a writers' conference in Pensacola, Florida. The flight from Madison to Chicago to Pensacola was hellacious—everything bad but the crash. I arrived with barely enough time to get to the conference before I was scheduled to speak. Huge crowd, unfamiliar hall, frazzled nerves from the trip—I was a real mess. It was all I could do to stand up straight and force the first words out of my mouth. Experience carried me through the presentation.

Afterwards, several people came to the podium to chat. One woman complimented my presentation, adding, "I don't know how you do it. I would have been a nervous wreck speaking to such a large group, but you were totally at ease!"

Oh, lady, I thought. You have no idea.

9. Act in spite of your fear. Don't wait for the fear to leave you before you act. It doesn't work that way.

Courage isn't lack of fear. Courage is action despite fear. Don't pretend to yourself that you're not afraid. Let yourself experience your fear fully. Then rechannel that fear into energy and alertness.

You will begin in fear, but soon a gentle calmness will replace that fear.

10. Protect yourself from the worry contagion. The more you learn about controlling and redirecting your worry, the more aware you'll become of others' fretting and stewing. You may find yourself surrounded by colleagues who sing the "ain't it awful" blues most of the time.

If so, don't buy into their negativity and their false sense of urgency. Don't try to fix the worriers' problems. Don't try to argue them out of their worrying. Remove yourself from the blather if you can and let it roll off you if you can't.

Do It Yourself

Reading a ten-step plan for ridding yourself of worry won't do you any good unless you actually apply the steps. Work through a present worry, including one of these three steps:

- Take action immediately to remove the cause of the worry.

- Create an action card, noting exactly what you intend to do and when you intend to do it.

- Decide that you aren't going to take any action. Write down your reasons for deciding not to act.

Five Forms of Worry and Five Ways to Deal with Them

1. Worry festering out of ignorance. You can't imagine anything good coming from your present situation. You can see only bad options or no options, no way out at all.

Instead of worrying, learn. Seek information. You just don't know enough yet to see your choices, and worry is preventing you from even looking.

As new information allows you to posit possible actions, resist the reflex to reject any of them. Develop as long a list of possibilities as you can. When you've assembled your list, choose the best option or choose not to act.

2. Worry lurking in the future. You're worried about a problem but can't do anything about it now, leaving you with no way to dispel your anxiety.

Instead of worrying, defer. Write down the specific time when you'll take action. Then set the problem aside. Every time the worry returns, gently remind yourself that you'll handle it at the appointed time.

3. Worry focused on the past.

"If only I had..."
"How could I have...?"

But you didn't. Or you did. It's done or it isn't done. Either way, it's over.

Instead of worrying, release. Is there anything you can do to make the situation better now? If so, write down the action with the specific time and place you'll do it.

If there's nothing you can do, let it go. Don't wallow in regret. As fear looks to the future, remorse dwells in the past. They are the same crippling response facing in opposite directions.

> Instead of worrying, learn. Seek information. You just don't know enough yet to see your choices, and worry is preventing you from even looking.

4. Worry feeding on inertia. Action deferred can be worry compounded. The longer you put off the confrontation, the stronger your worry may become—and the harder it will be for you to overcome it.

Instead of worrying, act. Even a "mistake" is often better than doing nothing. If you can't act now, write down the action you'll take and where and when you'll take it.

Deal with it and get on with it.

5. Worry thriving on evasion. Decisions carry price tags. Whatever choice you make, it may cost you something. If you don't want to face those consequences, you may simply put off the decision. Your worry will rush in to fill the vacuum you create with your lack of action.

Instead of worrying, pay the price. Calculate the true cost of your decision as best you can—in time, energy, money, and damage to relationships.

When you decide on your course of action, decide also to pay the price—and then do so, promptly.

What to Do When It's More Than Worry

The techniques we've outlined here will get you through most worries. But we need to differentiate between worry and a genuine anxiety disorder, such as obsessive-compulsive disorder or agoraphobia.

Between 1 and 2 percent of all Americans suffer panic attacks regularly, and as much as 30 percent of the population may experience at least one in a lifetime. Symptoms include dizziness and rapid heartbeat and may become debilitating.

People with obsessive-compulsive disorder receive unwanted thoughts they are unable to dispel and engage in repetitive behavior they are unable to stop. Such behaviors frequently involve cleaning (compulsive hand-washing, for example) and checking (going back dozens of times to make sure the front door is locked).

Sufferers from agoraphobia (literally "fear of the marketplace") experience panic attacks in public settings. The condition may progressively worsen, until the agoraphobic can't leave the house, a specific

> Instead of worrying, act. Even a "mistake" is often better than doing nothing. If you can't act now, write down the action you'll take and where and when you'll take it.

room, even one corner of that room. Some become paralyzed for hours at a time.

These conditions stem from biochemical predispositions of the brain. Sufferers can't simply "snap out of it," and the steps outlined in this chapter won't raise anyone out of a genuine disorder.

However, a combination of medication and behavioral therapy can alleviate or even eliminate symptoms. Get help if the fears get too big.

Ira finally stopped blaming his mother and got to work on his worry.

At first he felt pretty stupid, making out little "worry cards," listing his concerns and what he would do about them.

And at first, just as he suspected (and worried), the cards didn't seem to do any good. No matter what he wrote, the worries kept returning. But he was determined and kept filling out the cards, as if he expected them to do him some good.

One morning, about a month into his experiment with the worry cards, Ira woke up refreshed and alert and realized that he had actually deferred a worry, avoiding late-night sleeplessness. When the little voice in his head murmured, "Are you sure?" he was able to say, "Nope. But I'm going to go ahead anyway."

He may never be worry free, but every time a worry card works for him, he reduces the anxiety he feels the next time he faces a challenge.

Time-Management Tips

1. Accept and name the cause of your anxiety.
2. Rechannel or diffuse the worry by considering the possible consequences.
3. Decide exactly what you're going to do about the source of your anxiety and when you're going to do it—or decide to do nothing. But decide!
4. Act on your decision.
5. Stay away from worriers. Worry is contagious.

Don't Get Mad or Even: Just Get On with It

In this chapter, you'll learn:

- Why you get angry
- The hidden element that makes you even angrier
- Three reasons why you need to get rid of your anger
- Three ways to redirect your anger
- Three ways to let it go completely

Hal always blamed his temper on his red hair.

"I inherited both from my father," he'd say with a laugh.

But nobody laughed when Hal blew his stack, which happened often enough to make everyone who worked with him wary of bringing him bad news.

In fact, folks pretty much avoided talking to him about any subject that might make him lose his cool, especially when he was under the gun of a deadline. It just wasn't worth the grief.

Hal figured out that folks were avoiding him and that he wasn't getting the information he needed to do his job effectively. But until a kind—and brave—coworker told him why he had gotten so far out of the loop, Hal didn't even try to curb his temper.

In Chapter 30, we talked about various stressors in our lives, including the Bozo factor, people who annoy us. Now we'll take a closer look at your anger—and how you can eliminate it. Here are three good reasons why you should.

> Anger makes you sick. All that adrenaline, with no place to go and nobody to fight.

1. Anger makes you sick. All that adrenaline, with no place to go and nobody to fight.

You still get the primitive fight or flight response when you're angry or frightened. Your heart starts pumping faster, and the adrenaline and other activators start to flow.

Fight or flight saved us as a species when we lived in primitive environments full of physical dangers. But in modern life, fighting or running away is seldom an appropriate response. So instead of slugging the boss or running screaming from her office, you stifle your murderous impulses and turn all that anger inward. That's the stuff headaches are made of, and as we've seen, such internal distress can create serious health problems over the long haul.

2. Anger makes you stupid. People seldom make good decisions when they're mad. We say and do things we later regret, even though they feel so good at the time.

You can't think straight when you're angry. Your perceptions become distorted, and your thought process short-circuits.

There's a reason why *mad* means both "angry" and "crazy."

3. Anger makes you unpopular. We may fear people who blow up at the slightest provocation, but we don't respect them, and we certainly don't want to be around them.

A reputation for having a short fuse will hurt you in personal relationships and will thwart you in your career advancement.

Sick, stupid, and unpopular are not ways you want to be. If that isn't enough, anger wastes a hell of a lot of time, the time you spend:

- Being angry
- Expressing your anger
- Getting over your anger
- Making amends for your anger
- Trying to fix the things you messed up while you were angry

A streetwise time manager simply can't afford to get angry. Don't stuff your anger. Don't vent it. Don't get mad at all.

Impossible? Not at all. As soon as you understand the nature of your anger, you'll understand how you can eliminate it.

Three Reasons Why You Get Angry

1. Loss of control. You get mad when the world doesn't act the way you think it should or want it to. Just watch folks at a football game when the referee's call goes against the home team!

At these moments, you're reminded that you can't script your life. People, natural forces, and machines will act contrary to the way you want them to.

2. Thwarted goals. The loss of control becomes more serious when the outcome affects your desires. The signal turns to red just as you approach the intersection. The customer rejects your sales pitch. Your child refuses to eat breakfast. In each case, your progress is blocked. You don't get what you want and need, and so you get mad.

3. Moral outrage. Somehow we manage to cling to the notion that life is supposed to be fair—no matter how often experience

Caution

We're not talking about simply stifling or stuffing your anger. Stuffing eliminates some of the social consequences of anger but doesn't help the physical and psychological ones.

In fact, a lot of folks suggest that you vent your anger to keep healthy and happy—as long as you pick a socially acceptable outlet, of course. (Punch a wall rather than a face?)

But venting tends to feed rather than dissipate anger. Screaming just makes you madder, giving your system feedback that the threat still exists and it should keep pumping the venom. Bad idea.

teaches us to the contrary. It makes us angry when things don't work out the way they "should." In life, in fiction, and in football, we want the "good guys" to win. We want virtue to be rewarded and bad behavior to be punished.

When this doesn't seem to be the case, we get angry. Large, distant events make us a little angry—the murderer who goes free because of a legal technicality. Small, personal events make us even more angry—a coworker who takes credit for your work and gets away with it.

Three Madness Enhancers

These three elements will tend to make you madder easier and stay madder longer.

1. Lack of sleep. We're not sure yet what the long-term effects of sleep deprivation are, but as a culture we seem bent on finding out.

One thing we do know—being tired makes you grouchy. Things that wouldn't ordinarily bother you when you're well rested can make you mad when you aren't.

2. Scheduling frenzy. The more the delay costs you, the madder it will make you.

When you're overscheduled, racing to make the next appointment, the guy who makes you miss the traffic light will make you much madder than he would if you weren't in a hurry.

3. Hot buttons. We've all got them—and our kids seem to know where they are instinctively. We call them pet peeves—issues or actions that make us see red, even though they might not necessarily bother other folks.

Some folks can discuss religion calmly. Other folks can't. Just as you learn where other folks' hot buttons are, you must learn to acknowledge your own—and then avoid situations where those buttons are likely to get pushed.

So, if you can stay well rested, tame your to-do list, and recognize your hot buttons, you'll go a long way toward defusing your anger. But you won't be able to go the whole way. You'll still get angry. Here's why.

The Hidden Element Fueling Your Anger

To some extent, you get angry because you think you're supposed to. Anger may seem to be the appropriate, even the "natural," response in a given situation because you grew up with someone who got angry in that situation. You reinforced the connection between the stimulus and your anger response every time you reacted with anger. It came to feel automatic, no less a fact of nature than hunger or thirst. You now assume you don't have a choice about getting angry.

It's not true. You get to choose. If anger really is at least in part a habit—and it is—then you can learn not to get angry.

Do It Yourself

Revisit that list of ten events or people that made you angry recently. See if any of our three "anger enhancers" contributed to your anger.

How to Redirect Your Anger

Anger gives you energy, tons of energy. If you could somehow redirect it to something positive, you'd have a powerful force working for instead of against you.

Let's use a common, everyday urban anger provoker—getting stuck in rush-hour traffic—to illustrate three ways to use the anger instead of letting it carry you places you don't want to go.

1. Take action. Don't just sit there sputtering. Do something! We're not talking about leaning on the horn, screaming, making obscene gestures, or getting out of the car and trying to slug somebody. That's venting, and it's major league stupid. It does nothing to improve the situation, it fans the anger flames, and it makes those around you even angrier. It will also make you look like a jackass.

Is there anything positive you can do to improve the situation? (Take an alternative route?) Can you use the time while you're stuck? (Pull out a book and read it? Argue with the talk radio host?) Can you convert the wait into a rest? (Deep breathing? Fantasy?)

Ironically, by using your anger, you'll lose it. When you act, you remove one of the primary causes of your anger, the sense of loss of control over your life.

Sometimes you don't just feel out of control. There really may be nothing you can do about being stuck in bumper-to-bumper traffic, for example. At those times, you might create a purpose.

2. Create a purpose. Patience is a virtue. It's also, for some of us, a seeming impossibility. If patience is a problem for you, convert that bumper-to-bumper traffic jam into an opportunity to develop your patience. Really put your mind to the task. After all, you'll never become more patient if you don't work at it, and you can't work at it without events that test that patience.

There, now, don't you feel grateful for that traffic jam/opportunity?

Of course not. But you can still use it.

3. Learn a lesson. No matter what else you do with that anger, use it to burn a relevant lesson into your brain. See the pattern in the predicament. Will this route most likely be jammed again tomorrow at the same time? Is there some circumstance causing the jam today that will cause another jam tomorrow? Plan your strategy for avoiding the jam now. (Alternative route. Different departure time.)

Redirecting your anger can improve your health, your mental outlook, and your time efficiency greatly. But often you won't be able to use your anger in any way. For those times and, ideally, for every anger-provoking situation, you need to learn to let your anger go.

A Three-Step Process for Diffusing Your Anger

1. Catch yourself. Before you can handle your anger, you need to anticipate it so that you can get the kettle off the flame before it boils over. Understand your anger and when it's most likely to occur. Be ready to grab that anger the moment it begins to well up in you.

2. Count to 10. Once again, your dear old mama was right. It really does help if you count to 10 (or 20, slowly) before you act.

As you count, breathe—slowly, deeply, gently. It's almost impossible for the body to whip itself into a mad fit if your breathing remains regular. You'll feel the anger subside in you as you breath.

3. Visualize. Ideally, you want to wind up smiling by the end of this step. Laughing out loud is a bonus.

When you're angry, you're taking yourself very, very seriously. Silly is the opposite of angry and is its sworn enemy. If you can turn this situation from dire to foolish, you won't be able to get angry about it.

Visualize a caricature or symbol of the person or thing needling you, the sillier the better. Put your boss's head on the body of a jackass. Turn the car in front of you into a tortoise with crutches. Now imagine the image blowing up into a million fragments (violent, aggressive option) or floating away in a huge, shimmering bubble (gentle, nonaggressive option).

Picture yourself getting mad. Turn yourself into the Tasmanian devil or some other ridiculously angry critter. My favorite fit-thrower is the Yosemite Sam cartoon character, so I picture myself as old Sam, hopping from foot to foot and screaming "Tarnation!"

I know how silly this sounds. But it works. It really does work.

You're not going to get fitted for a halo for that hot head of yours the first time out. This will take weeks of practice before you start to get the hang of it. But if you keep after it, you're going to notice one fine day that you didn't even bother to start to get mad in a situation that would have had you boiling just a few weeks before.

When that happens, you'll be in control of yourself and your situation, and that's the essence of streetsmart time management.

Hal began his temper-abatement program with a brave gesture of his own. One on one, he owned up to his colleagues, admitting that his tendency to blow was making life tougher for everybody. He even promised to put five bucks into the office party fund every time he erupted.

By going public with his intention to control his temper, Hal shamed himself into taking the task seriously and working at it with focus and dedication. Everyone around him became his cohort.

Do It Yourself

Imagine yourself back in one of those top-ten situations you listed a while ago. Go ahead and let yourself remember the anger you felt then. Now see if there are ways you could take action, create a purpose, or learn a lesson while in that situation.

Try the same exercise with as many of the other nine situations as seem relevant. Thinking about your options now will help you be able to see them next time you really are mad.

Hal applied the techniques for redirecting and defusing his anger. He felt the bite in his pocketbook every time he failed.

He started seeing results within two weeks, and so did everyone else in the office.

Now, almost eight months later, Hal can remember how angry he used to get, but he no longer feels that anger.

Time-Management Tips

1. Anger makes you sick, stupid, and unpopular.
2. You can choose not to be angry.
3. Stay away from situations that are likely to push your hot buttons.
4. Don't fume. Take positive action.
5. Anticipate your anger and diffuse it with deep breathing, positive visualization, and laughter.

Make Time to Think

In this chapter, you'll learn:

- Why you shut down your own creative process

- Three ways to embrace your creative inspirations

- A Five-step process for becoming creative on demand

- Three ways to brainstorm solutions to creative challenges

Chapter 34

Jeremiah figures that maybe he's just getting old. Something has to explain why the creative juices seem to have dried up.

He used to be the creative genius of the firm, the guy everyone could count on for the big idea, even on the tightest deadline. He used to thrive on those ah-ha! flashes of inspiration, which he often received while jogging, biking, or driving to work. These flashes were often unusable, sometimes silly, but just often enough they provided the solutions he had been wrestling with for days.

Now it occurs to him that it's been a long time since he's had an inspiration more substantial than "Buy kitty litter."

He wonders if he really has to face the prospect of living the rest of his life this way.

Creativity is one of the first casualties when we allow ourselves to get too busy.

You rush from appointment to appointment, challenge to challenge. The phone rings—another disaster. You run faster and faster to keep even—never mind get ahead. There's no time to plan; you simply react.

In a moment of quiet despair, you realize that you haven't had anything resembling an original idea in weeks.

Where did your creativity go?

It didn't go anyplace. You're still thinking. In fact, you couldn't stop it if you tried. Go ahead. Sit in a corner and not-think for five minutes. How about a minute? Five seconds? Can't do it, can you? Zen masters need years of practice to learn to empty the mind.

Ah, but those aren't pearls of wisdom rattling around in your poor, distracted head, you say? More like the rattling of loose change in an aluminum can?

Listen closer. Your wisdom, your intuition, your creativity are right where they've always been, just beneath the surface of conscious thought. You just haven't had time to listen.

You have almost infinite capacity for inventiveness and creativity. But when you get caught in the time trap, you leave no time for reflection or for the incubation that yields flashes of insight.

Do It Yourself

Not convinced that you're a creative dynamo? Consider this. Everyone dreams. We don't always remember our dreams, of course, and some folks hardly ever remember their dreams, but we all do it. In our dreams, we make wild associations, suspend the laws of physics, ignore all the waking guidelines imposed by our ethics and morality.

Make a point of remembering your dreams for a few nights. You can do this by waking yourself a half an hour earlier than usual and immediately writing down the dream you're experiencing. You'll encounter your creative "wild mind," a dreamscape your conscious, rational mind won't even be able to understand.

Why You Shut Yourself Off from Your Good Ideas

Creative breakthroughs often derive from mistakes. Those ubiquitous Post-it notes were one such blunder, a glue that failed to adhere as firmly as intended. Velcro was another flop, the military's attempt to create a fastener that could be "unzipped" without making any noise.

Often the genius idea comes disguised as irrelevancy. The folks at Pringles potato chips had no luck trying to devise a better bag for their chips, one that would keep the chips fresh and prevent crumbling. They found their answer only when they expanded the search from bag to container and began looking at crazy stuff like tennis ball cans.

Invention often comes from dogged determination, as when Thomas Edison tried out hundreds of different materials before discovering that tungsten would glow without burning up when he allowed an electric current to pass through it.

How can you afford to try out hundreds of wrong answers? Maybe the question should be: how can you afford not to?

When you're busy, you stop seeking creative breakthroughs. You don't even welcome them if they somehow manage to thrust up through the wall of conscious thought and insist on recognition. Instead, you dismiss them as interruptions. You've already finished that project and need to get on to the next one. There's no time to go back and rethink it.

But instead of rejecting, you must embrace.

> Creative breakthroughs often derive from mistakes. Those ubiquitous Post-it notes were one such blunder, a glue that failed to adhere as firmly as intended.

Welcoming the Ah-Ha!

The history of humanity is filled with dramatic creative breakthroughs.

Archimedes discovers the displacement theory while sitting in the bathtub one day observing the level of water in the tub fall as he stands and rise as he eases himself back into the water. Kekule dreams about a snake biting its own tail and discovers the structure of the benzene ring after failing for years to uncover it in the lab. Coleridge writes "Kubla Khan" in a trance. Paul Stookey insists that he was the instrument, that his beautiful composition, "The Wedding Song," played him and not the other way around.

Such breakthroughs come from the subconscious mind, which a man named Charles Haanel called your "benevolent stranger, working on your behalf." We all get them, but we may have shut ourselves off from them. To recapture the gift of inspiration even amid the chaos of life, you must:

1. **Listen.** Create silence and time. Calm the din. Sit still, if just for a moment each day. Let your thoughts drift without direction.
2. **Accept.** Don't reject the idea, no matter how foolish it may seem. There's no way to selectively welcome only the good ideas, the ones that are going to solve your problems. If you try to cut off the bad ones, you lose touch with them all and choke off the creative flows. And besides, you might not be able to tell a good thought from a bad one until you've lived with it for a time.
3. **Note.** When you receive a breakthrough, note it exactly as it came. Don't try to process, shape, apply, or direct it. Let it be what it is before you make it be something else.

Creating the Ah-Ha on Demand

Can you really be creative on demand? You not only can, you have to.

Creative breakthroughs don't always or even usually come as surprise nudgings from the subconscious. In your world of constant deadlines and endless to-do lists, they are more often the product of a conscious process of problem solving.

You'll never find the time for this conscious process. No one will give you that time. You're going to have to make the time.

Here's a five-step process for making sure your creativity time yields the results you need.

Step 1. Make a creativity appointment. You've got a report to write, a presentation to prepare, a problem to solve. It will require more than just effort and time. You need inspiration.

> Creative breakthroughs don't always or even usually come as surprise nudgings from the subconscious. They are more often the product of a conscious process of problem solving.

Make an appointment to meet with that inspiration and do some brainstorming. I'm serious. Get out the calendar or the day planner and mark off a couple of one-hour sessions just for thinking.

If you don't schedule the time, the thinking you need to do just won't happen.

Schedule that appointment at least a day and preferably longer ahead of time, and plan the session to coincide with a phase of the day when you're most alert and awake. Clear the time of all interruptions.

Step 2. Tell your subconscious what you want. I know of a top executive who took his staff on a working retreat to a ski resort. He held meetings with them all day Friday, and at the end of that time, he spelled out the problem to be solved at Monday morning's meeting, admonishing them to prepare thoroughly for the session. Then he turned them loose for a weekend on the slopes.

They, of course, gave the problem no conscious thought whatsoever—which is just what he figured would happen. He knew that the problem would lodge in the subconscious of at least some of his advisors, and when the brainstorming began on Monday morning, they would surprise him—and themselves—with insights they didn't even know they had.

Such is the power of the subconscious mind.

You can bring that same power to bear on a brainstorming session of one. And you don't need a ski resort to do it.

Review the problem and the solution you're after. Be sure you've defined the problem clearly and specifically, but don't limit the scope of the potential solution. (You don't want a better potato chip bag; you want a way to keep chips fresh and intact.) Then put the problem out of your conscious mind. If you catch yourself brooding on it, send it back to the subconscious.

Step 3. Stay alert. Every student of advertising has heard the story of the fellow who comes rushing into the tire store, clutching a newspaper in his hand.

"This is amazing," the fellow tells the salesperson. "Just this morning I decided to buy four new tires for my car, and here's your ad in the morning paper advertising your prices. What a coincidence."

Make an appointment to meet with that inspiration and do some brainstorming. I'm serious. Get out the calendar or the day planner and mark off a couple of one-hour sessions just for thinking.

> Along with the conscious research you may need to perform to get ready for your meeting with the muse, stay open to information all around you that may prove helpful.

It's no coincidence. The ad had been running in the paper for years. The fellow just never saw it until he needed tires, and then the ad jumped out at him.

Advertisers use this story to explain the need for frequency: if you want your ad to be effective, you have to keep running it. But it also illustrates a principle of selective perception. When your mind becomes focused on a topic, you begin to notice material relevant to that topic. A casual conversation overheard in the elevator, a remark made over lunch, a small item on the back pages of the newspaper, a report on the evening news—suddenly the world seems to be conspiring to feed you information to help you.

Along with the conscious research you may need to perform to get ready for your meeting with the muse, stay open to information all around you that may prove helpful.

Step 4. Play with the possibilities. It's time to think. You've kept that appointment with yourself, clearing the calendar of all the demands on your time. You've done your best to make sure you won't be interrupted.

You sit at your computer, or you lie on a couch with a notepad and pencil, or you walk through a park with a tape recorder in hand. All right, you tell your subconscious. What's the answer?

And nothing happens.

Now what? You've fought hard for this thinking time, and now you haven't got a thought. Relax. You've got all the thoughts you need. Your subconscious isn't holding out on you. You just asked the wrong question.

Instead of seeking the answer, take a few minutes to try out as many answers as you can. Here are three ways to do it.

Play "How Many Ways?"

Make a list of as many possible solutions or approaches as you can muster. Set a timer for ten minutes so that you don't have to worry about the passage of time, and just let fly. Don't stop. Don't edit, evaluate, or in any way censor your thoughts. If something pops into your head, capture it on your list, even if it seems ridiculous. (I should probably say especially if it seems ridiculous.)

Remember Edison; there are no failures in the creative process.

"If you want to have a good idea," advertising executive Alex Osborne admonished, "have lots of ideas." (Osborne also coined the term *brainstorming*, by the way.)

Draw a Tornado Outline

Write your subject or goal in the center of a large sheet of paper (or a chalkboard, flip chart, billboard, or whatever you're comfortable with). Free-associate key words, phrases, statistics, anecdotes, anything that seems relevant. Again, avoid censoring ideas. (This is like the bubble outline described earlier, except it's more of a free-association approach.)

When you're done, sit for a minute or so more, to see if any stray thoughts catch up to you. Then begin linking related material and numbering items, bringing order to the chaos. You now have a working outline for further work; the hardest part of the process is finished.

Create a Grid

Return with me now to those thrilling days of yesteryear, when the resourceful masked man and his faithful Indian companion rode the range, bringing law and order to the Old West.

Fran Striker wrote a fresh script for his Lone Ranger radio dramas every week for years. He had great characters to work with and a durable myth of good and evil to develop each week. But there are only so many pretexts for sending Tonto into town to get beat up, and only so many disguises for the Lone Ranger to don; after a time, Striker began to run dry.

He didn't panic. Instead, he made lists—lists of weapons, lists of disguises, lists of settings, lists of bad guys, lists of all the elements that went into his half-hour morality tales. He would then combine items from his lists, playing with combinations until he got something that seemed promising. This system kept the Lone Ranger riding for years.

This grid or matrix system works because inspiration often occurs when an idea or image from one frame of reference collides

> "If you want to have a good idea," advertising executive Alex Osborne admonished, "have lots of ideas."

with an idea or image from a totally different context, creating something new, surprising, and original.

"Fellow dies and goes to heaven. There's St. Peter, guarding the pearly gates and eyeing him suspiciously. St. Pete checks his scroll, scowls, then squints down at the supplicant and says, 'Smoking or nonsmoking.'"

One context, heaven, collides with another context, restaurant seating arrangements.

Inspiration strikes when the collision occurs spontaneously, without you consciously willing it to happen. But you can create the combinations consciously through the grid system.

Step 5. Stop before you have to. If you can't finish in one session, break while you're still in the midst of creating ideas and certain of where you're going to go next. If you wait until you're stuck or seem to have exhausted all the possibilities, you'll carry a negative impression, which can grow into dread and create a difficult start-up time when you return to the project. But if you've left your work confident of your next steps, you'll come to the plan with a positive frame of mind, ready to resume immediately.

Dorothea Brande spelled out a similar process for writers in a book called *Becoming a Writer* in the early 1930s. This method is solid, it's time-tested, and it works.

By actually scheduling your thinking time, you'll nurture, maintain, and increase your ability to solve problems and develop new ideas creatively. As you do, you'll recapture a hyperalertness and openness to possibilities, not just during those scheduled sessions, but during the rest of the time as well.

Instead of trying to find time to be creative or to fit creative thinking into your hectic life, you'll find yourself living in a constant creative state.

Jeremiah has decided he's not washed up after all.

He was more than a little skeptical about trying to schedule thinking. Like most of us, he always thought that inspiration just happened and couldn't be forced.

Do It Yourself

Reading about the creative process isn't the same as being creative. Now it's time to try the five-step system out on a problem or other creative challenge you're facing. Make your appointment and follow the steps outlined. You'll probably be self-conscious the first time out, and that awareness may inhibit you somewhat. Even so, you may get surprising, even spectacular, results.

The more you use this method, the better it will work for you, until the steps become an automatic part of your life.

But after several appointments with his muse, Jeremiah has redis-covered the creative energy and spark that he was afraid he'd lost.

As a bonus, he seems to be getting more of—or at least is becoming more aware of—the inspirations that break in at the oddest times.

Time-Management Tips

1. Pay attention to and acknowledge your inspirations—especially the silly ones.
2. Schedule specific times for creative thinking.
3. Play with possibilities before you settle on a decision.

How to Create a Values-Based Time-Management Plan

In this chapter, you'll learn:

- Why you may not be spending time on the things that really matter to you

- Why "quality time" doesn't work

- Ways you can put your time where your values are

Chapter 35

Juanita has it all. So how come sometimes she feels as though she has nothing?

She's the modern ideal of everything a woman should have and be—married to a fine man, with two healthy kids. They own their own home, and she has a successful career as the top salesperson for a large Honda dealership.

She's a streetwise time manager, able to handle the hectic daily pace and even plan for those times when one of the kids gets sick and can't go to day care.

And still, she feels like a failure.

Something's missing from her life, and she's not going to be truly happy until she figures out what it is and does something about it.

"I wish I'd spent more time at the office."

History has never recorded these as anyone's last words. I'm fairly sure it never will.

"I wish I'd spent more time with my family" is a much more likely deathbed sentiment.

Here's how Americans responded when asked in a recent national survey to list the most important elements in their lives. The number listed next to each item indicates the percentage of people surveyed who listed it among their top three priorities. (So obviously the numbers add up to more than 100 percent.)

PRIORITY	PERCENTAGE
Family life	68%
Spiritual life	46%
Health	44%
Financial situation	25%
Job	23%
Romantic life	18%
Leisure time	14%
Home	11%

If you aren't spending large chunks of time on the three elements you've listed as the most important priorities in your life, there are three possible explanations:

Do It Yourself

List the three things in life that mean the most to you. Taken together, they might be your reason for living.

Got your list? Now next to each of the three note the amount of time you spend on it each week.

Shocked?

1. Important things don't necessarily require a lot of time.
2. You're mistaken about your priorities.
3. You aren't putting your time where your priorities are.

Let's examine each explanation.

Does the Way You Spend Your Time Truly Reflect Your Values?

The Myth of "Quality Time"

Two strong social forces combined to move Harriet Nelson, June Cleaver, and other American housewives out of the kitchen and into the work force.

First, we began to require two salaries to keep up with our increasing material expectations. In 1985, less than 2 percent of American homes had CD players in them, and only about 7 percent had answering machines. By 1996, two thirds of our homes had CD players and 63 percent had answering machines. These are our new "necessities."

At the same time, women began giving public expression to the notion that being "just" a housewife didn't allow them to develop fully or to take their place as equal partners with men in society. They didn't just need jobs; they wanted careers.

As more and more former stay-at-home moms took jobs outside the home, the myth of the superwoman developed. "You can have it all" translated into "You must *do* it all!"

Surveys noted that the distribution of housework didn't change in many homes even when the woman took an outside job. After a full day's work at the office, many women came home to another full day's work.

The term *quality time* was born.

As women joined their husbands in having less and less time for the kids and for their partners, social thinkers (that is, freelance magazine writers) developed the theory that a little bit of very good time together would compensate for the lack of lots of time together. The

> By 1996, two thirds of our homes had CD players and 63 percent had answering machines. These are our new "necessities."

more we talked about quality time, the more we came to believe in its reality.

But quality time is a sham, a hoax, a cruel delusion. Instead of quality time, we simply have less time, and what time we've got is really "pressure time."

If you can honestly tell me that you can schedule a meaningful conversation with your adolescent son or daughter, or that lovemaking by appointment doesn't lose a little something in spontaneity, I'll believe in quality time. But relationships don't work that way. You can no more force a teenager to talk before he or she is ready than you can convince a cat to play Scrabble.

There's no hurrying or scheduling meaningful moments, breakthrough conversations, wonderful gestures. They occur in the midst of the muck, often when we least expect them. If you aren't spending time with a loved one, you're going to miss many of those moments. And you'll be putting much too heavy a burden on the time you do have together. Quality time turns into tension time.

Are You Mistaken about Your Priorities?

If you aren't spending much time on family or spiritual life or health maintenance, for example, then maybe these aren't really the most important things in your life.

Could you be wrong about your own priorities? Well, sure. In the incredibly complex interactions of conscious mind, subconscious motive, and psyche, we're perfectly capable of masking our true motivations from ourselves even as we might seek to hide them from or misrepresent them to others.

Also, the process of writing a list of priorities is different from the process of living your life. Your list could reflect the things you think of when asked to make a list, and not necessarily your priorities as you live them.

You might have listed the elements you think you're supposed to list, the elements it's acceptable or right to value most highly. You really wanted to list "making a pot of money" as your number-one priority, but somehow you just didn't feel right doing so. You knew that "family" was the "right" answer.

> Quality time is a sham, a hoax, a cruel delusion. Instead of quality time, we simply have less time, and what time we've got is really "pressure time."

It's possible that you misrepresented your priorities—on a list that only you will see, in a book designed solely to help you make decisions about how you spend your time. It's possible—but it isn't very likely.

If you'd like to go back now and change your list to accurately reflect your values, that's OK. It's your list. But I suspect you got it right the first time.

Which brings us to the third possible explanation: that you aren't putting your time where your heart is.

Why Aren't You Spending Time on the Important Stuff?

Actually, there are three rather simple explanations, and none of them requires that you be a beast, a hypocrite, or a fool.

1. Time spent making money is time spent on the family. You aren't just working for VCRs and second cars. You're working to feed and clothe your children and to keep a roof over your family members' heads. You're working so that the government won't have to take care of you. You're working so that you'll be self-sufficient even when you're too old to work (or pushed out of a job because of a mandatory retirement age).

If you're lucky, your vocation may also be an avocation, even a passion, helping you to grow and develop intellectually. You may have been able to integrate your spiritual life and your work life. It isn't necessarily a strict either/or choice.

2. Working at your job is easier than "working at" your family. Jobs often comprise well-defined tasks. They aren't necessarily easy or even pleasant, but they're clear. You know what you're supposed to do, and you know what it's supposed to look like when you finish. Something outside yourself tells you when you've done well and when you need to work harder.

Knowing exactly how to "have a good family life" or to "be healthy" can be a lot harder, and the product of your efforts here is often intangible.

> Knowing exactly how to "have a good family life" or to "be healthy" can be a lot harder, and the product of your efforts here is often intangible.

3. Social pressure rewards traditional concepts of work. Even when you begin telling yourself that other aspects of life are important, too, you don't slack off on the job expectations in the slightest. Somehow you're supposed to devote more time to family without taking a minute from work—more of that "you can do more with less" and "work smarter not harder" nonsense, the underpinning for a belief in quality time.

How to Live a Values-Centered Life

You aren't a monster or even a hypocrite. You're simply a time-pressured American without enough hours in your day for the important things in life. That explains it, but it doesn't fix it.

What can you do to make or find or create time for family, for spiritual growth, for health maintenance?

"There's right and there's wrong," John Wayne as Davy Crockett told us in *The Alamo*. "You gotta do one or the other. You do the one, and you're living. You do the other, and you may be walking around, but you're dead as a beaver hat."

If only life were that simple. But to do the right thing, you have to know the right thing to do.

Knowing the right thing to do, then, must dwell at the core of any real time-management program.

Your values, your definition of the right way to live, are inside you. It's time to get them out so that you can live by them.

The rest of this chapter is one big *do-it-yourself* project.

Step 1. Create a personal mission statement. Most businesses and organizations have one—although the employees and members may be unaware of it. The mission statement is much more than policies and procedures governing day-to-day activities (though daily activities should reflect and contribute to the mission). The mission statement describes what the organization wants to be and what it wants to accomplish. Ideally, every member of that organization should contribute to building the statement and then work to embody it.

What's your mission in life? Why are you living? What do you hope to be and do with your life? What values and assumptions underlie your core mission?

> Knowing the right thing to do must dwell at the core of any real time-management program.

Spend some time with these questions. Let them dwell in your subconscious. Come back to them again and again. Be ready always to change and renew your answers as you grow in experience and wisdom.

Then you're ready to move on to a critical second set of questions:

- How will you act on what you believe?
- How will your life reflect your values?
- How can you live to fulfill your mission?

Step 2. Define values in terms of actions. Let's suppose that, like two thirds of all Americans polled, you listed "family life" as among your top three priorities in life.

What actions can you take—and what actions will you avoid—to live out that value?

My father once turned down a chance to take a new job for more money because the new job would have required a great deal of travel. "I wanted to be home at night to hear your prayers," he explained to me much later.

For my father, raising his sons translated into being there to tuck us in at night. It also meant checking our math homework, coaching a Little League team, serving as an adult Boy Scout leader, taking us fishing and to ball games, and lots of other activities, all of which took time and commitment. I know he enjoyed doing these things with us, but I also know now how tired he must have been sometimes, how much he might have longed to sit on the porch with his feet up instead of going out and practicing baseball with his son, the would-be all-star.

Core values translated into daily doing. My father lived his commitment.

What does a commitment to "spiritual life" mean in terms of activities? It could mean going to church weekly (or daily, or monthly, or sometimes), reading and reflecting, participating in a prayer group, going on a week-long silent retreat. What does it mean to you? When you answer this question, you have created the possibility that you can live out this value in your life.

Step 3. Schedule for your values. If you don't get it on the schedule, it isn't going to happen.

> What does spiritual life mean to you? When you answer this question, you have created the possibility that you can live out this value in your life.

> As you seek to change the way you live, remember one of the lessons we learned about stress: all change, including change in personal habits, is stressful.

That's the difference between a New Year's Resolution to "lose 10 pounds" and a Monday–Wednesday–Friday 7 A.M. appointment to take an aerobics class at the local Y.

Put it on the day planner. Be as conscientious about keeping that appointment as you would be about an audience with the president or a quarterly evaluation with the boss.

Step 4. Go gently into that new life. Conscientious, yes. Firm in resolve and consistent in action, you bet! But judgmental and unforgiving, never!

As you seek to change the way you live, remember one of the lessons we learned about stress: all change, including change in personal habits, is stressful.

Old habits are hard to break, and daily life patterns are the most deeply ingrained habits of all. (To illustrate this truth for yourself, simply try putting on your pants "wrong leg" first.) You're going to forget, and you're going to slip back into old ways.

You're also going to be overpowered by life at times, no matter how carefully you've planned and how well you've anticipated.

Don't berate yourself. Gently remind yourself and do differently next time. Slowly the new way will become the "right" way, the "natural" way.

Give yourself credit for what you do; don't just blame yourself for what you fail to do. If you finish fifteen of the seventeen items on that to-do list, rejoice in what you've done. Those other two items are what tomorrow was invented for.

Do one thing at a time, with all of your energy, your attention, your heart.

And finally, with all the planning and evaluating and scheduling—*don't try to do too much.*

Time management isn't about maximizing the number of items you can check off in a day or a life. It's about living fully, productively, joyfully—by your definitions of these terms.

I'll end this with these words of philosopher/theologian Thomas Merton:

The rush and the pressure of modern life are a form,
perhaps the most common form,
of its innate violence.
To allow oneself to be carried away by a multitude of
conflicting concerns,
to surrender to many demands,
to commit oneself to many projects,
to want to help in everything
is to succumb to violence.
The frenzy of the activist neutralizes work for peace.
It destroys the fruitfulness of work,
because it kills the root of inner wisdom
which makes work fruitful.

Quality time with the family just wasn't enough.

After long, heartfelt discussions with Ted, Juanita cut back her hours at the dealership, trading some of the money she was earning for time to be home with Ted and the kids.

Ted and Juanita have declared Sunday as Family Day, with time for a leisurely breakfast together, church, and an outing. Work doesn't intrude because they won't allow it to.

Perhaps she has a bit less of the American Dream now than she used to, but now she has something that eluded her before—a sense of satisfaction in a full and happy life.

Time-Management Tips

1. Create a personal mission statement.
2. Translate your values into specific actions.
3. Schedule time for the activities that support your values.

Glossary

Adrenaline addiction: The unhealthy habit of believing that we work better under pressure, playing chicken with deadlines, and trying to beat the clock.

Age of Leisure: A new era for society in which people would work less and enjoy life more, according to predictions in the '50s and '60s that turned out to be wrong as people opted for a higher material standard of living and created instead the Age of Anxiety.

Ah-ha: A dramatic, creative breakthrough, usually coming through the subconscious and the gift of inspiration that we usually neglect because we're too busy *doing* to let ourselves think.

Biorhythm: The natural cycle of the ebb and flow of energy—physical, mental, and emotional.

Block: An aversion to an activity or a particular aspect of that activity that slows us down or stops us completely. A state of partial or full psychological paralysis caused by fear or pain or a lack of desire, willpower, or discipline.

Bozo factor: The degree of annoyance that we allow other people to add to our stress levels and take away from our enjoyment of life.

CL: An extreme of the time-management continuum, characterized by being *cluttered* and *late*, usually also tolerant of ambiguity, chaos, and failure. *See* **TP**.

Clutter control: The art of maintaining a practical balance that meets your individual needs, an equilibrium in your ecosystem between wasting time with stacked desks and piled floors and losing time in the obsessive pursuit of perfect organization.

Committee: An infamous black hole that sucks away time, often providing too little in return on that investment.

Divergent thinker: A term used by Dru Scott in *How to Put More Time in Your Life* to refer to people who work better amid clutter— and worn as a badge of distinction by many people who simply can't get organized.

Emergency: A feeling of extreme urgency that we too often catch from other people and accept without question.

Endorphins: Nature's "feel good" chemicals, released when you exercise.

Errata: Mistakes in printing or writing.

Erratta: Mistake made while correcting mistakes.

Eustress: The ideal level of stress for your life.

"Got a minute?": Three of the most dangerous words in the English language.

Important: An activity that touches your core values, the motivations that guide your life. *See* **Urgent.**

Information Age: A time in which we all agree to believe that having more information can somehow compensate for having less time to make use of that information.

Insidious cycle of work and speed: A term used by Juliet Schor in *The Overworked American* for the lifestyle of working longer in order to buy more things, a cycle that can be broken through a decision to "reclaim leisure."

Lakein question: A simple technique for prioritizing activities, proposed by Alan Lakein over twenty-five years ago in *Time Management: How to Get Control of Your Time and Your Life*, based on three criteria—"Is this what I *want* or *need* to be doing *right now*?"

Lifestyle: The total of all the choices you make about how you use your time.

List addiction: The unhealthy state of allowing our to-do lists to run our lives, instead of controlling them to manage our time.

Meeting addiction: An insidiously easy way of losing time by instinctively trusting in the old adage, "the more the merrier," and scheduling to gather with others to deal with any situation—and systematically stake out and subdivide our time.

Minivacation: A break that you allow yourself in order to keep time from managing your life, to relieve the stress and fatigue, and to recover your sanity through any of the many short, simple techniques that put "the power in the pause."

Moment management: The fine art of taking control of the many small decisions of life, making good use of the minutes that make up the hours that make up our lives.

Motion sickness: A physical and psychological dependence on activity—constant and fast-paced—that can become as powerful as any chemical addiction. The excitement of life in the fast lane can make people forget about why they're out traveling that road at all.

Multitasking: The practice of doing several things poorly at the same time.

Noise pollution: An environmental hazard that invades us and distracts us, sucking away bits of time.

Omnivore: A term used by John Robinson in his study of how Americans use their time, for "doers," people who make full use of their free time, as opposed to "sitters."

Pareto Principle: The theory that 80 percent of the results come from 20 percent of the effort, named after Vilfredo Pareto (1848-1923)—who ironically has earned over 80 percent of his fame from less than 20 percent of his work.

Penny time: Term used by Marshall Cook in *Streetwise Time Management* for the minutes that many people squander although they obsess over "pound time," the hours composed of all those minutes.

Perfection: A myth that causes too many of us to lose too much time too often—and generally end up with more problems and frustration than improvements.

Positive visualization: The technique of preparing mentally for an activity, using the subconscious mind to help us concentrate on succeeding.

Pound time: Term used by Marshall Cook in *Streetwise Time Management* for the hours that many people worry about losing, even as they fail to control their use of minutes–"penny time" that adds up to "pound time"–and become "pound wise and penny foolish."

Procrastination: The technique of putting something off until a time (a) when it will be too late to do it, (b) when it will be even more urgent and stressful and overwhelming, or (c) when you will have even less time than now to do it. Procrastination is to time management what credit cards and borrowing are to financial management: we may get what we want now, but we pay for it later.

Quality Time: The myth that you can somehow schedule meaningful interaction with another human being. Most harmful application: the myth that a little bit of "Quality Time" will make up for the lack of "Quantity Time."

SARME: A five-step process for reading more effectively: **s**cout the material, **a**sk questions about it, **r**ead it, **m**ap the key information in it, and **e**tch the information into your memory by reviewing it.

Speed Sickness: Moving too fast for too long, damaging physical, mental, and psychological health.

Stress: Your internal reaction to a stressor.

Stressor: A source of irritation, anxiety, or conflict.

Take a Meeting: A trendy way of saying "Meet with me" that leads us to casually and instinctively accept impositions on our time.

Technology: The science of creating devices to allow us to do more with our time, which generally leads us to expect that we should be able to do even more in even less time–and often makes it necessary to do so.

Thrashing: A computer term for overload, when there are too many commands for the computer to follow any of them, a term appropriated by Anne McGee-Cooper in *Time Management for Unmanageable People* for the similar human phenomenon of having so many things to do that we end up doing nothing–totally thrashed.

Time: Potential life.

Time management: Making conscious decisions on how you will use your time.

Time management, streetwise: To get more out of your time by making the day-to-day decisions that let you live as you like, do what you want and need to do, and still have time for the things that make your life worth living. Streetwise time management is about more than speed; sometimes it's about stopping altogether.

Time management, traditional: To follow the advice of every efficiency expert and obsess about cramming more activities into your time.

To-do list: A way to remember what we need to do—and too often a way to yield control over our time to a piece of paper.

TP: An extreme of the time-management continuum, characterized by being *tidy* and *punctual*, usually also organized, detail-oriented, and perfectionist. *See* **CL.**

Two-minute drill: A term used in football for the art and science of cramming as much activity as possible into the final 120 seconds of the game, in the hope of snatching victory from the jaws of defeat, a strategy that for too many people becomes a way of life.

Urgent: An activity that demands your immediate attention. *See* **Important.**

Values-based time management: An approach that balances quality of life and quantity of time, basing the use of time on what matters, one's priorities in life.

Find more on this topic by visiting BusinessTown.com

Developed by Adams Media, **BusinessTown.com** is a free informational site for entrepreneurs, small business owners, and operators. It provides a comprehensive guide for planning, starting, growing, and managing a small business.

Visitors may access hundreds of articles addressing dozens of business topics, participate in forums as well as connect to additional resources around the Web. **BusinessTown.com** is easily navigated and provides assistance to small businesses and start-ups. The material covers beginning basic issues as well as the more advanced topics.

✓ **Accounting**
Basic, Credit & Collections, Projections, Purchasing/Cost Control

✓ **Advertising**
Magazine, Newspaper, Radio, Television, Yellow Pages

✓ **Business Opportunities**
Ideas for New Businesses, Business for Sale, Franchises

✓ **Business Plans**
Creating Plans & Business Strategies

✓ **Finance**
Getting Money, Money Problem Solutions

✓ **Letters & Forms**
Looking Professional, Sample Letters & Forms

✓ **Getting Started**
Incorporating, Choosing a Legal Structure

✓ **Hiring & Firing**
Finding the Right People, Legal Issues

✓ **Home Business**
Home Business Ideas, Getting Started

✓ **Internet**
Getting Online, Put Your Catalog on the Web

✓ **Legal Issues**
Contracts, Copyrights, Patents, Trademarks

✓ **Managing a Small Business**
Growth, Boosting Profits, Mistakes to Avoid, Competing with the Giants

✓ **Managing People**
Communications, Compensation, Motivation, Reviews, Problem Employees

✓ **Marketing**
Direct Mail, Marketing Plans, Strategies, Publicity, Trade Shows

✓ **Office Setup**
Leasing, Equipment, Supplies

✓ **Presentations**
Know Your Audience, Good Impression

✓ **Sales**
Face to Face, Independent Reps, Telemarketing

✓ **Selling a Business**
Finding Buyers, Setting a Price, Legal Issues

✓ **Taxes**
Employee, Income, Sales, Property, Use

✓ **Time Management**
Can you Really Manage Time?

✓ **Travel & Maps**
Making Business Travel Fun

✓ **Valuing a Business**
Simple Valuation Guidelines